Moulton
College

NORTHAMPTONSHIRE

Profit through Skill

THE COMPLETE
ENCYCLOPEDIA OF
ORCHIDS

THE COMPLETE
ENCYCLOPEDIA OF
ORCHIDS

Informative text
with hundreds of photographs

ZDENĚK JEŽEK

REBO
PUBLISHERS

A list of symbols used

Size of the plant:

☐   – miniature

⊡   – small

▣   – medium

■   – robust

Growing:

☹   – extremely demanding

😐   – considerably demanding

☺   – not demanding

Photo on p. 3: *Rhynchostylis gigantea,* var. *virapandahui,*
        p. 298: *Orchis tridentata*
        p. 304: *Epipactis purpurata*

© 2003 Rebo International, b. v., Lisse, The Netherlands
© 2003 Rebo Productions CZ, Ltd.,
Obchodní 106, Čestlice, 251 70 Dobřejovice

Text by: Zdeněk Ježek
Translated from Czech to English by: Lea Hamrlíková
Photographs: Zdeněk Ježek 364, Libor Jankovský 200, Petr Starý 30,
Jindřich Šmiták 22, Aleš Knoll 21, Jarmila Matoušková 20, Václav Klát 9,
Jiří Troneček 6, Libor Kunte 6, Jan Gloser 2 and Čestmír Čihalík 1
Graphic design: Studio Granit
Editing and production: Granit, Ltd., Prague, The Czech Republic
Proofreading: Jarmila Pešková Škraňáková
Typography: Amos typografické studio, spol. s r. o., Prague, The Czech Republic

1st edition 2003
004321201

ISBN 90 366 1589 5

Contents:

Introduction

Queen of the Realm of Plants

Orchid. A word that still invites attention and commands respect even among complete botanical laymen, despite the fact that these beautifully blooming plants are no longer as rare and remote as they once were. In our minds, orchids are still associated with the smell of exotic places; they are a symbol of nobility, luxurious beauty, as well as a certain myth of unattainability. It is no wonder, if we consider that up until a century ago, the lay public could only find out about orchids second-hand from the testimonies of a small number of orchid hunters, who would undertake perilous journeys to unexplored tropical regions to find them. Growing orchids that had been found there and transported to Europe in a very complicated way was, until the end of the 19th century, a very exclusive and expensive hobby of a small number of well-heeled individuals. In the 20th century, especially in the past few decades, new developments in transportation, computer technology, and the introduction of new construction and insulation materials have made it possible for orchids to become a common part of our lives. Great improvements have also taken place in the hybridization and breeding of orchids. As a result, orchids can be purchased literally on every corner nowadays—at a reasonably low price and in a stunningly wide range of colors and shapes. Orchids abound in stores both as fresh-cut flowers and potted flowers. The lay public is still not ready to admit that orchids cannot only be easily obtained, but also quite successfully grown in our homes on a long-term basis, without expensive devices and technological tools. A conviction lingers on that the cultivation of orchids in apartments is a privilege of only the most experienced and best-informed experts, while the fact is that growing a large number of "domesticated" botanical species and modern orchid hybrids (which often far surpass their original "wild" parents in beauty) is quite easily manageable.

Characterization of Orchids

A prosaic origin of the name

The noble and exotic-sounding term "orchid" has a very prosaic and "low" origin. It is derived from the Latin word "*orchis*" meaning testicle, suggesting the similarity of the tubers of some of the terrestrial European orchids to a part of the male genitals. The use of the name "*orchis*" for orchids dates back to the third century BC, when Theophrastus (a disciple of the famous Aristotle) first used it in his book "History of Plants". The term "*Orchis*" is now used to describe a particular European genus, and the name of the entire family—*Orchidaceae*—is also derived from it.

Orchids—What Are They?

We have already touched upon the fact that orchids are perennial plants, and members of *Orchidaceae*–the largest family of plants. The estimated number of orchid species living in the wild runs to 25 thousand. This astonishingly high number of species can be explained by the relatively "young age" of the genus: the first angiospermous plants appeared on the earth as far back as 130 million years ago, while the first representatives of the family *Orchidaceae* did not come until 50-60 million years later. Thus, orchids apparently haven't yet "found" their final appearance and they are still subject to

Left: *Alamania punicea*, a precious inhabitant of cloud forests in Mexico

The remarkable blossoms of *Dendrobium eximium*, an Asian orchid

Orchis, a genus of European orchids, lent the name to the entire family—*Orchidaceae* (the photo shows a specimen of *Orchis morio*).

Orchid blossoms are symmetrical along only one geometrical plane (the photo shows *Paphiopedilum charlesworthii*, a rare Venus's shoe).

a fairly rapid evolution. This is suggested, for example, by the genetic instability of the members of the family. Many species of the same genera, and even representatives of different orchid genera interbreed in the wild without much trouble, giving rise to a large number of new hybrids that are often very different from their parents, fully viable and perfectly capable of further reproduction. An overwhelming majority of hybrids came to existence in the past 100 years through human intervention; by deliberate and not always appropriate selection and crossbreeding, humankind has taken the evolution of orchids into its own hands. In total, there are another 25-30 thousand both natural and especially artificial orchid hybrids, a number comparable to the amount of the botanical—"pure"—species alone. The exact inventory of all orchids present on the surface of the earth will most likely remain unknown, as the regions that have not yet been sufficiently explored may still contain a lot of surprises. In addition, random interbreeding may result in the creation of other brand-new "species". Furthermore, many still undiscovered species are bound to disappear owing to the ever-more intensive and unregulated devastation of rainforests and other natural localities. Although a general (while still fitting) characterization of orchids is very complicated, there are four basic features of orchids that, admittedly, can be found with other plant groups individually but which apply all at once only in the case of the representatives of the family *Orchidaceae:*

- the flowers of orchids are bilaterally symmetrical;
- the pollen grains are grouped into sticky masses termed pollinia (which is related to their complicated reproduction—see the following text);

- the seeds are very minute and contain only undeveloped embryos with no nutritive material;
- in natural conditions, seeds can germinate only when symbiotic fungi are present.

Double Lifestyle

The family *Orchidaceae* got its name from the small group of terrestrial orchids growing in the Temperate Zone. This is rather paradoxical, since an overwhelming majority of the family members live in the tropical regions, and in a completely different way. For there are not only terrestrial orchids (growing in the ground), but also epiphytic orchids (living on other plants—mostly trees, tree ferns or cacti). In addition, there is also a small group of lithophytes, i.e. orchids growing on rocks. The terrestrial representatives of the family can naturally be found everywhere, not only in the Temperate, Subtropical and Torrid Zones. In contrast, epiphytes can survive only in regions where temperatures never drop to freezing point.

As with the vast majority of plants in general, terrestrial orchids grow in the ground and use their roots to obtain nutrition and water from the soil. Apart from the tropical genus *Paphiopedilum*, very popular with growers, this group contains all European orchids. The chapter entitled "Terrestrial Orchids of the Temperate Zone" will discuss them in more detail.

Nevertheless, a greater proportion of orchids are epiphytes. There is an erroneous conviction spread among the lay public that epiphytic orchids are para-

The inconspicuous appearance of European terrestrial orchids makes them little known among the lay public (the photo shows a specimen of *Dactylorhiza majalis*).

Together with other epiphytic plants, orchids often form "aerial gardens"—surprisingly large and weighty communities in the treetops (the photo was taken in Cuba).

Solitary trees in the vicinity of water reservoirs are the home of hundreds of orchids (the photo shows a robust *Schomburgkia tibicinis* and other epiphytes).

sitic upon their host trees. This opinion is likely to have originated in the minds of Central Europeans, who compared orchid bunches to the fresh green bushes of the well-known mistletoe (*Viscum album*) growing on treetops in the Temperate Zone. Mistletoe does profit from the vessels of the trees but it has nothing at all in common with orchids. *Orchidaceae* are completely independent as far as their nutrition is concerned, and they use trees merely for support; they grow over them and do not encroach upon their tissue. If they do any harm to the trees at all, it is second-hand damage caused by creating shade and by the orchids' weight. For it is a fact that orchids often form (along with other epiphytes from other families) weighty communities, known as aerial gardens, in the treetops. Epiphytism of orchids seems to be a result of the very recent origin of this family. Its representatives did not appear on the earth until the time when the surface of the earth had already been "taken" by other rival plants. However, the surfaces of these plants, especially trees, remained vacant for occupation. Orchids therefore chose trees to climb up in search of light. And they do so to this day, at the same time providing for their nutrition and water themselves (or, rather, with the help of symbiotic fungi—see further text).

Curious Seeds

The odds that an orchid seed will take root and mature on a tree—a place with very severe life conditions—are very small (some estimates are as high as 1:100,000,000!). Orchids thus needed to adapt and ensure the production of a sufficient number of seeds

to offset the unfavorable probability ratio: and they succeeded! All representatives of the family are able to produce enormous amounts of seeds (a single ovary can contain up to 5 million seeds!). However, if all the seeds are to fit into the ovaries, they need to have an appropriate size and weight. Therefore, orchid seeds underwent a radical miniaturization to turn

A well-developed ovary of a *Cattleya* orchid contains between four and five million minuscule seeds.

Natural germination of orchid seeds is rare in greenhouse conditions. The photo on the left shows a year-old seedling of *Maxillaria* sp., after spontaneously germinating on a grapevine trunk in a greenhouse; the photo on the right shows the same specimen after 10 years of cultivation.

into extremely tiny embryos. In fact, they are nothing but primitive clusters of several cells weighing no more than a few millionths of a gram. The embryos are covered with a thin coat (termed "testa") and their parents equipped them with no nutritive material whatsoever. If this is the case, we need to ask: how can they germinate? As usual, nature found a way and sent symbiotic fungi to help.

A Mysterious Symbiosis

All orchids are partly dependent on cooperation with highly specialized species of fungi—this cooperation is somewhat similar to the relationship of the roots of some European trees with fungi, the fruiting bodies of which are traditionally collected for consumption. After they ripen, the seeds of all orchids need to reach conditions favorable for both their existence and the existence of the fungal filaments (known as hyphas) as soon as possible. If that happens, the seed swells up, the embryo cells begin to divide and create miniature pseudo-hair roots. Any possible development of the seedlings without the presence of fungi is terminated in this phase. For it is only the fungus that can provide for a further supply of carbohydrates and perhaps also vitamins and hormones. The fungal filament penetrates the bottom part of the germinating seed and begins to nurture it. Gradually, a sphere-shaped "protocorm" develops from it, which soon turns green and grows an apical bud at the top. At the base, the first genuine roots spring out, into which the filaments of the symbiotic fungi "move house," and they usually stay put for the rest of the orchid's life. The relationship between the specialized fungi and *Orchidaceae* has not yet been fully explained, for it is not quite clear what the plant actually has to offer to the fungus, and what stimulates the fungal filaments to penetrate the orchid roots. What is for sure, however, is that the hyphas thickly cover the orchid roots and through their skin they penetrate the living cells, where they form tiny ball-like shapes that are subsequently consumed by the orchid tissues. In summary, the fungi provide the orchids with some organic ma-

terial, and according to present knowledge, their relationship is more likely a symbiosis of both rather than parasitism of the orchid on the fungus.

The next developmental stage of the orchid/fungus coexistence differs from case to case. Some orchids are able to achieve full "independence," once they have formed a sufficient assimilation apparatus; other orchids remain dependent on the fungi more or less for the rest of their lives, which complicates their transplantation, breeding, etc. A specialized group of orchids known as saprophytes cannot do without fungi at all, as they contain no chlorophyll and therefore have no other way of obtaining all their nutrients than through the fungal filaments (*Neottia nidus-avis*, a well-known European orchid, is a case in point).

The complicated development of the seedlings, coupled with the stunted metabolism of orchids, considerably prolongs their ontogenesis: it can take 2-3 years from the germination of a seed to the first anthesis of the adult specimen (in the case of hybrids of the *Phalaenopsis* species), but usually it takes 7-10 years, and in some cases even as many as 15 years!

The Distribution of Orchids in the World

Orchids live practically all over the world, with the exception of deserts and areas of perpetual ice. An overwhelming majority of them (90%) are found in the tropics—mostly in Asia (10,000-15,000 species), and also in Central America (1,000 species), South America (6,000-8,000 species) and Africa (2,000 species). The rest of the world is poorer in orchids (700 species in Australia, 200 species in North America, 200 species in Europe).

Not all the orchids in the tropical areas are necessarily thermophilic—it all depends on the altitude of their occurence (e.g., in the Himalayas, some species of the genus *Coelogyne* can be found as high as 3,000 m above sea level, and in the South American Andes, representatives of the genera *Lemboglossum* and *Odontoglossum* live at an altitude of over 13,000 ft/4,000 m). Therefore, when looking for a new species for your collection, you always need to

An overwhelming majority of orchids grow in the Tropical Zone, mainly in the upper levels of rainforests (the photo on the left is from Puerto del Aire, Mexico).

find out whether you are dealing with a lowland, sub-montane, or montane species.

The Structure (Morphology) of Orchids

The appearance of orchids somewhat defies the usual ideas of what a plant should look like. Moreover, there are a large number of variations and modifications within the family, resulting from adaptation to various environmental conditions. The further text will there-fore focus on the most common peculiarities of the structure of orchids—the knowledge of which will help you understand the extraordinary life of orchids and facilitate their cultivation in artificial conditions.

The Importance of Roots

Roots are perhaps the most important organ of the members of the family *Orchidaceae*. With epiphytic species, they serve more functions than is common with classical terrestrial plant species. They serve not only as a mechanical tool for anchoring the plant to the trees and in the earth: they are used for absorption and storage as well (they contain important fleshy tis-sues serving as storage space for water and nutrients). And more than that—the roots of many species even contain the green coloring matter of "leaves" (chloro-phyll), thus serving other functions—those of assim-ilation. (Some species have gone so far as to form no leaves whatsoever—see details mentioned in connec-tion with the species of *Chiloschista, Polyrrhiza* and *Microcoelia*). The roots are also an environment for the development of symbiotic fungal filaments.

Orchid roots are covered with skin cells capable of growing perpendicularly to the axis of the root—once a root approaches the surface of the skin, they can grow, firmly and flatwise, into the crevices. A very firm adherence takes place all along the surface of the root, which reliably supports the often very heavy

The fleshy roots of orchids perfectly accrete to the support. When the roots are dry, a layer of velamen makes them almost shiny white (the photo shows the roots of *Cattleya loddigesii*).

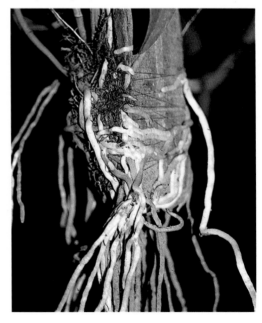

Typical representatives of orchids with a monopodial stem are those of the Asian genus *Vanda* (the photo was taken on the coast of the Andaman Sea, Thailand).

clumps of plants, securing them against falling. The existence of aerial roots that hang down freely into space, has been questioned by some botanists; in their opinion, this phenomenon only occurs if a plant has insufficient life space and is therefore searching for a new support.

It is only the young root tips that absorb water and minerals; the older parts are later covered with another speciality of orchids, known as velamen (i.e., a layer of dead thick-walled cells filled with air). The velamen gives the dry roots their white color, serving as an insulant and thus facilitating water savings. In wet weather, the velamen absorbs water and transmits more light to the chlorophyll that is, to a limited extent, functional even in older roots.

Two Types of Stems

There are two very different types of growth of orchid stems: monopodial and sympodial. The stem of monopodial orchids is developmentally older, it resembles the same organs of other plants of many families, and it grows in one direction from one active bud on the end. The leaves grow in two rows opposite

Sympodial orchids sprout annual shoots from a trailing rhizome, perpendicularly to the direction of its growth. The herbaceous shoots gradually turn into firm pseudobulbs and a subsequent activation of a standby lateral bud ensures further horizontal growth (*Miltonia* sp.).

each other. A typical example of this orchid type is the genus *Vanda* with elongated internodes, or the genus *Phalaenopsis*, whose internodes are, in contrast, significantly shortened. The inflorescence of monopodial orchids always develops from the lateral buds of the stem. The stems gradually grow away over the years, often lignifying in the lower part, they shed their leaves and subsequently die.

The sympodial growth of the stem is much more interesting, developmentally more modern and original in the realm of plants. This type of stem follows the surface of the support and is often completely buried in the substrate—we are in fact dealing with a rhizome with shortened or long internodes. A shoot grows out of the apical bud of the rhizome once in each season. It has its own roots and leaves. After a short rest and maturing of the shoot, the rhizome continues to grow out of a lateral bud formed next to the apical bud. There is not usually only one lateral bud—there are about 1-2 backup buds, in case the "main" bud cannot burgeon (owing to an obstacle, damage, etc). These buds were termed "sleeping buds", and they are used for vegetative propagation of thick clumps of orchids (see the chapter "Vegetative Propagation"). Strong plants sometimes begin to reproduce vegetatively by themselves, when one of the backup sleeping buds becomes activated. The rhizome splits in two, which results in the forming of two shoots instead of just one. In the course of several years, the end part of the original rhizome dies away, giving rise to two independent daughter plants at the place of the split. The inflorescence of sympodial orchids is formed either at the tip of the shoot (*Cattleya*), on the side (*Cycnoches*, *Dendrobium*), or out of special rhizome buds on the base of the stem (*Lycaste*).

Pseudobulbs

It is typical of most sympodial orchids (with the exception of, for example, the genus *Paphiopedilum*, which looks monopodial but is in fact sympodial), that the entire shoots or their bases swell up to form special storage organs known as pseudobulbs. These can vary both in shape (round, ovoid, spindle-shaped) and size (for example, the size of the pseudobulbs of the petite representatives of the genus *Bulbophyllum* does not exceed 0.08 in/2 mm, while the pseudobulbs of *Grammatophyllum speciosum*, the biggest orchid in the world, can grow to up to 6.5-9.8 ft/2-3 m in size!). The surface of the pseudobulbs is smooth, with lengthwise or crosswise grooves, or constricted. Interestingly, in the genus *Schomburgkia*, these organs are hollow and serve as a dwelling for ants. The pseudobulbs remain on the plant for several years, assimilating and serving as a storage space for nutrients and water.

Even Leaves Can Decorate

Orchid leaves usually maintain a belt-like, oval or elliptic shape. The structure of the leaves always corre-

Extremely fleshy leaves often substitute the reduced pseudo-bulbs and serve as water storage (*Pleurothalis teres*).

sponds to the environment in which a particular orchid species occurs (this piece of knowledge can in turn be used in growing new and not-so-well-known orchid species). The leaves of the plants growing in a wet and shady environment are thin and flabby, and not very resistant to a decrease of air humidity. A brief exposure to direct sunlight is often enough to destroy them completely. In contrast, the leaves of orchids growing in stations that are temporarily very dry and heavily insolated are fleshy, tough and covered with a thick skin. Their succulent tissues serve as storage for water. Between the two extremes that have been mentioned, there are of course many different transitional cases. The leaves of some species can even assume a decorative appearance and are sometimes embellished with silvery spangles (genera *Macodes* and *Ludisia*), or spots that were formed through the presence of anthocyan colorings (*Psychopsiella limminghei*, *Oncidium cramerianum*), or uneven distribution of chlorophyll (what is known as marbling of the leaves of the genus *Paphilopedilum*). With most orchids, the leaves remain attached to the pseudobulbs for several years (evergreens), or they are shed annually, with new leaves growing on newly developed pseudobulbs. (*Bletia*, *Calanthe*, *Catasetum*, etc).

Extraordinary Flowers

No other plant families have flowers that abound in such a variety of shapes as orchids. Orchid flowers come in an incredible number of variations and modifications, characteristic of particular orchid genera and species. In spite of this variability, most orchids have certain morphological features and flower parts in common. The flowers usually consist of six flower "leaves", known as tepals. The three outer tepals (termed sepals) function at first as a protection for the whole flower (the outer wall of the buds) and are green. Only after blooming do they get their color. Two out of the three inner tepals are called petals and are identical in shape, size and color. There is no scientific reason for using the terms "sepals" and "petals" to denote the orchid tepals, but they are commonly used in practise. The third inner tepal is transformed into a "lip", or *labellum*. It is broadly expanded and conspicuoulsy colorful, and forms a dominant feature of the flower. Its function is both to attract pollinators and serve as a landing field for them. With "Venus's shoes" (the genera *Capripedium*, *Phragmipedium* and *Paphiopedilum*), the lip is transformed into a hollow slipper. The lip sometimes sports a spur-shaped prolongation filled with nectar. In flower buds, the lip is nothing but a medial upper tepal. It is not until the last stages of the development of the flower, and right before its opening, that a phenomenon known as resupinantion, characteristic of most orchids, occurs: the ovary twists along the longitudinal axis and the entire flower makes a 180 degree turn. The lip then finds itself in the lower part of the flower. In orchid flowers, the original six stamens have been reduced to only one (most species) or two (for example, the genus *Capripedium*). The stamen (stamens) unites with the styles of the pistil to form

Some orchids have a lip turned into a showy hollow slipper (*Cypripedium macranthum*).

13

Hundreds of thousands of seeds are generated by ovaries during a very long, complicated process (a fertile cluster of *Phragmipedium lindenii*, a Venus's shoe from Ecuador).

an unusual shape called a column. It looks like a little dip, with the surface often sticky, to facilitate the attachment of the pollen. The pollen of the anther is stuck together with a sticky substance (viscin) into club-shaped masses called pollinia—another great specialty of the family *Orchidaceae*.

The Mysterious Origin of Orchid Seeds

The assemblage of pollen into lumpy pollinia is vital for orchids, as it is the only way of transporting at one go a sufficient amount of pollen grains to ensure effective fertilization of the flowers and the subsequent development of a gigantic number of minute seeds. Tiny, firm peduncles with a sticky bat at the end protrude from the pollinium. The pollinator (usually a flying insect) is attracted by the beauty, and not rarely the fragrance of the flower, and makes a visit during which the pollinia stick to its body. When it lands on the next flower, it delivers an entire "package" of pollen. If the transported pollinium makes it to the stigma, a definite pollination and fertilization of the flower is ensured.

These are still not all the unique features of the sexual life of orchids. Nature was faced with yet another problem, one regarding the enormous production of seeds. As we know, one egg in the ovary is necessary for the forming of each seed. After pollination, the egg merges with the penetrating pollen tube, giving rise to an embryo and seed casing. If orchids were to produce in each ovary an amount of eggs corresponding to the amount of the final production of seeds, they would probably die of exhaustion. That is

why in the family *Orchidaceae*, the eggs do not develop before the pollen is deposited on the stigma and the pollen tubes have penetrated the ovary! The development of the bearers of male genetic information is halted there, until the eggs are "ready". The process from pollination to fertilization is thus radically prolonged and can take up to 280 days! In the meantime, the tiny lower ovary balloons up, growing several times bigger in size and turning into a triangular or sextangular pod. After the seeds mature, the pod turns yellow, its valves begin to burst, the seeds spill out and are dispersed by the wind.

Cultivation and Care

Environmental Needs of Orchids

The cultivation of most terrestrial orchid species in amateur conditions is practically impossible (their special needs are discussed in detail in the introductory part of the chapter "Terrestrical Orchids of the Temperate Zone"). The following text will therefore focus on a group of *Orchidaceae* that is most interesting from an orchid cultivator's point of view: the tropical epiphytes.

The main conditions necessary for the survival of all plants, including epiphytes, are certain levels of humidity, temperature, light and nutrition. A limiting

Highly specialized species are sometimes the only plant inhabitants of locations with extreme conditions; the *Paphiopedilum* Venus's shoes thriving without rival vegetation in the cracks of sun-baked vertical rock walls (Thailand) are a good example.

Unique metabolic and anatomical adaptation enables orchids to survive even in apparently impossible conditions (a *Cattleyopsis lindenii* on a sun-drenched bare palm tree trunk in Cuba).

factor of the life of epiphytic orchids is not only a certain level of surrounding **humidity**, but also its oscillation, which is no less important. The morphological structure and the survival strategies of orchids are adapted to both regular and irregular changes in the water supply during the day and in course of the season. The water supply for overcoming drier periods is stored in succulent tissues of the ballooned roots, stems and leaves. Although this arrangement enables many orchids to overcome without much trouble periods of drought lasting up to several months, certain limit levels must be maintained at all times. Besides humidity, another often crucial condition for the survival of an orchid is the air circulation, and the fluctuation of daily and nightly temperatures. An optimum **temperature** is important not only for the development of an orchid itself, but its temporary decrease (taking various amount of time), along with the decrease of humidity, is often necessary for the induction of the flower. It is therefore crucial for the cultivator of a particular species to have a thorough knowledge of the altitude and temperature characteristics of the place where it naturally occurs. In the artificial cultivation, temperature affects the plants in joint action with the intensity of light. Therefore, if orchids cultivated in the temperate zone cannot get a sufficient amount of light in winter, their suffering can be mollified to some extent by reducing the temperature—the plants do not use up as much energy by breathing and, "half-asleep", they survive dire times and live to see a more favorable time of the year.

Orchids' needs of **light** are also very diverse. Rainforest species require significantly less light than alpine orchids. Experienced cultivators can infer how demanding a particular species is in regard to light from a single look—from the outward appearance of the plant (the size of pseudobulbs, the consistency and surface of leaves, the texture of roots, etc.).

Nutrition plays a less important role compared to the previously mentioned factors, although it should not be underestimated. In contrast to terristric species, epiphytic species have a much smaller chance of obtaining minerals. The only source of minerals is rain water containing dust particles, and humus accumulated in the epiphyte colonies, excrement of animals, and their dead bodies. There is an interesting phenomenon observable in the tropics with regard to nutrition: orchids do not grow on just any tree—they "pick out" their hosts with great care! For example, they do not occur on eucalyptus trees, but they can often be found on oaks. Sometimes young trees of a particular tree species host orchids that are completely different from the ones hosted by adult trees of the same species (often only a few yards away). This is related, apart from the different lighting conditions of each tree, to the quality of the tree's rhytidome, its capacity for releasing and retaining nutrients, accumulating humus etc. Some trees make it downright impossible for orchids to grow on them by discharging certain substances preventing the development of fungal filaments and orchid roots.

When cultivating orchids, you want to satisfy the environmental needs of the plants as well as you can. It is impossible to give one simple and uniform set of instructions for cultivating such a diverse group of plants as *Orchidaceae*. All there is left to do is to learn some general rules for cultivation that are applicable both to those members of *Orchidaceae* grown in a "classical", traditional way (namely, the widely popular and advertised hybrids of the genera *Cattleya, Cymbidium, Laelia, Oncidium, Paphiopedilum* and *Phalaenopsis*), and the smaller, "pure" botanical species, the size of which makes them more suitable for amateur growers—owners of small greenhouses, floralia, glass cases, paludaria and epiphyte cases. Other special skills for the cultivation of orchids are a question of patience, experience, sense and observing skills of every orchid lover.

Space for the Cultivation of Orchids

Before starting or extending a collection of orchids, one should always take time to think about how much money and time one is willing to devote to orchids. The selection of suitable orchid species and the purchase of the appropriate devices for their cultivation ought to be based on that decision. An average person interested in growing orchids is no longer limited by any technical or material complications. Scientific and technological progress has resolved all the pitfalls associated with choosing the most suitable material for building a cultivating device that would include a reliable and economical heating system, a perfect regulation and programming of temperature, the manner and frequency of watering etc. The limiting factor nowadays tends to be rather the content of the wallet of each lover of exotic plants. Few people can afford the construction and energy-consuming operation of spacious orchid greenhouses. Cultivation of orchids can, sadly, be a rather upmarket hobby. Luckily for amateurs, there are still a lot of alternative methods—for example, cultivation of orchids in indoor glass cases, window greenhouses, or in the open on the window sill. The latter method is getting the green light nowadays—thanks to the emergence of many resilient and vigorous hybrid orchids. The desire to keep the queen of the realm of plants at home can thus be satisfied without a substantial financial sacrifice. An overwhelming majority of orchids need both higher air humidity and at the same time a sufficiently intensive air circulation. A matter of course must also be maintaining optimum temperatures and an appropriate lighting for the plants. That is why they have to be cultivated in enclosed or partly enclosed spaces, in which the aforementioned growth factors can be controlled and administered. The golden rule to remember is that the more spacious a particular cultivation equipment is, the better. Small glass cases that do not allow for sufficient ventilation can be used for growing very few species. The choice of species that can be cultivated

using the appropriate equipment increases radically with the increasing size of the device, thanks to the fact that inside the device a certain microbiotope is formed, with its own air circulation, and with more humid, drier, warmer and cooler spots. All the cultivator needs to do then is to find these "minilocalities" suitable for certain orchid species, and she is "home and dry": if a particular species does not prosper in a certain location, it can be moved elsewhere. In small spaces, you can try to fine-tune the microclimate by the use of technology (air humidifiers, additional artificial lighting, in-built ventilators). However, the intensity of illumination or the power output and intervals of starting up the ventilators and vaporizers cannot be clearly defined; this is where the cultivator's patient testing—often quite painful, especially for the plants—has to come in.

Selecting a Suitable Species

Especially with epiphytic orchids, an unwritten rule applies that the smaller the plant, the more demanding and less immune to cultivation errors it is. Large species can sometimes endure even long-lasting cultivation errors but small orchids cannot. The choice of minispecies for cultivation in epiphytic cases is thus limited to the most resilient few. Finding your way through the vast number of orchid species is not

Owners of small cultivation equipment—indoor glass cases or greenhouses—should focus on species that are small but of an interesting appearance (a *Pleurothalis subulifolia* with succulent leaves, barely 1 in/ 2.5 cm long).

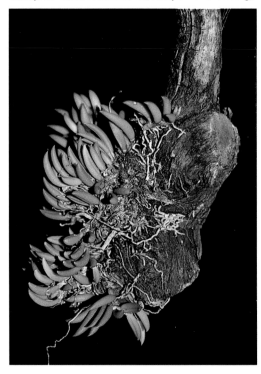

easy, although books can help. Not everything can be found in books, however. They list the basic rules that you have to keep but what counts most is practice—patient effort, and to some extent also the cultivator's sixth sense—a good sense of plants and an ability to notice the changes in the state of their health and physiology. In any case, beginners, or even more experienced cultivators, when planting orchids in new cultivation spaces (especially the small in size), should pay extra attention to the choice of plants and use the well-tried, more common, "pioneer" species. Only later is it advisable to choose rarer and more sensitive (and also more expensive) plants. But be careful: the opinion, often almost dogmatically endorsed, that any orchid hybrid is significantly less demanding for cultivation than its "pure-bred" parents, does not apply without exception, and in many cases it seems to be a gimmick.

Division of Orchids by Temperature Requirements

Division of orchids by temperature requirements can help you pick out an orchid for cultivation. The members of the family are divided into three groups with different temperature needs—**thermophilic**, **intermediate** and **cryophilic**. It is not possible to place every single orchid in one particular group—due to great environmental plasticity, there are many plants whose temperature needs vary. Apart from that, their optimum winter and summer temperatures may be radically different. An experienced orchid cultivator should be able to make a rough estimate about which category a species belongs to, what temperatures are suitable for it and how to grow it correctly, at the moment of first contact with the plant—and from its appearance alone.

Thermophilic plants from tropical lowlands are usually greener, their tissues are only slightly succulent—the flat leaves are flabby and have little resistance to drought. Such orchids need to be provided with higher temperatures and humidity all year round, and sufficient shade in the summer. They grow and bloom without a substantial period of rest and are better able to tolerate longer overwatering (although they certainly benefit from an occasional careful drying-out of the root environment). Lowland orchids are most suitable for the usually shady glass cases and boxes with limited air circulation. Species from mountainous areas of the Tropical Zone are termed "**intermediate**". They are of a more tough and compact build, their pseudobulbs are bigger, their leaves are firmer, and their color can be more or less yellowish. The further their home is from the equator and the higher above sea level, the less demanding they are in terms of temperature, while their need for air circulation and sunshine increases. Besides that, you need to ensure a certain regular drying out, because the air humidity in the wild maintains a much higher daily and yearly periodicity. Natural localities face regular rains and droughts. A period of drought is accompanied by shortening of daylight (even though the intensity of sunshine increases thanks to the cloudless sky) and a decrease of night temperatures. These factors induce the forming of flowers. Unless you provide the plants with this kind of dry (and sometimes rather drastic looking) period during artificial cultivation, you will never see the flowers. Intermediate orchids are doubtless the most suitable orchids for amateur greenhouse and indoor collections.

With the extremely **cryophilic** species from alpine locations, it can be difficult in the summer to maintain the low temperatures that they are accustomed to (i.e., 65-72°F/ 18-22°C). A possible solution might be to hang the orchid bunches outside the greenhouse and in the semi-shade of fruit trees, under gazebos etc. Plants kept in this way, however, need more frequent misting. In winter, alpine species present us with another problem that is hard to solve: the lack of sunshine. That can be partly compensated for by lowering the temperature to a certain bearable level.

Supports, Substrates and Containers for Cultivating Botanical Orchids

Small botanical species are usually cultivated epiphytically, without a substrate, that is, suspended on a support. Various things can serve as a support:

Representatives of the genera *Odontoglossum* and *Lemboglossum* are the most popular cryophilic orchids grown under cultivation.

17

a piece of pine bark, or cork bark (which is even better but more expensive and harder to get), a nicely-shaped "head" of grapevine, or other branches or tree stumps with bizarre shapes. Tufts of fern roots used to be popular as well. Thicker sticks of *Sambucus nigra* (elderberry) have been recommended lately for their good results. Well-matured, 4-7 year-old elderberry wood should be cut in winter and, for easier handling, it should be cut lengthwise in two halves. Before use, the sticks need to dry out well. *Sambucus nigra* has a soft, highly-absorbent bark that is popular with the roots of most orchids. Fix the plants with a nylon fishing-line or strips of cut-up nylon stockings, either on an empty surface or into a layer of moss (*Sphagnum* moss). For more robust or more hygrophilous species, you can put a handful of epiphyte substrate underneath the moss sheet, and attach the plant on top.

Botanical and hybrid species can also be cultivated in epiphytic baskets made of wood or plastic; with the genus *Stanhopea*, which shoots the inflorescence vertically downward, this is the only possibility. Naturally, you can use flowerpots as well—orchids grow more in a flowerpot, because they have a greater supply of nutrients and the substrate remains moist for longer. However, the moisture considerably increases the chance of losing the roots. Especially when temperatures plunge down in greenhouses, mold instigators breed excessively in the moist substrate of flowerpots and baskets, and the plants lose both their roots and new shoots. Sticking to the more natural looking, epiphytic way of cultivating orchids is better also for esthetic reasons.

The choice of the combination and proportion of the substrate components for cultivating orchids in baskets or flowerpots is an individual decision of every cultivator. It depends on his or her experience, humidity in the greenhouse, availability of substrate materials and the type of cultivation containers. The following ingredients are used in cultivation mixtures: pine, poplar or cork bark crushed into pieces of various sizes, Agroperlite, Styrofoam or plastic foam torn up into pieces of various sizes, dry peat moss cut up into pieces, peat (make sure it is not too acidic!), oak wood chips, or coconut shells—ground or pressed—that are becoming ever more popular. The final mixtures should be airy, permeable, mold-resistant, poor in nutrients, and they should enable the plants to root well. It is always important that the mixture stay moist for some time after watering, but not overly moist. Therefore, you need to ensure good drainage, for example by cutting up a big round hole in the bottom of the flowerpot and covering the hole from inside the pot with a small plastic basket, or by filling up the bottom part of the flowerpot or basket with bigger pieces of bark, Styrofoam etc. If you transport an orchid that is well rooted in a certain mixture, into a different environment (purchase, exchange), it sometimes loses its roots very soon due to

mold. More rarely, it may suffer from insufficient moisture. The reason is that a substrate adapted to a particular watering regime in one greenhouse may not be suitable for a different greenhouse. In any case, when acquiring new specimens, it always pays to replant them in a substrate containing a mixture of proven quality (that way you also get rid of the risk of spreading certain diseases and pests through your collection).

Watering and Temperature Regime

In the preceding text, we already touched upon the relation between the optimum moisture and temperature. Both function in close coaction that cannot be underestimated. The general rule is: the warmer the environment, the more frequently you can (and must) mist and water the plant. What also matters is the intensity of ventilation, which can dry up the plant in a fairly short time during hot months. That is why in this period you need to mist the plants up to several times a day. Again, a number of local conditions are of crucial importance, such as the spacial position of the greenhouse, shading, ventilation possibilities, the amount of room inside the greenhouse etc. Use water that has been warmed up or left to stand to match the air temperature in the greenhouse. Mist the plants wet, until they start dripping excessive water. In summer, it is advisable to mist them at least twice a day— early in the mornings and in the early evenings (if you expect warm nights). After the evening misting

Nanodes megalospatha from Ecuador is an example of an extremely moisture-loving orchid. Its clusters grow in permanently wet moss growth on the trunks of rainforest trees, and therefore must never be allowed to dry up completely.

session, switch on the inner ventilator. The plants will thus have enough time and favorable conditions to absorb water into their tissues. In winter, cut down on watering because of the insufficient amount of sunshine, lowering the temperature to 61-65°F/16-18°C. If the plants are overly dehydrated, raise the temperature and give them a good watering. The best tool for misting the plants is a manual spray pistol, which enables you to regulate the rate of flow by adjusting the jet. In an ideal case, it is connected to your home "waterworks", which will ensure a permanent level of water during discontinuous misting, thus giving you a chance to focus on each plant or group of plants individually.

The only type of water recommended for watering is rainwater. Using distilled water is too expensive and puts the plants through the exhaustive process of discharging some elements from their tissues (if you want to prevent that from happening, add a solution of complete fertilizer to the distilled water). Well water or river water is unsuitable due to the high content of salt. The worst of all is of course tap water for drinking. It is too hard and, if fresh, it contains a lot of chlorine, which is harmful to the plants. Simply leaving it to stand does not help, for even though you do get rid of a part of the chlorine, the water will still keep its dissolved salts. After boiling, only magnesium and carbonates condense, but acidic chlorines and phosphates do not. Naturally, the salinity of the water differs between different regions. Hard water prematurely uses up the substrate, which results in the need for frequent replanting.

Lighting Regime

Owing to their tropical origin, the average requirements of orchids for light are quite extensive. Expecially in winter it is necessary to provide the plants with the maximum possible amount of light—greenhouses should be covered with no protective coat of paint or other screen. Epiphytic glass boxes and cases should be placed as close to a window as possible. These devices should unquestionably be equipped with fluorescent tubes or other strong sources of light, switched on for 10-11 hours a day on dark and gloomy days. On the other hand, in summer it is important to protect the plants under glass from being scorched by direct sunlight, and from overheating the environment inside the glass case. The most expensive and most effective are automatic louvered shades: a sensor responds to the intensity of the fallen sunlight by regulating the tilt of the slats, thus ensuring that the flowers receive light of an appropriate intensity. Less affluent cultivators usually make do with sparse reed nets, or better still, military dazzle nets. Painting the glass with a layer of slaked lime is not recommended.

Fertilization

Thanks to their economical and slow metabolism, the requirements of orchids for mineral nutrition are rel-

The group of orchids with the lowest need of light includes species of the *Phalaenopsis* genus (the photo shows a white-flowered hybrid).

atively low; still, they need to be side-dressed during growth. The ideal choice is a solution of a complete fertilizer that contains—besides the main growth elements of nitrogen, magnesium, potassium, and phosphorus—a mixture of other microelements. There are many more or less suitable agents and preparations out there, whose suitability needs to be checked in each individual case. The intensity of fertilization depends on the season of the year, and the physiology and health of the plants. During the period of full growth, fertilize twice a month and if desired, you can indulge the plants with a little extra nitrogen, best of all in the form of a nitrate. Toward the end of the season, when new shoots are maturing and flowers begin to form, you limit the supply of nitrogen and replace it with phosphorus and potassium. The concentration of the fertilizer should match the lower limit recommended by the producer for indoor plants. You can alternate the use of artificial agents with the application of natural fertilizers, for example a fermented solution of cow pat: Place a fresh or dry piece of excrement taken from "healthy" grazing land in a container with rain water. Leave the cow pat to ferment and then mist the plants with the tincture. Of course it needs to be diluted before use, to the point of looking like a cup of weak tea. This unusual fertilizer provides the plants not only with nutrients, but also some important humic substances. Toward the end of the growing season, limit the use of cow pat to a minimum, until you stop fertilizing completely. Also the intervals between side-dressing with an artificial fertilizer should get longer and longer, until you apply only a minimum amount during the period of vegetational standstill.

Use a nylon fishing-line to attach the orchid clusters to a wooden support, such as a stick of elderberry. As soon as the plants take root, it is recommended to remove the line (*Nidema boothii*).

Replanting

Strictly speaking, we cannot talk about replanting as such in relation to orchids grown on suspended supports. A more accurate term to use in this case would be replacing old supports with new ones. Once every few years, the supports fall apart owing to the natural aging process. It is sometimes partly caused by the use of unsuitable water for watering, the weight of the growing bunches and the action of the roots. The plants therefore need to be reinstalled. You do so at a time when the plants do not form flowers or new shoots. Remove the orchids carefully from the old supports and cut off a substantial part of dry used-up roots. At the same time, split overgrown bunchy plants into smaller parts—but not too small, for then it takes too long for them to "catch their breath" and begin to grow at a normal pace and rhythm. After removing the plants from the old supports (and after splitting them, if desired), leave them in a dry and shady place in the greenhouse without watering them, to protect the unhealed wounds from infection. Fresh

cuts can be covered with charcoal. Only then do you attach the plants to new supports and hang them up. The plants cultivated in epiphytic baskets and flowerpots ought to be replanted more frequently. The interval between each new replanting varies according to the speed of growth of a particular orchid, the makeup and quality of the substrate and the water for watering. It is again up to every individual cultivator to decide how often to replant. A general recommendation would be, however, not to leave a plant in one substrate for more than 2-3 years.

Propagation of Orchids

It is every cultivator's objective not only to keep his or her plants in good shape and bring them to bloom, but also to propagate them. New plants can thus enrich a collection, serve as a backup in case of death of a specimen, or be used in exchanges. There are two ways to go about it: generative (sexual) and vegetative (asexual) propagation. Each has its own advantages and drawbacks.

Generative Propagation

As we have already mentioned, generative reproduction of orchids is extremely complicated, and it requires an active cooperation of certain kinds of fungi for their seeds to germinate. These fungi cannot be successfully cultivated, so in artificial conditions they are replaced with what is known as "aseptic sowing in vitro". The basic principle of this method is an effort to give the germinating orchid seeds—by means of nutritional soils (media)—the substances they get from symbiotic fungi in the wild. Nutritional soils contain both anorganic and organic material, the most important of which are minerals, carbohydrates, hormones and vitamins. Because the soil has to be tough, it is fortified with agar (gelatine extracted from seaweed). It is chiefly the presence of carbohydrates and organic substances that causes the nutritional media to rot by the action of mildew, yeast and bacteria, for which it provides an ideal place to live. That is the reason why the soils need to be sterilized

Early developmental stages (protocorm) of a terrestrial orchid *Orchis morio* cultivated in vitro.

by high temperature immediately after mixing up, and why all further manipulation with seeds and germinating plants takes place in aseptic ("infection-free") conditions with the aid of laboratory technology. Since the germinating plants are cultivated in laboratory glass, the whole method is termed "in vitro", meaning "in glass".

The whole process of aseptic sowing is rather complicated and can be successfully carried out only by well-equipped laboratories. Before the invention of sowing "in vitro" (the beginning of the 20th century), orchid cultivators and especially orchid breeders had to rely on sowing seeds into flowerpots containing mother plants, which provided the necessary infection by fungi filaments. But this method was highly unreliable and it rarely had satisfactory results. Even today, one hardly ever hears about a rare success in, especially older, greenhouses, namely a spontaneous germination of seeds and the subsequent growth of some orchid species. The photograph on page 10 presents a ten-year-old specimen of the species *Maxillaria*, which was cultivated by exactly this method!

Vegetative Propagation

An advantage of vegetative propagation carried out in the traditional way is the relatively high speed with which new plants are produced. A disadvantage is the limited number of newly produced specimens as well as the fact that they are genetically identical and therefore useless for mutual hybridization. Another drawback is a certain degree of risk of spreading infection and mold into the cuts during the division of the bunches.

Vegetative propagation can be used especially with sympodial orchids. If you want to propagate a plant whose rhizome has not branched yet, cut off the sufficiently grown front (younger) part that has an active top. The rear part will shoot out again from the backup buds. Many orchids form tiny daughter plants on the top of the pseudobulbs or even on the faded flower spikes. Long, jointed pseudobulbs, for example of the species *Dendrobium*, can be cut into pieces, the wounds treated with charcoal and placed slantwise into damp moss. The sleeping buds will "wake up" and give rise to new plants.

Monopodial orchids can be propagated vegetatively only to a limited degree. It is especially difficult in species with very short stems, for example the genus *Phalaenopsis*. Only some botanical species and subspecies of this genus have a capacity for spontaneous creation of young plants at the ends of flower scapes, whereby almost all the possibilities of vegetative propagation of these Asian orchids are exhausted. In orchids of the species *Phalaenopsis*, *Vanda* and some others, vegetative propagation takes place even when their growth tips are destroyed. The plants then shoot again from the sleeping buds, often forming up to 2-3 daughter individuals that can be separated after

Some orchid species grow daughter plants on faded flower spikes (an unknown species from Ecuador).

a while. The representatives of monopodial species with elongated stems (*Vanda*, *Holcoglossum*, *Ascocentrum*, etc.), can be vegetatively propagated by sprigging. Cut off the top part of the plant and let it root in a standard substrate; the lower part will then spontaneously form new shoots (often more than one).

Cloning

There is another highly effective way of propagation, one known as explantation. It's a cloning type of propagation of orchids which works by cultivating their dividing tissues, termed "meristemic cultivation in vitro". It is in fact a simpler version of cloning animal species—so widely popularized nowadays; the complete method had been successfully mastered much earlier—in the 1950s. This highly effective technique is based on removing and transferring the meristem—the dividing tissue—from an individual plant into sterile conditions in vitro, its subsequent multiple propagation, and a final transfer of the new small plants back into the natural environment. After being cut off from the plant, the meristem is cultivated in a liquid nutritional solution and influenced by certain hormonal substances. Soon it begins an exponential and undifferentiated division and the test tubes containing tissues are placed into a slowly rotating cylinder to prevent the formation of root and apical buds. As soon as the callus (a special cluster of cells) grows big enough to be able to divide, it can be cut into several pieces that can subsequently be cultivated. This approach can be repeated for an indefinite number of times. It is easy to get the daughter plants from the cultivated tissue: first of all, alter the cultivation medium and terminate the rotation. Soon after that, new orchids begin to form, which can later be transferred into a non-sterile environment and cultivated in a traditional way. The meristem cultivation technique is valuable especially for the producers of cut orchid flowers—one exceptional specimen can give rise to an enormous amount of identical versions, in a relatively short time. The explantation method has not yet been successfully used with the genus *Paphiopedilum*, but it has been used with the genera *Cattleya, Cymbidium, Dendrobium, Oncidium, Odontoglossum, Miltonia, Vanda*, and with many orchid hybrids that have exceptional flowers or are interesting in some other way.

Diseases and Pests

A greenhouse environment is, of course, very suitable not only for orchids, but also for a lot of diseases and pests. In general, the best way to fight harmful agents is keeping the cultivated plants in good health. That can only be achieved by consistent adherence to and meeting of the environmental needs of the cultivated plants. Diseases and pests usually begin to occur in neglected cultures as a consequence of incorrect watering, ventilation, and fertilization habits, and other cultivation errors. If you observe the rules, you will not very often need to use the "crutch" of chemical intervention, which should be resorted to only in extreme cases. However, a prerequisite of effective chemical treatment is a precise diagnosis of the pest or disease. Depending on their origin, there are four types of diseases: those of fungal, bacteria, viral and physiological origin. In addition to these, the negative activities of a whole army of animal pests must be taken into account as well.

There are a lot of effective pesticides available nowadays for destroying animal pests and fungal diseases; by using them reasonably you can keep the pathogenes within bearable limits. What you should fear more than fungal infections, which can be easily destroyed by fungicides (just take extra care not to destroy the symbiotic fungal filaments in the roots!), are invasions of animal pests. Pests that are the most harmful for plants are: slugs, mites, aphids, thrips, mealybugs, weevils and scale insects. The range of pesticides is constantly changing. When applying the pesticide, it is advisable to follow the instructions for use and repeat the spraying several times at short intervals in order to destroy all the generations of pests that are coming out one by one from hardy eggs. It also pays to use various agents alternately; using only one agent may result in producing resistant populations of pathogenous organisms. A type of protection termed biological protection is also worth mentioning. It consists in the deliberate planting of the pests' natural enemies in greenhouses

(for example, spidermites are planted against weevils). After a while, a natural balance may form in a culture, and the pests do not overpopulate. But if a pathogen that has no natural enemy in a culture overpopulates in a greenhouse, you have to resort to pesticides again. They destroy everything—the pests and their predators, and you can start again. Eggs of particular species of "protection" organisms are offered every spring by specialized companies.

Bacterioses are usually caused by a long-lasting damp coldness. The time to watch out is especially the fall when greenhouses are not heated yet and temperatures drop radically if the weather gets bad. One solution may be to intensify ventilation and limit watering temporarily. A source of infection of bacteriosis can be old, biologically noxious rain water, an unsterilized substrate, etc.

There is no "medicine" available so far for viral diseases of orchids. The only way of fighting them is a careful examination of new acquisitions to prevent spreading infection through your collection. If that happens, you have to destroy the sick specimen and thus prevent the infection from spreading onto the other plants. Sometimes, however, the viral infection is only latent—"sleeping"—in the plant and is not observable. Therefore you need to be very careful, especially when cutting into living orchid tissues (for example, during the flower harvest or vegetative propagation). Scissors and knives should be disinfected after each use (e.g., by running them through a flame) to prevent the plant juice containing viruses from spreading in the tissue of another individual. Viruses can also be spread by slugs and plant lice. Smokers, who should never be smoking when handling the plants, can even spread tobacco virus. The symptoms of a viral infection are deformations of foliage and flowers, color break streaking, chlorotic streaks and spots, and slow growth. The last on the list are diseases of physiological origin. They cause disorders in the metabolism and development of orchids. They are caused mainly by long-lasting deviations from optimum growing conditions and from the ecological requirements of the plants. The lack of some biogenic and trace elements causes disorders in the production of chlorophyll, the plants become dwarfed and their roots and newly-forming buds necrotize. Insufficient lighting causes the orchids to stretch and reduces chlorophyll, whilst too much light disables chlorophyll, the leaves turn yellow or red, and scorched; too much coldness results in the deformation of the center of growth, flower buds etc. The only cure for such troubles is maintaining optimum growing conditions.

Hybridization and Breeding of Orchids

The preceding text already tackled the fact that orchids are, in terms of their development, a very young family of plants and that their genetic instability is

An instance of an excellent intergeneric primary hybrid *Brassocattleya* Binosa (*Cattleya bicolor* x *Brassavola nodosa*)

therefore literally endless. Viable individuals can originate not only through breeding of various species within the same genera, but also through hybridization of apparently quite dissimilar and distant members of different genera. Clearly, the closer the genera are to each other genetically, the easier hybridization becomes; this knowledge is used also for a taxonomical evaluation of relations within a family. Hybridization is possible even between genera that have a completely different morphology—i.e., between sympodial and monopodial orchids. A hybrid "classic"—Veitch's *Epiphronitis* Veitchii (*Epidendrum radicans* x *Sophronitis coccinea*)—is a case in point. Interestingly, orchids that are older in their development can be hybridized with each other only very rarely; for example, all the effort put into hybridizing *Paphiopedilum* and *Phragmipedium*—two very similar genera of Venus's shoes—have so far been futile. An important issue in the hybridization of orchids is which of the parent plants assumes the role of the mother (i.e., it accepts pollen and creates seeds in pods) and which plays the role of the father, for the features of the mother usually dominate over the qualities supplied by the other sex. If you hybridize the same species reversely (that is, if you switch the role of the mother and father), the resulting hybrid usually comes out having a completely different appearance! Amateur growers are advised to focus in their breeding attempts on forming primary hybrids (that is, hybrids of two botanical species). The offspring of such combinations tend to be more uniform and stable. In hybridization and repeated hybridization of multiple hybrids, the situation is different—

the resulting offspring branches out very intensively. In order to achieve specimens that are in some way interesting, you need to cultivate a large number of seedlings into bloomable size, and then choose among them. This is, of course, a very space-demanding business. As almost all hybrids of primary origin are capable of further sexual reproduction, human hands might gradually give rise to two-generic (for example, *Brassolaeliocattleya* or *Sophrolaeliocattleya*) or multiple-generic hybrids. Many hybrids that have become classics by now have very long and precise genealogies—for they were created by a gradual combination of ten, twenty or more generations of ancestors of various parents. Apart from the increasingly more rare botanical species, supermarkets and flower shops now offer a wide choice especially of orchid multihybrids that had been cultivated in laboratories of the world's leading companies, and bred to have beautiful flowers and low cultivation demands. Dozens of original species and simpler hybrids could contribute to their creation.

The history of hybridization is as old as orchid cultivation itself. The first hybrids to grow in European greenhouses were members of the genus *Cattleya* as far back as 1852. A more widespread propagation of hybrid orchids was prevented by problems with sowing their seeds—it was very rare to achieve the stage of a seedling. After the discovery of antiseptic sowing (Knudson 1922), the quality of artificial hybridization of *Orchidaceae* reached a superlative level. A contribution to the progress in hybridization was also made by the method of meristemic cultures, which ensured a sufficient speed and volume of propagation of the best orchid clones. To date, the number of all hybrids of the family (with a small contribution from natural hybrids) is estimated to be at least 25,000!

However, humans do not only hybridize different orchid species and genera; it is also necessary to hybridize plants of the same species—for specimens of the youngest, and therefore genetically unstable,

Primary hybrids of closely related species need not be very different from their parents in appearance, but they tend to be more sizeable (a hybrid *Lycaste lanipes* x *L. ciliata*)

species are those which especially tend to form mutations. While in the wild, these deviations are suppressed and gradually disappear; orchid growers are able to stabilize them by further appropriate hybridization, and maintain the new positive qualities (it is usually their color or size of their flowers). Some collectors can thus specialize in, for example, collecting different types and forms of a single orchid species. Some of these forms are typical enough to get their own names and terminologies, as do interspecies and intergeneric hybrids.

Thanks to F. K. Sander, a famous English businessman and botanist, all newly-formed hybrids have been registered in a multivolume and continuously updated "Sander's List of Orchid Hybrids" ever since the dawn of orchid breeding (in 1869). Each new entry contains the name of the hybrid, both parent plants and the name of the breeder. Newcomers are evaluated on a global level and once a year the best of them receive prizes. A disadvantage of Sander's List is the fact that it does not mention the sex of the parents—as has been said, hybrids from the same parents whose sex roles were switched may look completely different. Although a lot has already been accomplished in the field of orchid hybridization, the job is far from done. No matter how scientific and organized the breeding of orchids pretends to be, there is still enough room left for empirical experiments by "crazy" amateur enthusiast experimenters—and it may well be that some more as yet unknown secrets of the world of orchids are waiting to be revealed by them...

The Most Significant Groups of Hybrid Orchids

Nearly all the members of the family *Orchidaceae* can be hybridized with each other; however, some more significant groups of orchid hybrids stand out over the others—mainly due to the priceless service they have done to the world's ornamental and productive gardening.

Among the best known and the most popular with both commercial and amateur growers are hybrids of the genus *Cymbidium*. These plants have a long-standing tradition—their undemanding temperature requirements and the fact that they bloom in winter made them, until very recently, the only substantial source of orchid flowers used for cutting. Not even after the cut flowers market became globalized (through better opportunities for commerce and especially for travel) were these flowers swept away from flower shop counters. One of the assets of the *Cymbidium* genus hybrids are robust, erect or semi-erect inflorescences of relatively large flowers of many shades of pastel colors. The flowers are not only very stiff but also exceptionally durable—they will hold out for up to two months on the plants, and for only a little less time in vases placed in cooler rooms! A disadvantage of these orchids is their robust size (the streaky leaves are sometimes over 3.3 ft/ 1 m in size), which prevents amateur growers from getting larger numbers of *Cymbidia* for their orchid collections. Large-scale market gardens cultivate only the best clones of the *Cymbidium* multihybrids, propagated by meristemic cultures.

Colorful hybrids of the genus *Cymbidium* are available in stores mainly in the winter.

Hybrids of the genus *Paphiopedilum* come in highly diverse shapes and colors. The photo on the left shows a hybrid *Paphiopedilum* Harrisianum cultivated for 130 years, now an absolute classic.

There is also a great tradition of breeding the popular genus ***Paphiopedilum***; and there are entire interest groups of enthusiasts who hybridize and describe an endless stream of new cultivars of this genus. There is an abundance of outstanding and distinct members of the genus to bring them satisfaction. Plus, new species (in other words, new sources of genetic information) are being continuously discovered in the

wild. To date, over 13,000 hybrids of the genus *Paphiopedilum* have been cultivated! Hybrid Venus's shoes are among the most handsome orchids—their large wax-hard leaves are distinguished by an interesting shape and color, as well as a remarkable durablity. For their noble appearance and color they are sometimes regarded as a kind of orchid aristocracy. Their positive qualities include fairly low

The tried-and-true beauty of *Paphiopedilum* Maudiae— a classic among hybrids.

The most productive and least demanding Venus's shoe hybrid, *Paphiopedilum* Lathamianum

Phalaenopsis hybrids speckled with dots are highly sought-after by cultivators.

their outstanding flowers; of late, however, they have been appearing in bouquets less often owing to their fragility, to give way to the cheaper and equally beautiful hybrids of the genus *Vanda* and the species *Dendrobium phalaenopsis*. However, they have become an object of interest both for amateur growers and producers of potted flowers. Hybrids of the genus Phalaenopsis are perhaps the most suitable orchids for open-grown cultivation in modern apartments. They are well equipped for that—their succulence makes them tolerant of dry apartment air without much trouble; they are thermophilic and therefore do not mind higher temperatures in winter (rather the opposite). Their low lighting requirements are not insignificant either. From the producers' perspective, what matters is also the record-breaking short time span between sowing the seeds and achieving bloomable plants—this time span has been shortened to 2-3 years! Most of the original cultivars had white and pink to purple flowers, but recently multihybrids with yellow, star-shaped, striped and dotted flowers have taken center stage. Small-flowered hybrids that originated for example from the genus *P. equestris* are also making it back onto the market.

Perhaps the largest group of hybrid orchids are hybrids of the orchid subtribe *Laeliinae* (a group associating "close relatives"—the genera **Cattleya, Laelia, Schomburgkia, Brassavola, Rhyncholaelia,**

The striped flowers of this *Phalaenopsis* hybrid are among the prettiest.

cultivation demands and a relatively short time span between the sowing of the seeds and the first bloom (4-5 years); a disadvantage that needs to be mentioned is the fact that some bunches are not very robust and that every cluster of leaves shoots out only one flower spike. The genus seems to be undergoing something like an "overbreeding" nowadays, in that some multihybrids' genealogies are excessively complex, while they can hardly compete in appearance with the historically first primary hybrids or hybrids with only modest genealogies, a lot of which have remained unrivaled and are still popular with cultivators. One of them is a Venus's shoe of the name P. Harrisianum (a hybrid of the genera *P. barbatum* x *P. villosum*), which was cultivated in 1869 as the very first intergenous hybrid of the genus *Paphiopedilum*. Another cultivar similar to P. Harrisianum is the still notable white-and-green cultivar P. Maudiae, and also P. Lathamianum—a cultivar not very remarkable as to its color, but easy to cultivate and readily blooming. Hybrid Venus's shoes are universally employed nowadays as a source of cut flowers, potted plants suitable for open-grown cultivation in apartments, and, last but not least, as undemanding and spectacular gems of specialized collections.

In the 20th century, the plants of the genus **Phalaenopsis** were bred chiefly for the cutting of

Brassocattleya Pernosa, a hundred-year-old primary hybrid, is also popular with growers of small epiphytic orchids.

Sophronitis and others). The members of all the listed genera are characterized by outstanding flowers on the one hand, and easy hybridization on the other hand. The first hybrids were cultivated by crossing various *Cattleya* orchids with each other and with orchids of the genus *Laelia*. In the course of time, species of the genera *Brassavola* and *Rhyncholaelia* "joined the club". The overall number of all the hybrids often created by multiple hybridization of the original species of the entire subtribe is now estimated to be 12,000-13,000! Usually the large-flowered hybrids have been bred to bear showy flowers of lavish shapes in the following colors: purple, white, white with a contrasting lip, red, yellow and orange, bluish, greenish, and others. They used to be used as a source of exclusive cut flowers, and their even bigger upswing was prevented by a relatively small number of flowers per inflorescence (i.e., low productivity), a usually short flower spike rendering them useless for classical bouquets, and in many cases the enormous size of the plants. Nowadays, the hybrids of the subtribe *Laeliinae* are popular mainly with amateur growers; besides the assets already mentioned, it is also important that they do not have high cultivation demands. Nevertheless, they do not tend to be on offer in flower shops and supermarkets very often, and the

Every orchid admirer knows numerous *Cattleya* hybrids.

The gorgeous and exceptionally durable flowers of this primary *Miltonia* hybrid (*M. spectabilis* var. *moreliana* x *M. clowesii*) will glamorize any collection of epiphytic orchids.

only places you can find them are specialized orchid companies.

Breeding of the genus **Dendrobium** has not yet gained sufficient appreciation and development; still, two suggested directions can be observed in it. The first one is a thorough breeding of the individual species *D. phalaenopsis*, which is becoming an ever-more popular source of cut flowers worldwide. A large number of different cultivars of distinct colors and shapes of this species have been created, but most of them are grown exclusively in farms in Southeast Asia and Hawaii. Commercial plants do not thrive in Europe, and therefore only the cut and cooled inflorescences are imported here. Hybrids of the species *D. nobile*

and the like have a similar function—they only serve as beautiful specimens for amateur collections and orchid shows. Since the genus *Dendrobium* includes a large number of distinct species of various shapes, the sphere of the cultivators' activity is in the case of this genus potentially very large.

Hybrids of the genus **Vanda** are also very beautiful and very popular. But amateur cultivators stand in awe of them. No wonder: the overwhelming majority of the relatively pricy cultivars are not eager to bloom in these latitudes, and their growth is very lazy. Most generic and intergeneric hybrids are grown in Thailand, Hawaii and other tropical countries, and their outstanding blossoms are cultivated for cutting.

As many as 1,500 hybrids within the genus *Vanda* have been registered. But orchids of the genus *Vanda* are easily hybridized with related genera—there are hybrids known as *Ascocenda* (*Ascocentrum* x *Vanda*), *Renantanda* (*Renanther* x *Vanda*) and *Rhynchovanda* (*Rhynchostylis* x *Vanda*). Importers of orchids to Europe have begun to include the interesting inflorescences of these plants in their offers.

The genus **Renanthera** as such is widely used for thoroughbreeding of cultivars suitable for the cutting of flowers of interesting colors. Apart from intergeneric hybrids, special hybrids known as *Renanthopsis* (*Renanthera* x *Phalaenopsis*) are worthy of remark: they help (so far without much success) introduce red-colored flowers into the fairly dull and unchanging community of hybrids of the genus *Phalaenopsis*. Their cultivation and use are similar to those of hybrids of the genus *Vanda*.

Hybrids of the genus **Oncidium** have so far played a secondary role—owing to the fact that the flowers of the original species are rather small and do not gain in size or change their shape even through hybridization. If you ever come across hybrids of *Oncidium* at all, it will most likely be the primary hybrids of the basic species, sold as potted plants in supermarkets. More attractive for amateur growers tend to be the colorful epiphytic hybrids of the genus *Tolumnia* (which has recently been excluded from the genus *Oncidium*). It is mainly the species *T. variegata* that has been used for creating tiny succulent plants.

Stores frequently offer potted plants with the tongue-twisting name **Vuylstekeara**. These are hybrids created between the genera *Cochlioda*, *Miltonia* and *Odontoglossum*, characterized by richly red, flat foliage. Their big asset is, apart from an almost kitschy attractiveness, the extraordinary durability of the flowers. However, they are rarely cultivate for cut flowers. Even the parent genus of **Miltonia** is often used for producing hybrids in flowerpots—the large flat flowers resemble pansies in appearance. Approximately 350 intergeneric hybrids within the genus have been registered, with the best of them being propagated large-scale by explantation cultures. The plants are not very suitable for epiphytic cultivation and thrive better in flowerpots. The range of potted orchids includes also hybrids of the genus **Odontoglossum** (**Lemboglossum**), the number of which exceeds 1,800 and which tend to be somewhat more demanding and suitable only for well-tended orchid collections. The genus *Odontoglossum* has served as a basis for the widely sold potted cultivars known as *Odontioda* (*Odontoglossum* x *Cochlioda*) and *Odontonia* (*Odontoglossum* x *Miltonia*).

The Conservation of Orchids in the World

Orchids are an extremely endangered group of plants all around the globe. As highly specialized organ-

isms, they find it very hard to cope with the radical and drastic human interventions into the wild nature. The reason for their demanding requirements for the immutability of the ecological conditions of the environment is their symbiotic relation with fungi, and the complicated process of germination of orchid seeds. Any slight change in the plants' environment may harm or completely destroy the fungal hyphas on which the plants' existence depends. For that reason, orchids can die out even in a relatively unharmed area that appears completely "healthy" at first glance. Morever, a process known as "cultivating the land" is becoming widespread at a rapid rate throughout the tropical region. Thousands of hectares of rainforests and mountain forests are being insensitively lumbered and turned into dry, erosion-ridden, cultivated semi-steppes, or, less destructively, into monocultural ground covers of fast-growing and often unindigenous wood species. The autochthonous vegetal societies thus dissapear irretrievably along with entire natural ecosystems. Only a small number of orchids has a chance to take root in secondary stations—for example, on fruit trees, in parks, on balks, or in planted forests with an

Some orchids "move house" from cutover rainforests to secondary locations, such as trees in fruit orchards (the western slope of the Andes in Ecuador). The species make-up of the resulting societies cannot compare with the richness of the original vegetation communities.

artificial, humanly designed combination of woods. But people also endanger orchids directly: *Orchidaceae* are martyrs to the desire of humans to surround themselves with exceptional, attractive and beautiful things. "Hunters" of new ornamental plant species have had their eyes on *Orchidaceae* for many years, and the orchid trade has assumed global and mass dimensions. The interest of numerous specialized amateur collectors who hunt for the rarest orchids, no holds barred, is also harmful for them. Considering the often desperate economic situation in the Third world (i.e., places where an overwhelming majority of orchid collection items occur), there is no wonder that many newly-discovered or otherwise "high-profile" species are becoming completely extinct in the wild soon after their popularization, and the plants only eke a living in collection greenhouses. The more limited the geographical range is of particular attractive plants in the wild, the rarer they are, and so much the worse for them! The so-called experts and scientists also represent a threat for orchids, because they feel entitled to handle orchids any way they like, pleading the excuse of being personally qualified and among the chosen few.

To mitigate at least partially the negative and sometimes devastating effect of human activity on the world population of orchids, the whole family *Orchidaceae* was entered on the CITES lists. CITES stands for Convention on International Trade in Endangered Species. By ratifying it, a country commits to introduce certain laws and measures for controlling, limiting and even prohibiting international (and also intrastate) trade with some endangered plants and animals. On account of the high degree of endangerment, all botanical species of orchids, with no exception, have been listed in "Appendix 2"— a category of plant and animal species that "are not currently threatened with extinction, but may become so unless trade is strictly regulated to avoid over-exploitation." Even more endangered and much more strictly protected are the species enetered in "Appendix 1", including all the "pure-blooded" representatives of the genera *Paphiopedilum, Phragmipedium*, and some species, such as *Dendrobium cruentum, Cattleya trianae, Laelia jongheana, L. lobata, Renanthera imschootana* and *Vanda coerulea*.

It is practically impossible for an ordinary nature enthusiast to privately collect any orchid species in the wild and transport them across the border. Unless you obtain the appropriate export and import permits, or also, if necessary, a phytopathological certificate, it is prohibited to transport even plants grown in artificial cultures. Very strict controls are imposed even on field collections by botanical gardens employees, and they require a large number of permits. Unfortunately, although the international conservation of orchids has brought some improvements, it has by no means been followed through. Many measures that have been taken either didn't hit

home, or worse, had the opposite effect! For example, certain species became so attractive by being entered into the "Appendix 1" list that the remainder of their populations soon fell prey to merciless invasions of collectors and smugglers. In countries where orchids grow in the wild, companies known as "cultivation farms" have sprung up like mushrooms, which often "launder" illicit collections of botanical species under the guise of artificial cultivation of hybrid orchids. Many individuals (including employees of botanical gardens) then do not pay these companies for actual plants, but merely for documents necessary for exporting orchids, which they subsequently collect by themselves in the wild nature of the particular country, and pass them off as artificially cultivated hybrids. Perhaps the most endangered species of today are Venus's shoes of the genus *Paphiopedilum* (mainly the new species that are often found in sporadic and small localities in some areas in communist China and Vietnam that have until recently been inaccessible), and some orchids growing in small populations in Brazilian mountains along the coast of the Atlantic. It seems that humans will absolutely never learn, and not only in the world of orchids...

Ways of obtaining collection plants

Even though "wild" collections of the family *Orchidaceae* by individuals and companies are prevented by strict conservation measures, there are still many legal ways left of obtaining orchids for your own pleasure. You can buy orchids of various shapes and in various places (all the plants on offer ought to come from artificial cultures). Even the orchid trade is controlled by the firm hand of the market economy, and everything is a matter of supply and demand. People who do not want to dig too deep into their pockets to buy an orchid have to settle for quality hybrids in flowerpots. They are available both in flower shops and supermarkets. Although most of these multiple hybrids can be converted to the epiphytic way of cultivation, this can prove difficult owing to their rather robust size and paradoxically also their excessive vitality, which will soon "make sure" that they do not fit into the small cultivation equipment. Getting your hands on botanical species and "pedigree" hybrids is more complicated and often much more expensive. "Pure" plants are offered by various private companies; addresses of sellers are available in magazines about plants. A lot more contact information is available on the Internet, but a certain degree of patience is recommended in searching for them, as there are tens of thousands of links available on the worldwide web, rendering the situation rather chaotic. Many orchid species can be ordered abroad; transportation costs may be an obstacle, however, and it is therefore advisable to place bulk orders. Other ways include exchanges of propagated species between individual growers. The

Places like this one, with hardly any human intervention, are quickly disappearing from the face of earth (Rio Pastaza in the eastern foothills of the Ecuadorian Andes).

plants can also be purchased at specialized orchid shows organized in big cities in spring and fall. Organizers of such events usually arrange the selling of extras—the sellers being the orchid growers themselves, who are able to provide potential buyers with expert advice and consultation. Orchids are available for purchase also at the ever-more popular terraristic fairs.

Tropical Orchids

This chapter will introduce you to over 500 tropical orchids—either epiphytic orchids, which form the overwhelming majority of orchids presented, or ground growers (known as "terrestrial"). All the important facts concerning orchids have been discussed in the previous chapters, and the only thing left to mention is a note on the terminology of the representatives of the gigantic family *Orchidaceae*. The genetic instability and the incredibly high number of species cause problems not only for the systematics of newly discovered orchids, but also in the taxonomy of those orchids that have been well known for a long time. To place some members of the family *Orchidaceae* correctly in the taxonomical system is often a hard nut to crack not only for amateurs but also for experts. They find differences, for instance, in the structure of the flowers and other organs, in their genetic equipment, ecology etc., that are hardly noticable to a layperson's eyes. Many species are often repeatedly renamed and transfered from one genus to another. Even within individual species we can sometimes find a great many deviations and variations, which can be raised by contemporary taxonomical methods to new "pure" species. However, their validity is very debatable in many cases and depends only on the subjective evaluation and opinion of any given expert. An ordinary orchid lover should not worry too much about these problems, and stick to the old traditional nomenclature instead, and especially enjoy the unique beauty and exotic shapes of the various species of the queen of the realm of plants—whatever their names are at a given moment...

Acacallis cyanea □ ■ ☺

INTERMEDIATE

A very handsome orchid, but very rare in collections. Its unifoliate pseudobulbs are reduced and covered with bracts, the flower spike is arched over and bears 3-7 rather large and ornamental flowers. The somewhat shell-shaped lip is brown-and-red, with bluish tepals pointed at the ends. The cultivation has no special features: the species is grown epiphytically in semishade on a twig or a piece of bark. It blooms in early summer and comes from the Rio Negro river basin in Brazil.

Ada aurantiaca ■ ☺

CRYOPHILIC-INTERMEDIATE

The genus *Ada* includes only two species, which resemble the representatives of the genus *Odontoglossum* in appearance. From the cultivator's perspective, it is mainly its richly colored flowers that are valuable. Its pseudobulbs are up to 4 in/10 cm tall, with 1 to 8 in/2-3 to 20 cm long belt-shaped leaves. The flower spike does not overtop the leaves and is arched, with up to 15 extraordinary flowers deployed on it. All the tepals are thin and pointed and their orange-red color attracts attention from a distance. Cultivation is not very easy—the plants are demanding in a similar manner to the cryophilic species of the genus *Odontoglossum*. A summer stay in overheated greenhouses is a sure way of destroying the orchid. The species is therefore recommended only for cultivators who are able to provide their plants with cool conditions, or transfer them to a garden in the summer. The plants thrive in semi-shade, provided that they get appropriate ventilation and sufficiently frequent misting. The flowering season comes between January and March, and the orchid's original home is in the midlands and highlands of the Colombian Andes.

Left: *Ada aurantiaca*

Acacallis cyanea

Aerangis carnea

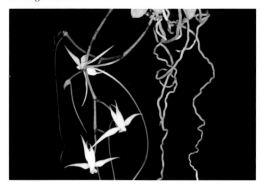

Aerangis carnea ▫ ☺

INTERMEDIATE-THERMOPHILIC

All of the approximately 70 members of the genus *Aerangis* come from the tropical regions of Africa (including Madagascar). These are small, mostly epiphytic orchids with surprisingly large and beautiful flowers, arranged in racemes of several flowers on each; they are usually white and open wide. The lip is flat and resembles the other tepals in appearance. In spite of their unquestionable beauty, these orchids are not included in collections as frequently as they deserve to be. This is also surprising because their cultivation is not very complicated: they are grown epiphytically on a bare slab of wood or bark, or in flowerpots with a very permeable substrate. Another possibility is placing them in a basket made of soft plaiting. The plants require warm moisture and semi-shade. After the flowers fade away, and

Aerangis citrata

also in winter, it is recommended to "hold them up" a little by placing them in temperate conditions and cutting back watering. *A. carnea* has white flowers equipped with a conspicuous spur, and it flowers in the fall and in the winter.

Aerangis citrata ▫ ☺

INTERMEDIATE-THERMOPHILIC

This species differs slightly from its closest relatives by the color of the flowers—they are waxy and pale-yellow. In cultivation and during the winter flowering season, the yellow fades considerably, as in the case of the specimen in the photograph. *A. citrata* has a long, thick stem up to 4 in/10 cm tall, bearing 6-10 egg-shaped leaves that are about 6 in/15 cm long and 1.2 in/3 cm wide. The ends of the leaves are, somewhat atypically, almost symmetrical, with a single point at the ends. A large number (up to 30) of smallish flowers grows on an overhanging spike that is up to 8 in/20 cm long. The waxy and pale-yellow to whitish flowers are embellished by a 1.2 in/3 cm long, yellowish spur. The cultivation requirements are the same as with the other members of the genus. It blooms in early spring and it occurs in the wild in Madagascar.

Aerangis kirkii ▫ ☺

INTERMEDIATE-THERMOPHILIC

A characteristic feature of the flowers of all the representatives of the genus *Aerangis* are their fairly

Aerangis kirkii

long spurs containing nectar to attract pollinators. The white flowers of the species *A. kirkii* are likewise equipped with arched spurs, up to 1.6. in/4 cm long. In a similar manner to the other *Aerangis* orchids, the leaves of *A. kirkii* are unsymmetrically ended (along a horizontal axis)—the tip of each leaf assumes the shape of round lobes of various sizes, divided from each other by a central nerve. The leaves are typically arranged in two rows. The plant blooms in winter and spring and comes from Madagascar.

Aeranthes ramosa   ⊡ ▣ ☺

INTERMEDIATE-THERMOPHILIC

The representatives of this genus come from the African south—most of the total of 40 species grow in Madagascar. All the members of the genus have dramatically shortened monopodial stems, and their tepals are often almost transparent and run into long pointed tips at the ends. The short stem of *A. ramosa* bears a total of 5-7 leaves that are 6-10 in/15-25 cm long and are arranged in two rows. The wiry flower spike grows to the length of 12 in/30 cm and bears 1-2 green-and-yellow flowers of a curious, almost glass-like appearance. Their tepals and lip are pointed at the ends. Part of the ca 1.5 in/3-4 cm big flowers is a spur with a blunt end. The rules of cultivation are the same as with the genus *Aerangis* (see *A. carnea*). The plant blooms in the fall and comes from central and eastern Madagascar, just like its close relative, *A. grandiflora*.

Aerides   ▣ ☹ ☺

THERMOPHILIC

The genus *Aerides* is closely related to the genus *Vanda*, and shares the same ecological requirements and the structure of green body parts: an elongated stem that keeps growing at the end bears two thick rows of firm and resistant succulent foliage. The smallish flowers grow in multiple, thick, overhanging, cylindrical racemes and are very richly colored. The flower lip is equipped with a conical, spur-shaped protuberance that is usually bent forward. Cultivating the botanical species, and also some hybrids, of the genus *Aerides* is traditional mainly in the United States; in European collections, the *Aerides* are very rarely found. The plants are grown in a similar way as in the case of the genus *Vanda*. They require a warm to very warm environment with a maximum possible amount of diffused light, relatively infrequent misting and very good ventilation. Ideal seems to be cultivation in small wooden baskets with a handful of coarse epiphytic substrate inside. The succulent structure of *Aerides* argues their ability to resist drought, which enables them to thrive when open-grown in well-lighted apartments. The genus *Aerides* includes over 60 orchid species (the species *A. houlletiana* in the photograph is an example), growing epiphytically or on rocks. These Asian orchids have a very wide area of occurrence: it reaches up to Southern China and New Guinea in the northeast, although most species can be found in the Himalayas, Burma, the Phillipines and Indonesia.

Aerides houlletiana

Alamania punicea

Alamania punicea   ⊡   ☹

CRYOPHILIC-INTERMEDIATE

A walk through a thick, well-grown oak forest can indeed be a very pleasant experience. And all the more so, if everywhere you look you see brick-red clusters of orchids peeping at you like Chinese lanterns hanging on the dark tree tops! No mere fantasy, for this is exactly what it looks like when you find the rare and beautiful orchids *A. punicea*. The species *A. punicea* resembles the genus *Sophronitis* a little in appearance; its pseudo-bulbs are very reduced, with their lower halves pressed against the support and ended with 1-2 reddish, dark green and slightly thickened leaves. The orange blooms grow in clusters with several heads on each, they can be

Amesiella philippinensis

0.8 in/ 2 cm across at most, and they literally shine into space. Although you could hardly find an orchid lover who would not like to grow this orchid, it is very rare in cultivation. The problem is that in order to prosper, it needs a very specific environment of the tropical mountain forest—a constant breeze that is not very warm, an almost permanent fog, rain and a lot of light. These conditions can rarely be provided in artificial cultures. *A. punicea* blooms in March to April and comes from Mexico.

Amesiella philippinensis   □   ⊡   ☺   ☺

INTERMEDIATE-THERMOPHILIC

A tiny epiphyte with a short stem and singular flowers—what more can an orchid grower wish for! The shortened stem is covered with up to 2.2 in/5.5 cm long thick leaves arranged in two rows, and the very short flower spike bears 1-3 exceptionally large flowers (up to 2 in/5 cm in diameter). The tepals are white, the inside of the three-lobe lip is honey-brown. The cultivation is the same as with the genus *Angraecum* (the monotypic genus *Amesiella* was excluded from it in 1972). The plant blooms in spring and comes from the Philippines.

Ancistrochilus rothschildianus

Angraecum distichum

Ancistrochilus rothschildianus □ ■ ☺

INTERMEDIATE-THERMOPHILIC

Characteristic of the small and not very well-known genus *Ancistrochilus* are wide conical pseudobulbs, up to 1.2 in/3 cm tall, with 2-3 leaves. The short flower spikes bear 3-4 big showy flowers. The purple lip is three-lobed and extended into a narrow bent pointed protuberance. The tepals are narrow and pointed, and purplish white. *Ancistrochilus rothschildianus* is an epiphytic orchid that requires similar conditions to those of the indeciduous *Dendrobia*—warm semi-shade, plentiful watering and fertilization in the summer, and a temperate environment with the maximum amount of light and careful reduction of misting in the winter. The flowers appear on the plant in the summer. The species occurs in the tropical west of Africa.

Angraecum distichum □ □ ☺

THERMOPHILIC

A tiny orchid with the appearance of a strange trailing succulent—its physical parameters and shape distinguish it radically from the rest of the genus. *A. distichum* has overhanging or trailing stems, 4-6 in/10-15 cm tall, with thickened leaves, 0.4. in/1 cm in size at most, arranged in two thick rows. Individual white flowers grow out of the axils of the leaves and they have a hood-shaped lip with a spur pointing backward. The species is popular with growers as a curiosity and a miniature "complementary" orchid that will not adorn a collection with its flowers but with its interesting and rather rapidly growing bunches. Cultivation is not complicated—the plant will settle for a suspended slab of bark or a twig with a handful of moss, occasional misting and semi-shade. In the winter, provide the plant with a somewhat cooler—temperate environment and reduce

misting. The orchid blooms in late summer but flowers can sometimes appear in other seasons as well. *A. distichum* comes from the tropical west of Africa.

Angraecum germynianum □ ■ ☺

THERMOPHILIC

In contrast to the previously mentioned species, *A. germynianum* has an appearance typical of the entire genus: members of the genus *Angraecum* are usually of a bigger build, with a more or less elongated stem covered with two thick rows of leaves. The flowers shoot out either one by one, or more often in clusters, and they are white. The most beautiful feature of the flower of the species in the photograh is its shell-shaped lip with a conspicuously extended spur; these are also characteristic traits of the genus. Cultivation of all the members of the genus is fairly simple. The most robust plants need to be planted in flowerpots with a coarse epiphytic mix; smaller species are happier if attached to a slab of bark or twig. Provide larger supports for the climbing species. Other cultivation rules are identical with the care of the species *A. distichum*. The species *A. germynianum* blooms in the fall and early spring, and it comes from the tropical west of Africa.

Angraecum germynianum

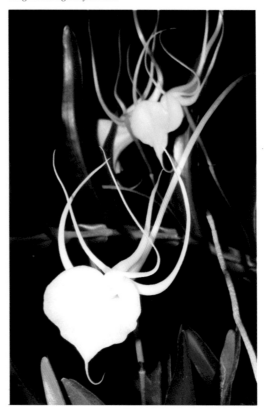

Angraecum scottianum

of over 40 in/1 m. The leaves are tough, in the shape of a narrow belt, and up to 12 in/30 cm long. The spikes are arched over and bear 2-4 star-shaped flowers. Their size is almost surprisingly large for an African orchid—the flowers are often over 5 in/12 cm in diameter! All the tepals including the lip are snow-white, widening at the base and narrowing at the top into a pointed tip. Another notable feature is unquestionably their giant greenish spur, which can grow up to a truly record-breaking length of 12 in/30 cm!

A. sesquipedale should be cultivated in the same way as the related species; its size makes it suitable only for growers who dispose of spacious cultivating equipment. It blooms in the winter and its home is in what is left of wild nature on the island of Madagascar.

Anguloa uniflora

CRYOPHILIC-INTERMEDIATE

The small genus *Anguloa* includes no more than 10 "good" species—they are easily distinguishable from closely related orchids by their characteristically structured and only partly open flowers. The members of this genus are in some languages called "tulip" orchids, apparently for their obvious likeness to the flowers of the famous spring bulbous plants. The species *A. uniflora* has rather robust pseudobulbs with 2-4 flabby leaves, fimbriated lengthways. Individual flowers that are later carried up on long flower spikes,

Angraecum sesquipedale

Angraecum scottianum

THERMOPHILIC

This species has a thin, overhanging stem that is up to 12 in/30 cm long and covered with terete leaves of about 4 in/10 cm in length. The white and relatively big (up to 2.4 in/6 cm) flowers are borne singly or in pairs. They have a snow-white and typically shell-shaped lip with a long, narrow spur pointing backward. The other tepals are yellowish. The species is rather easy to cultivate (see previous representatives of the genus), it blooms in late summer and in the fall. It was discovered in the Comoro Islands.

Angraecum sesquipedale

INTERMEDIATE-THERMOPHILIC

The genus *Angraecum* is one of the largest groups of African orchids—it includes up to 200 epiphytic, lithophytic and even terrestrial species. The most typical, best-known and the most often cultivated species is *A. sesquipedale*, even though it is not very suitable for amateur collections where space is limited because it is rather robust. The species has a thick, lignifying stem that is densely covered with leaves, and grows to a size

Anguloa uniflora

reason why various synonyms are used to describe this orchid in different publications (for example, *A. africana, A. congoensis, A. gigantea, A. humilis*). The partite pseudobulbs are really huge—they reach lengths of up to 24 in/60 cm and are embellished with a tuft of 4-7 lanceolate, leathery and very long leaves. The flower panicles grow terminally—i.e., from a growth top between the leaves. The inflorescence is up to 12 in/30 cm long and consists of 10-15 flowers that are 1.2 in/3 cm in size. The three-lobe lip has a characteristically shaped triad of yellow keels; the tepals are yellowish and covered with brown spots. Cultivation is easy: the epiphytic orchid thrives when placed in a temperate environment and provided with standard watering, fertilization and ventilation. It blooms in early spring—from March till May—and comes from extensive areas in the west, east and south of Africa.

Ansellia nilotica

are formed at the base of the pseudobulbs. The flowers are greenish to purple-white, covered with fine purple dots and embellished with a yellowish spot in the centers. The tepals assume a typically helmet-like shape on the upper part of the flower, and on the lower part they form a chin-like protuberance that is impossible to overlook. Cultivation is not very complicated: cultivate the plant epiphytically in a temperate environment, and in winter indulge it in a somewhat cooler period of rest. It blooms in late spring and in the summer and occurs in the wild in the South American Andes between Colombia and Peru.

Ansellia nilotica   ■ ☺

INTERMEDIATE

The variable *A. nilotica* has an interesting taxonomical history: the originally described 6 species of the genus were gradually reduced to only one. That is the

Arachnis flos-aeris

liaged. Likewise, the inflorescences are often sparse in flowers. *Arachnis* orchids have highly genus-specific flowers with falcate tepals and a chin-shaped spur at the base of the lip. Plants of this genus are, either in their botanical forms or as parents of many hybrids, grown for cut flowers—especially in farms in Thailand, Malaysia and Hawaii, where they are grown under the open sky. The species *A. flos-aeris* can be quite un-wieldy, as its continuously growing stems reach heights of up to 13 ft/4 m and the inflorescences can grow to be 5 ft/1.5 m in size! The gradually blooming showy flowers are up to 3.6 in/9 cm in diameter and are green-and-yellow with brown spots. This species photographed in Borneo blooms from August to November and is also native to mainland Malaysia, Sumatra and Java.

Arachnis flos-aeris ▣ ■ ☺

THERMOPHILIC

The Asian genus *Arachnis* has a very fitting name, for its flowers bear an obvious resemblance to spiders (the Greek word "*arachne*" means spider). The plants are closely related to the genus *Vandopsis*, except for the stems of *Arachnis* orchids are very thin and sparsely fo-

Ascocentrum ampullaceum ▣ ■ ⊗

THERMOPHILIC

This species represents another stem-growing genus from tropical Asia. Their likeness to the tiny representatives of the genus *Vanda* makes *Ascocentrum* orchids extremely popular among orchid lovers. Even their rather high and often unpredictable cultivation needs have done little to diminish this popularity. *A. ampullaceum* is a pleasantly tiny plant—its stem can reach the height of 6-7 in/15-18 cm with two thick rows of foliage. The leaves can grow to be

Ascocentrum ampullaceum

Ascocentrum miniatum

longed light shock, which causes them to stagnate, grow no roots and often not blossom for years. *A. miniatum* is similar to *A. ampullaceum* in terms of its habits, but its leaves are narrower and its flowers are yellow, yellow-orange and orange-red. There is no difference between the cultivation requirements of the two species. Give the plants maximum warmth and sunlight; the environment does not need to be very moist—the plants are quite happy even when grown out in the open on sunlit apartment windowsills. Make sure to prevent the leaves from being scorched by direct sunlight if grown in a glassed, poorly ventilated environment. Watering must correspond to the state of the roots and season of the year; decrease it in winter, along with temperature. Grow the plants in epiphytic baskets filled with a coarse growing mix, or attach them to wooden supports. The plants can be propagated vegetatively by removing sufficiently matured lateral shoots. *A. miniatum* blooms in May and June and can be found in Malaysia, Java and Borneo.

Ascocentrum semiteretifolium

THERMOPHILIC

Not all the representatives of the genus are as attractive in appearance as the two previously mentioned species. *A. semiteretifolium* is one of the small-flowered epiphytes suitable only for the staunchest enthusiasts of thermophilic "*Vanda*-like" Asian orchids; besides being inconspicuous, they are very difficult to cultivate. *A. semiteretifolium* also differs from its closest relatives in its sparse, fleshy leaves that are almost orbiculate in cross-section. Sometimes partly open flowers, 0.4 in/1 cm in size, grow in sparse short inflorescences and are purple red, with a tinge of white on the outside. Grow them as you would the previously mentioned species. *A. semiteretifolium* blooms between February and April and comes from Thailand.

Ascocentrum semiteretifolium

4 in/10 cm long, are exceptionally firm and tough, and are resistant even to direct tropical sunshine. The flowers grow in dense, erect inflorescences that can reach the height of up to 4 in/10 cm. They are up to 0.8 in/2 cm long and their shiny cerise-pink color is pleasing to the eye. *A. ampullaceum* is an avid sunbather—in the wild it can even grow on completely barren rocks facing south. This causes problems in cultivating not only *A. ampullaceum* but all the other *Ascocentrum* orchids as well: the plants literally starve in the winter, and in the summer they seem to struggle when exposed to too much daylight, which may result in their slow growth and unwillingness to bloom. Tend to the plants as you would to the genus *Vanda*. The flowering season for *A. ampullaceum* comes in late spring, and the species makes its home in the lower elevations of the Himalayas, Burma and Thailand.

Ascocentrum miniatum

THERMOPHILIC

Ascocentrum orchids are very difficult to cultivate: their seedlings obtained in European laboratories grow extremely slowly after being transferred to a normal environment, and imported flowers are quite lazy and unwilling to adapt. They experience pro-

Aspasia lunata

Aspasia variegata

Aspasia variegata   ▣ ☺

INTERMEDIATE

This species has, in contrast to the previous species, slightly bigger pseudobulbs and smaller belt-shaped (up to 6 in/15 cm long) leaves. The flowers are showy, up to 2 in/5 cm in size, with a ruffled three-lobe lip adorned with purple, and with two yellow spots in the center. The tepals are greenish, with brown lengthwise dashed lining. The plant's ecological needs are almost identical with those of *A. lunata*, except that it is perhaps a little more thermophilic. It should be grown epiphytically on a piece of bark or twig of an appropriate size. It blooms in early spring and it was discovered in northern Brazil, Guiana and Trinidad.

Aspasia lunata   ▣ ☺

INTERMEDIATE

The small genus *Aspasia* numbering approximately ten members grows epiphytically or lithophytically, and resembles the genus *Odontoglossum* in appearance. The species *A. lunata* is popular among growers for its showy-colored flowers. It forms a somewhat trailing rhizome with distanced pseudobulbs that reach 2 in/5 cm in height and bear two leaves at the top and several smaller leaves at the base. The flowers are up to 1.6 in/4 cm in size and grow individually or in pairs on short flower spikes. The lip is flat and white with pink-purple venation and a spot in the center. The green tepals covered with brown spots harmonize well with the lip. Cultivation is manageable even for a novice orchid lover: the plant thrives if attached to a wooden support and placed in semi-shade, with a normal dosage of misting and good ventilation. You can reduce temperature somewhat in the winter. In early spring—April to May—the species blooms eagerly. *A. lunata* comes from Brazil.

Baptistonia echinata   ☺

INTERMEDIATE

A rare epiphyte, closely related to the genus *Oncidium*. The only representative of the whole genus is a very sought-after collector's item for its interestingly shaped flowers. The pseudobulbs are cylindrical, only 1.2-4 in/3-10 cm across and with 1-2 leaves at the top. The leaves are prolonged, and up to 6 in/15 cm long. The overhanging flower spikes often branch out and bear numerous flowers—many more in the wild than when cultivated (see the rather small specimen in the photograph). The tiny flowers are partly open, usually yellow, with a dark purple lip. The epiphytic method of cultivation is more advisable than flowerpot cultivation; the plants prosper in semi-shade on a cork slab with a little moss. After the pseudobulbs mature, you

Baptistonia echinata

should allow for a brief drier period of rest. The flowers appear in the winter and in the spring. The plant was discovered in Brazil.

Barkeria lindleyana   ■ ☺

INTERMEDIATE

Barkerias are very attractive orchids when in bloom. The species *B. lindleyana*, nevertheless, is not recommended for small amateur collections, as it is extremely bulky. The plants of this species do not form pseudobulbs and their foliage grows on a rather thick lignifying stem. The shoots of *B. lindleyana* reach lengths of up to 36 in/96 cm, and with an additional 36 in/90-cm long apical flower spike (!), the resulting plant is a true orchid giant! Growing sparsely on a clustered inflorescence are 5-20 purple-pink flowers, up to 2 in/5 cm in

Barkeria lindleyana

size each, with a white spot on the thick lip. In spite of its size (and weight!), the species grows epiphytically; therefore, if you pluck up the courage to cultivate it, the best way to go about it is to attach it to a large slab of bark. The plant requires plenty of diffused light, and a brief period of rest after fading in the winter. It blooms between October and November, and has been known to grow in higher elevations of Mexico and Costa Rica.

Barkeria skinneri   ■ ☺

INTERMEDIATE

This plant was introduced into culture in the "pre-historical" period of orchid cultivation, thanks to numerous botanical adventurers, who explored Mexico—the Promised Land of botany—in the 19th century. In the case of the species *B. skinneri*, they had a lucky hand: it is a rather small (in comparison with the previous species), attractive and easily cultivated species. Its stems are up to 16 in/40 cm tall; the leaves are narrow and lanceolate. The top of the mature shoot is a base for a wiry inflorescence with 5-20 purple flowers that are about 1.6 in/4 cm across; their tepals are rather narrow and the wide lip with a yellow spot is typically extended into a narrow end. The species can be grown both epiphytically and in flowerpots; however, if grown in flowerpots, it tends to assume undesirable proportions. The remaining cultivation rules are the same as with the previous species. *Barkeria skinneri* blooms in the winter and comes from higher elevations of Mexico.

Barkeria skinneri

Batemannia colleyi

Batemannia colleyi　　▣ ☺

INTERMEDIATE-THERMOPHILIC

All the species (a total of 5) of the genus *Batemannia* grow in the rainforests of the Amazon basin. The medium-height epiphyte, *B. colleyi* is very rare in cultivation. Its egg-shaped pseudobulbs are up to 2 in/5 cm long and quadrangular in cross-section. Two long lanceolate leaves are borne at the top. Sometimes even several overhanging inflorescences with 2-6 flowers, up to 6 in/15 cm across, grow out of the bases of the pseudobulbs. The leaves are fleshy and cream-white, with

Bifrenaria aureofulva

a tinge of brown. Grow the plants epiphytically or in flowerpots with a coarse epiphytic mix for adequate drainage. The flowers appear in early spring. The plant has a large geographical range—from Colombia, Venezuela and Guiana to Bolivia and Brazil.

Bifrenaria aureofulva　　▣ ▣ ☺

INTERMEDIATE

B. aureofulva does not differ very much in appearance from the following species and from other members of the genus. However, its golden-and-yellow-to-orange flowers in a sparse erect clustered inflorescence are, atypically, much smaller (0.8 in/2 cm) and only very slightly open. Grow them epiphytically on a piece of bark or twig, in semi-shade; provide good ventilation and the usual dosage of misting and fertilization. The plant enjoys a brief period of reduced watering and decreased temperature in the winter after fading. It blooms in the winter or early spring and is native to Brazil.

Bifrenaria harrisoniae　　▣ ☺

INTERMEDIATE

The orchids of this genus resemble the genus *Lycaste* in their morphology and type of blooming. The difference between them consists in the smaller size of the flowers and the fact that their lip is hairy. *B. harrisoniae* is the best-known species of the genus (that numbers a total of 20 species), and the most frequent in cultivation. The plant creates quadrangular pseudobulbs that reach a height of up to 3.2 in/8 cm and bear one broadly oval, tough, indeciduous leaf which can be up to 12 in/30 cm long. Between 2-3 yellowish flowers grow on erect inflorescences from the bases of the pseudobulbs. They are fairly large (2.8 in/7 cm), with a showy spur-shaped "chin". The lip is purple and covered with a thick layer of hairs. Cultivation is easy—see *B. aureofulva*. The

Bifrenaria harrisoniae

Bletia sp., Mexico

species *B. harrisoniae* blooms between March and May and grows in the wild natural environment of Brazil.

Bletia

INTERMEDIATE

The New World genus of *Bletia* includes about 50 terrestrial species of orchids. Their 2-4 long pointed elliptic leaves grow out of undergorund or surface bulbs, which die during the dry season without leaving a trace. The erect flower spike grows after the period of rest is over and bears 3-15 showy flowers of medium size. These popular orchids

are not difficult to cultivate: they require a sandy medium enriched with peat, semi-shade and a period of rest after the leaves fall. The taxonomy of *Bletia* is still full of confusion, and it is frequently mixed up with the orchids of the genus *Bletilla* that are similar in appearance and partly frost-resistant. They are, nevertheless, quite easy to distinguish—the flower spikes of *Bletia* grow out of old, leafless pseudobulbs, and not during the shooting of new shoots. The plant in the picture blooms in early spring and the photo was taken in Lagos de Monte Bello in Mexico; the genus of *Bletia* as such occurs all over tropical America.

Bollea coronaria

INTERMEDIATE-THERMOPHILIC

The genus *Bollea* has not been fully explored and enumerated; the seven species known so far have been found in temperate warm regions of South America. The plants resemble (and are closely related to) the genus *Huntleya* or *Pescatorea*—they have small pseudobulbs covered with two rows of robust, leathery, elongated leaves. Very showy flowers on short spikes grow individually from the axils of the leaves, with a conspicuous column and a blunt lip. The tepals of *B. coronaria* are burgundy red and the lip is covered with fringed protruberances. Grow *B. coronaria* as you would the following species. The flowering season comes usually in the fall. The plant on the photograph comes from Venezuela.

Bollea coronaria

Bollea hemixantha

INTERMEDIATE-THERMOPHILIC

The flowers of the species *B. hemixantha* are snow-white, the fleshy lip is deep yellow with the edge slightly fringed. Cultivation is fairly easy, if you make sure to provide the plants with a somewhat moist environment in the vegetation period. The plants in the wild grow in the deeper part of rainforests and therefore have to be protected from direct sunlight. The fine roots of both the epiphytic and terrestrial species are "accustomed" to a thicker layer of organic material and should therefore be grown in flowerpots containing a humic medium that is kept permanently a little moist. *B. hemixantha* blooms from the fall till the spring, and is most likely native to Colombia and Ecuador (the precise geographical range has not yet been discovered).

Brassavola cucullata

INTERMEDIATE-THERMOPHILIC

The genus *Brassavola* includes some highly distinctive orchids that attract attention even outside the flowering period with their narrow, highly succulent cylindrical leaves (that grow out of dwarf, thin, stick-shaped pseudobulbs). And when the gorgeous flowers appear, the plants look all the more attractive! The species *B. cucullata* is the longest and most arched of all *Brassavola* orchids. This characteristic applies both to the leaves and the flowers: the leaves

Bollea hemixantha

Brassavola cucullata

are narrow, with an orbicular cross-section and up to 14 in/35 cm long, and the yellowish-white flowers have arched tepals that reach a length of up to 4.4 in/11 cm. Likewise, the lip is ostensibly long and looks like a ribbon. And to add yet another elongated organ—each flower is borne by an ovary that reaches a length of up to 6 in/15 cm! *B. cucullata* is a sought-after gem of every orchid collection. In the wild it grows almost vertically on barren tree bark, wherefore it ought to be grown attached to a slab of bark or a thick stick. Flowerpot cultivation is unnatural and rather risky (the roots tend to mold). Over the summer, you can hang the supports with the orchids outside in semi-shade on a place protected from rain. After a few weeks of "fasting", the plant can even achieve the blooming period twice a year, if watered and fertilized regularly in the course of the year. *B. cucullata* blooms irregularly, but up to twice a year in cultivation. It is native to Mexico, other Central American countries and also Venezuela.

Brassavola martiana

INTERMEDIATE

A smallish and attractive, and thus rather popular collection orchid. The plant grows in a semi-arched or overhanging fashion. Its leaves reach lengths of up to 12 in/30 cm, they

are thin and round in cross-section. The rather short flower spike bears 3-8 showy flowers, 2-2.4 in/5-6 cm in size; their characteristic feature is the ruffled edge of the white lip. The other tepals are greenish-white. Grow the plant in the same way as the previous species. The flowers appear in the summer. *Brassavola martiana* comes from the warm Amazon lowlands of Brazil and Guiana.

Brassavola nodosa   ▫ ◼ ☺

INTERMEDIATE-THERMOPHILIC

Compared to other representatives of the genus, the species *B. nodosa* is smaller and most eager to bloom, a feature that rightly makes it the absolute favorite of all *Brassavola* orchids among orchid growers. Moreover, it is very undemanding and resistant to drought and cultivation errors. The inconspicuous pseudobulbs bear thick leaves that are semi-circular in cross-section and do not exceed a length of 6 in/15 cm—the drier and lighter the habitat of the plant is, the chubbier and shorter the leaves. 1-5 highly decorative greenish-white flowers grow on short flower spikes from the individual psuedobulbs. Cultivation is easy. Even though *B. nodosa* is not an overhanging species, we recommend that you attach it to twigs or bark slabs, because the roots are sensitive to overwatering. In winter or at a time when no new

leaves are forming, the plants enjoy a period of rest lasting several weeks. The flowers are then more abundant. *B. nodosa* has as its habitat the countries of Central America.

Brassavola nodosa

Brassavola subulifolia   ☺

INTERMEDIATE

The flowers of all the species of the genus *Brassavola* are intensely fragrant; since they give off their fragrance exclusively at night, pollinators will most likely recruit from the group of night butterflies. *B. subulifolia* is an erect or semi-erect orchid, its leaves are up to 8 in/20 cm long, the flower stalk is short (2.4 in/6 cm) and it bears 2-4 flowers. The flowers assume the shape of a symmetrical star and are unusually petite—up to 1.5 in/3-4 cm across. Small and undemanding as it is, the species could make a nice part of small orchid collections; however, it is not widely known, and hardly ever cultivated. The cultivation rules are the same as with the species *B. cucullata*. *B. subulifolia* comes from Brazil and Bolivia.

Brassia bidens   ☺

INTERMEDIATE-THERMOPHILIC

Here comes another matchless species! The species of the genus *Brassia* are of singular beauty—their flowers assume truly extraordinary proportions and appearance. And if you add the lovely colors and fragrance typical of the genus, the result is more than attractive for orchid lovers. The species *B. bidens* is a lithophytic (see photo) or epiphytic orchid with egg-shaped, elongated yellowish pseudobulbs that are up to 3.2 in/8 cm long. Some 3-8 flowers grow on each erect wiry spike. The yellowish tepals covered with pale brown spots are, as with the rest of the genus, extended, with thick lining. The lip is whitish and looks rather unexciting compared to the other flower parts. Grow it as you would the following species. The plant blooms in the winter and spring, and occurs in Venezuela and Colombia.

Brassia bidens

Brassia longissima

Brassia maculata

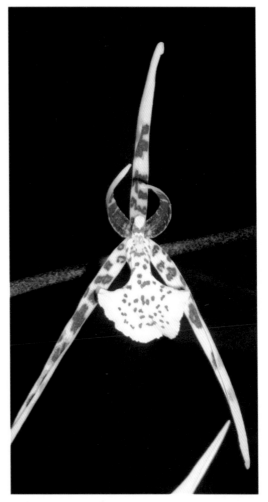

Brassia longissima ◼ ☺

INTERMEDIATE-THERMOPHILIC

This species has, judging by its generic Latin name, the longest something of all the members of the genus: the "something" happens to be its tepals (namely, the lateral sepals) which overhang downward and can be up to 8 in/20 cm long! The remaining flower parts have a slightly more modest appearance—the elongated heart-shaped lip is inexpressive and whitish, the other tepals are barely half as long as the previously mentioned record-breakers. The elegantly distributed brown spots that stand out nicely against the yellow backdrop provide additional embellishment. The erect inflorescence numbering 10-15 flowers grows out of the bases of the flat pseudobulbs, and can reach a length of 24 in/60 cm. The leaves are rather long, which makes *B. longissima* unsuitable for small collections kept in a limited space. Other than that, there are no catches as to its cultivation. It requires more light and, in order to achieve regular blooming in the spring or summer (May-July), a period of rest. Its geographical range is interestingly dispersed—the species comes from Costa Rica, Panama, and also Ecuador and Peru.

Brassia maculata ◼ ☺

INTERMEDIATE-TERMOPHILIC

This species is worth a remark even though its flowers are not so extended as those of *B. longissima*. Their cultivation requirements and the appearance of the green parts make the two species almost identical, but *B. maculata*'s pseudobulbs are a little bigger. The flower spike can bear up to 20 greenish flowers, each with a whitish, shiny-brown-dotted lip. The length of the extended sepals does not exceed 4 in/10 cm. *B. maculata* blooms from late summer to late fall. It was discovered in Cuba, Jamaica, Guatemala and Honduras.

Bulbophyllum

THERMOPHILIC

The genus *Bulbophyllum* is the largest of the entire family *Orchidaceae*. It is no wonder, as it numbers at least 1,100 species! The phrase "at least" suggests that the total number of *Bulbophyllum* orchids has not been, and perhaps never will be, exactly determined—new species are continuously discovered in the wild. And besides, even within the genus itself, there is a lot of confusion: owing to the great variation and heterogeneity of shapes, there is no precise list of distinctive features available. A common denominator of all *Bulbophyllum* orchids are their smallish round-shaped to egg-shaped flat pseudobulbs, with 1-2 leathery leaves at the ends (hence the Latin name of the genus). The pseudobulbs grow at greater distances from each other, from a firm trailing shoot, and create clustered or

Bulbophyllum sp., Thailand

Brassia mexicana

INTERMEDIATE

The only feature that significantly distinguishes *Brassia mexicana* from the rest of the genus are the solid purple-brown extended spots at the base of its tepals, and a few dark purple spots assembled in the center of the whitish lip. The appearance of the green parts, coupled with the ecological and cultivation needs of the species, make it a typical representative of the genus. *B. mexicana* blooms in the spring and comes, as could be expected, from Mexico.

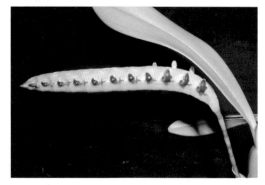

umbellifrous inflorescences. The overwhelming majority of flowers are small and ugly, with a tongue-shaped lip. From a cultivator's perspective, plants with such flowers are only interesting for curiosity-lovers. The genus used to include many species with miniature flowers arranged in comely umbellate inflorescences, but the vast majority of them were transfered to a somewhat artificial (and significant in cultivation) genus *Cirrhopetallum*. Several species of the genus *Bulbophyllum* have their tiny flowers arranged in two rows in a spiral-shaped arched spike, or on an enlarged flower axis (*B. falcatum*); others have lips adorned with attractive hair-like or brush-like pendants. To add even more variety, a few *Bulbophyllum* orchids boast individually growing, rather large and bizarre looking flowers—the best-known and longest-grown of them is the species *B. lobbii*. The great quantity of species within the genus does not allow for a universal set of instructions for cultivation; but the available species (mostly coming from orchid farms in southeast Asia) are not exceptional in this respect—their cultivation is manageable even by an inexperienced orchid grower who owns an indoor, moderately-lighted glass case. As *Bulbophyllum* orchids are epiphytic almost without exception, the plants are happier if attached to a bigger

piece of bark or branch, even in a greenhouse—for their trailing shoots "escape" from a flowerpot very fast. Attach them either to a barren piece of wood or place them in a thin layer of *Sphagnum* moss. The plants can even tolerate semi-shade and a poorly ventilated station, but in such an environment they bloom less abundantly and assume undesirable dimensions. The center of their occurence is in Southeast Asia, but some species come also from the tropical regions of America, Africa and Australia.

Bulbophyllum auriculatum

Bulbophyllum gadgarrense

Calanthe vestita

Calanthe

INTERMEDIATE-THERMOPHILIC

The genus *Calanthe* includes one immensely interesting "refugee": all of the 150 representatives of the genus grow in Asia, Australia and Africa, and only one of them strayed as far as the New World! Botanists divide this genus into two ecologically different groups. The members of the first group (*Eucalanthe*) have only reduced pseudobulbs with clusters of large indeciduous foliage. Their robustness prevents them from being very popular with orchid lovers. *Eucalanthe* orchids are epiphytes that vegetate all year round without a break; they require humous soil, semi-shade, countinuous watering and a warm to temperate environment. *C. arcuata* in the photograph represents this group. The other ecological group (*Preptanthe*) numbers more species and is more significant with regard to cultivation. *Preptanthe* orchids form large, annualy deciduous pseudobulbs, and the most widely cultivated and popular species *C. vestita* is no exception to this rule. There are three periods in the life of a *Preptanthe* orchid: vegetation, flowering and rest. Its life cycle is thus quite unique: the flower spike that reaches a length of up to 28 in/70 cm grows out of the side of a bare pseudobulb and bears many flowers; their dominant feature is a four-lobed lip. The plants bloom in the fall and in the winter, always after all the leaves have fallen. That is followed by a period of rest and a subsequent burgeoning of new shoots. Most *Preptanthe* orchids are terrestrial species that in-

habit humus-filled cracks in limestone rocks, if growing in the wild. Cultivation has some specifics: after fading, store the bulbs until spring in a dry, shady place (under a greenhouse table), and start watering them carefully only after they begin to burgeon. They are grown atypically—in ordinary garden soil, after adding a little humus and limestone grit. When the plants reach the peak of their growing period, keep them in semi-shade and provide plentiful watering and fertilization. When misting the plant, keep away from the leaves—misting the foliage is undesirable! As soon as new pseudobulbs are formed and the leaves start turning yellow, cut down on

watering. The photographs introduce four representatives of the *Preptanthe* group—*C. rubens*, *C. triplicata* and *C. vestita* var. *rubrooculata*. The latter species occurs in several color variations.

Calanthe arcuata

Calanthe rubens

Catasetum macrocarpum

Catasetum pileatum

Catasetum macrocarpum

CRYOPHILIC-THERMOPHILIC

The orchids of the genus *Catasetum* are very unusual plants indeed, for flowers on a single plant assume two entirely different forms—male and female. *C. macrocarpum* is a robust orchid forming
spindle-shaped pseudobulbs, which bear several
lanceolate deciduous leaves during growth. A cluster
of flowers grows out of the base of a pseudobulb, assumes a length of up to 18 in/45 cm (hence the Latin
name of the species) and bears 3-10 flowers that are
turned in the opposite direction. Their green-yellow
lip is enclosed like a helmet, convex and dark on the
inside. The male flowers are decorated with feeler-
like pendants, the female flowers are yellow on the
inside of the lip. Cultivation is not very complicated
and should include sufficient nutrition and watering
during the period of growth, followed by a cooler
and drier period of rest. *C. macrocarpum* can be
grown epiphytically, or in baskets or flowerpots. The
flowers appear in late summer and in the fall. The
species grows in the large tropical area of South and
Central America.

Catasetum pileatum

INTERMEDIATE

Catasetum orchids are famous for their remarkable
flowers dominated by a lip that is either wide open, or
enclosed in a helmet-like fashion. In the latter case, the
flowers are also turned in the opposite direction—the
lip thus forms something like a roof. In many species,
the flowers sport peculiar feeler-like protuberances. The
species *C. pileatum* is thanks to its whitish-yellowish
and bizarre-shaped flowers undoubtedly the most beautiful species of the whole genus. There are 3-6 flowers,
up to 4 in/10 cm across, growing on long spikes. The lip
is broadened to the point of looking like a satellite
aerial, and has a dark hollow in the lower part. Grow the
species as you would the previous one. *Catasetum*

pileatum may please you with flowers in August and
September. It is native to lower levels of Venezuela and
Ecuador.

Catasetum sp.

INTERMEDIATE

It is quite an event whenever an amateur admirer of orchids comes across a *Catasetum* orchid in bloom in the
wild. This is true in spite of the fact that the exact name
of the plant is usually impossible to determine; only experts are able to do that but not unless they have specimens of living plants or their herbarium items at hand.
And as picking orchids in the wild is prohibited by law,
the plants usually remain unnamed. This is the case
with the plants in the photograph that were found in
Mexico. If you are lucky enough to have a *Catasetum*

Catasetum sp., Mexico

Catasetum sp., Bolivia

Cattleya aclandiae

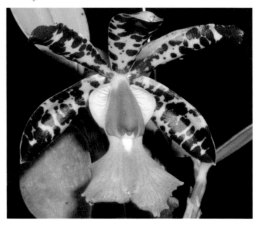

Cattleya amethystoglossa ■ ☺

INTERMEDIATE

The flowers of this species literally have the power to hypnotize—so unusual and interesting is their color. It is a shame that *C. amethystoglossa* is so unwilling to bloom in cultivation, and that it is quite unwieldy. The pseudobulbs reach a height of up to 32 in/80 cm and bear 2-3 leaves on the top. As with all the other *Cattleya* orchids, a flat flower sheath forms between the leaves on the maturing shoots, bursts after some time and puts out the flower spike. The inflorescence is rich—it numbers 5-10 flowers. The flowers are tough, up to 3.2 in/8 cm in diameter; the lip is rather small and mauve, with lateral lobes that have a tinge of white. The tepals are white to pinkish, with burgundy spots. Cultivation is the same as with the species *C. bicolor*. The plants bloom between February and April. They were first discovered in Bahia, Brazil.

Cattleya amethystoglossa

orchid in your possession, it is not too difficult to grow. Cultivation should include sufficient nutrition and watering at the time when new pseudobulbs are forming, and a subsequent cooler and drier period of rest. It can be grown both epiphytically and in baskets or flowerpots. The plants in the photograph bloom early in the year and come from Bolivia and Mexico.

Cattleya aclandiae ⊡ ■ ☹

THERMOPHILIC

This orchid holds a unique position among its relatives—it is the smallest of them all. That does not diminish its beauty, rather the opposite. The pseudobulbs are narrow, bearing 1-3 extended, oval leaves, and reach up to 6 in/15 cm in length. In sharp contrast to their size are the gaudy-colored flowers that can be as large as 4 in/10 cm in diameter. Each flower is crowned by a purple lip. The other tepals are green-and-yellow, spangled with large russet spots. Its proportions make *Cattleya aclandiae* a sought-after rarity with orchid growers; however, it is the most difficult to cultivate of all the *Cattleya* botanical species. It blooms between summer and fall, and is native to Bahia, Brazil.

Cattleya aurantiaca ◨ ☺

INTERMEDIATE

As the generic name suggests, this orchid is attractive mainly for the lively yellow color of its flowers. It is therefore very important for breeding new cultivars, although the petite proportions of the flowers are a disadvantage. The species forms club-shaped pseudobulbs that are only slightly thickened, up to 14 in/35 cm tall, and bear two leaves. A short flower spike bearing a raceme of up to 15 flowers pushes its way out from the flower sheath that occurs between the leaves at the end of the pseudobulb. The flowers are about 1.4 in/3.5 cm in diameter, and last for no more than 6-9 days. In its homeland, the plant often occurs on older trees on coffee plantations; in the virginal wild, it has been known to grow in the central part of Central America, between Mexico and Costa Rica.

Cattleya bicolor ◨ ■ ☺

INTERMEDIATE

An epiphytic or lithophytic orchid, a lover of cool, humid air—for in the wild it grows in stream canyons at medium elevations. The plants form slender, 60-cm-tall or smaller pseudobulbs that are not thickened, as is typical with *Cattleya* orchids. The flower spike bears up to 5 flowers that can be 4.8 in/12 cm in diameter and have a pink crimson lip and olive-brown tepals. They occur between August and September, and last for a maximum of 3-4 weeks. Cultivation is not very complicated: the best thing to do is to place the plant in an epiphytic basket and suspend it at a well-ventilated and rather humid and cool place in the greenhouse. During the summer months, you can suspend the plant from the crown of a fruit tree, but make sure to mist it frequently whenever the weather gets particularly sultry. *Cattleya bicolor* comes from Brazil, where it was discovered as far back as in 1836.

Cattleya bicolor

Cattleya dowiana var. *aurea*

Cattleya elongata

Cattleya dowiana var. aurea ▣ ☺

THERMOPHILIC

C. dowiana is the most spectacular and the most fragrant *Cattleya*, and among the prettiest orchids ever, as far as the contrast of its colors and shapes is concerned. The flowers are giant—up to 6.4 in/16 cm tall. What attracts attention is mainly the lip, which is purple in color, interwoven with yellow-and-golden streaks. The other tepals are broad, ruffled and deep yellow. The species requires a warmer environment compared to the other *Cattleyas*, and it should be grown in a flowerpot. It is native to Panama, Costa Rica and Colombia, where "*aurea*", its rare variety, was discovered in a mountain valley of Antiqua. *C. aurea's* lip is shot through with comparatively deep golden streaks, and the tepals are reddish at the bottom (see photo). As a bearer of valuable features, *C. aurea* is widely used in orchid breeding.

Cattleya elongata ■ ☺

INTERMEDIATE

This *Cattleya* orchid resembles *C. amethystoglossa* both in size and in appearance. That means it is quite bulky and therefore unsuitable for small amateur collections. As a bearer of a genetic quality that is alwyas welcome—namely long pseudobulbs—it is popular with orchid breeders. The long (up to 16 in/40 cm) flower spike bears 3-8 large flowers that are up to 3.2 in/8 cm in diameter. The three-lobe purple lip is surrounded with brownish-purple tepals that have wavy edges. In the wild, the species occurs in drier localities, and therefore it needs more light and air movement than is usual. It blooms in the spring, and it was discovered in Brazil, for example in Minas Gerais and Bahia.

Cattleya forbesii ▢ ☺

INTERMEDIATE

C. forbesii is one of the bifoliate *Cattleya* orchids, and its small proportions make it suitable even for collections limited in space. The pseudobulbs are no more than 10 in/25 cm tall, and bear 1-5 tough flowers (up to 4 in/10 cm in diameter) on erect flower spikes. The lip is white and wavy on the edge, yellow on the outside and shot with red venation on the inside. The tepals are olive-yellow. Cultivation could not be easier. The plants bloom eagerly between July and October. *C. forbesii* is native to Brazil.

Cattleya forbesii

Cattleya guttata

Cattleya iricolor

Cattleya guttata ■ ☺

INTERMEDIATE

Another robust *Cattleya*; the "unwieldiness" of the plants is counterbalanced by their resistance to cultivation errors, as well as their heroic blooming. The pseudobulbs reach the height of up to 28 in/70 cm and bear usually two, occasionally three leathery tough leaves. The flower raceme is erect and consists of up to 15 very tough flowers. The middle, circular lobe of the three-lobed lip is enhanced with purple color, the tepals are green and embellished with brownish-red dots. The plants stretch out excessively to form an unattractive shape, if grown in an excessively shady place. Otherwise the species has no other cultivation surprises in store. *C. guttata* blooms between September and December, and occurs in the wild only occasionally—in Brazil.

Cattleya intermedia ■ ☺

INTERMEDIATE

Along with the species *C. bowringiana*, this is the most widely cultivated bifoliate *Cattleya*. It is popular in spite of the fact that it blooms in the summer—a season that is unfavorable from a cultivator's perpective. The

Cattleya intermedia

pseudobulbs are rather large—up to 16 in/40 cm long. The inflorescence is made up of 3-7 pale pinkish purple flowers with purple venation and a yellow spot in the throat. Apart from its typical form, the species has several varieties and deviations that are significant both genetically and for cultivation. The popular albinos are worth a remark, as well as a flower anomaly termed *aquini*. Its petals are the same color as the lip, and it has been used by breeders to produce a large number of attractive hybrids (known as *aquini*-types). The species blooms between May and August and comes from Brazil.

Cattleya iricolor ▣ ☺

INTERMEDIATE

C. iricolor is not the finest looker, but it still deserves a little attention—if only for the interesting history of its discovery and re-discovery. The species was first found in Ecuador over a century ago. Then the orchid disappeared for many decades, to be re-discovered in the 1980s, and the cultivators and botanical gardens managers of today vie with one another in their efforts to get hold of it. The morphology of this orchid is the same as with the other bifoliate orchids—the flowers are smallish and grow on a fairly short flower spike in inflorescences numbering 3-7 flowers. The tepals are narrow and yellowish, the tube-shaped, extended lip is embellished with a purple ornament that resembles a rainbow (hence the species' name). Cultivation is not complicated; the plants need a period of rest for new shoots to mature.

Cattleya leopoldii

THERMOPHILIC

This is a highly popular species, but very hard to get, as it is not eager to grow in cultivation. *C. leopoldii* is closely related to the species *C. guttata*, but is distinguished by a smaller build and giant flower racemes that can number no fewer than 20 flowers! The color of the flowers is quite impressive: the lip is mahogany brown with a tinge of purple and with irregularly distributed red spots. There is even one very interesting and highly valued colorless (apochromatic) variety, the white lip of which is complemented by the myrtle-green of the other tepals. Cultivation rules are the same as those that apply to other *Cattleyas*. The species blooms between August and October. Its original habitat is in Brazil.

Cattleya loddigesii

INTERMEDIATE

This plant is quite small and easy to cultivate; in addition, it is an eager and beautiful bloomer—in short, it has all the important assets and is definitely suitable

Cattleya loddigesii

Cattleya leopoldii

for small amateur collections. The bifoliate pseudobulbs are up to 14 in/35 cm tall, and 2-5 flowers grow from flower sheaths on a short spike. They are up to 4 in/10 cm wide and have a three-lobe, thickly ruffled purple lip that is yellowish on the inside. The other tepals are shiny pink-and-purple. *C. stanleyi*, an albinic variety of *C. loddigesii* discovered in the wild, ranks very high on the hybrid popularity chart. The flowers of both varieties are tough and exceptionally durable, and are therefore cultivated for cut flowers. Cultivation is similar to that of the other intermediate *Cattleyas*. A drawback of the species is the fact that some specimens bloom in the summer—the flowers appear between June and November. *C. loddigesii* is native to Brazil.

Cattleya luteola   ☺

THERMOPHILIC

A unifoliate miniature species, suitable even for growing in smaller cultivation equipment. Admittedly, its
flowers are quite small (1.6 in/4 cm), but their color is
highly rated, as sulfur yellow is quite rare in *Cattleyas*.
The pseudobulbs of this genus reach up to 6 in/15 cm
in size, and a short spike numbers 2-5 flowers. The lip
is yellow with a white edge and an orange-and-red
marking inside the conspicuous tubular throat. *C. lute-
ola* requires a warmer, and at the same time more humid, environment for cultivation, which is a combination that some growers may find a bit difficult to
achieve. The species flowers in the fall and in the winter. It is an epiphyte and grows in Amazonia—north
and west of Manaos.

Cattleya maxima   ■ ☺

INTERMEDIATE

This species is included in collections much less often
than it deserves to be. The pseudobulbs are club-
shaped, flat, 10 in/25 cm in length and end in one narrow leaf that can be up to 8 in/20 cm long. The flowers tally with the generic name (for there are not too
many *Cattleyas* that could compete with this orchid in
height) and reach up to 6 in/15 cm in length. What is
more, there can be up to 8 flowers per one long spike.
The lip is long and tubular, with a wavy edge, and is
golden-yellow with deep purple to orange venation on
the inside. The other tepals are light purple, with ruffled edges. Cultivation is not difficult. The flowering
season comes at a favorable time for European growers: the flowers appear between October and January—a gloomy time poor in light. *C. maxima* comes
from the foothills of the Andes in Peru, Ecuador and
Colombia.

Cattleya mossiae var. *wageneri*

Cattleya percivaliana

Cattleya percivaliana

INTERMEDIATE

A species of singular beauty, perhaps one of the most beautiful of all orchids! Its only imperfection is the slightly dank smell of the flowers. The unifoliate pseudobulbs do not exceed a length of 6 in/15 cm; the leaves are 4 in/10 cm longer than the pseudobulbs. The flower spike is 10 in/25 cm long and bears 3-4 flowers that reach up to 4.8 in/12 cm in size. The color of the tepals ranges between pink and purple, the tubular lip is purple-and-red on the inside, yellow to yellow-and-orange in the gullet, and has ruffled edges. Cultivation is fairly easy. The flowers appear between January and March. *C. percivaliana* grows exclusively in Venezuela, in regions with a higher level of humidity.

Cattleya schilleriana

INTERMEDIATE

A small, "display-case" *Cattleya* species with large flowers. Bifoliate pseudobulbs barely reach the size of 4-6 in/10-15 cm. The flowers, up to 4 in/10 cm in size, appear singly or in pairs on a short spike. They have a three-lobe, pale purple lip with a brownish ornament. The tepals are green, with a tinge of red, and are thickly covered with purple-and-brown dots. Cultivation is easy. Epiphytic growing is recommended. Specimens of the species flower irregularly between February and July. *C. schilleriana* comes from Brazil.

Cattleya schilleriana

Cattleya mossiae var. *wageneri*

INTERMEDIATE

The full-colored variety of this species is not valued as highly as the albinic version *C. mossiae* var. *wageneri* that has pure-white flowers with a yellowish lip, and is hardly second to the white-flowered *Cattleya* hybrids. The pseudobulbs are unifoliate, quite thick, club-shaped and are topped with one thick, tough leaf. The flower spike bears up to 5 sizeable flowers. A typical specimen of the species is characterized by a particularly wavy lip with a yellow throat and purple venation. The other tepals are pale pink-and-purple. The species is undemanding in cultivation, and blooms between June and August. Its natural habitat is in Venezuela.

Cattleya skinneri   ◘ ▪ ☺

INTERMEDIATE

This orchid is the national flower of Costa Rica and is quite rare in cultivation. It is a fairly robust representative of the genus—its thick bifoliate pseudobulbs reach up to 10 in/25 cm in size. The narrower bases of the pseudobulbs distinguish it from a similar species, *C. bowringiana*. A short spike bears 3-7 purple flowers that assume the size of up to 4 in/10 cm, and have a plain, long tubular lip that is yellow on the inside. An albinic variety of this species, var. *alba*, has been known to exist, with pure white flowers that are greenish on the inside of the lip. The species thrives if given normal care—best of all in a flowerpot filled with a mix containing a high percentage of crushed pine bark. It blooms in the spring and comes from Mexico, Costa Rica and Guatemala.

Cattleya sp.   ◘ ☺

INTERMEDIATE

It might seem that in the taxonomy of the rather showy, big-flowered orchids of the genus *Cattleya*, there can be no room left for surprise. And yet, one can still come across interesting specimens in the wild: the plant in the photograph has been a subject of dispute among experts as to whether it is a generic or intergeneric hybrid, or even a new species. A bifoliate orchid with thin pseudobulbs that reach up to 14 in/35 cm in height is an epiphyte and its ecological needs are similar to those of the other Brazilian *Cattleyas*. It was discovered in 1999 in Brazil, near Rio de Janeiro.

Cattleya velutina   ◘ ☺

THERMOPHILIC

This species was discovered in the Parahiba valley between Rio de Janeiro and Sao Paulo, Brazil. It is *Cattleya* sp., Brazil

Cattleya velutina

Their lip has a wide-open central lobe and purple venation; the other tepals are russet and embellished with dark spots. When not in bloom, the plant resembles the species *C. bicolor*, except that its pseudobulbs are shorter and thicker. Grow the species as you would other botanical *Cattleyas*. *C. velutina* blooms in June and July.

Cattleya violacea var. *superba*

INTERMEDIATE

This attractive Amazonian species is very rare in cultivation, in spite of its singular beauty and small proportions; the reason is its slow growth and unwillingness to bloom. The bifoliate pseudobulbs can reach 8 in/20 cm in size, and the short inflorescence bears 3-7 flowers. The flat, tough leaves are up to 5.6 in/14 cm in diameter. The shiny purple tepals are complemented with red-and-purple three-lobe lip. Grow it epiphytically, or in a potted medium of coarse bark. The flowers appear on mature pseudobulbs between July and August. The species resides all over the Amazon basin, including Colombia and Venezuela, Brazil and Bolivia.

most likely completely extinct by now, owing to unregulated collection in the wild in the 1980s. This makes *C. velutina* a heavily guarded gem of every orchid collection. Apart from being rare, it is also very attractive and special for the beauty of its flowers.

Cattleya violacea var. *superba*

Cattleya walkeriana

INTERMEDIATE

This species stands out by the extraordinary way it blooms—the flowers do not grow out of the flower sheath on the top of the pseudobulb but out of a special leafless shoot. The unifoliate pseudobulbs are only 4 in/10 cm tall, and the inflorescence bearing 2-3 flowers does not outgrow it. The flowers are quite large (up to 4 in/10 cm in diameter) and purple. A white-flowered variety—var. *alba*—is also known to exist. The lip is flat, three-lobed, narrowed heavily at the base. Its dimensions make the plant a sought-after gem of small greenhouses and glass cases, except that it is hard to get. It should be grown epiphytically on a piece of bark or twig, as the roots are prone to mold. *C. walkeriana* blooms between December and April—the perfect time for cultivators. In the wild, it grows in Brazil.

Cattleya walkeriana

Cattleyopsis lindenii

Cattleyopsis lindenii

THERMOPHILIC

C. lindenii is quite rare in cultivation. This is ascribed mainly to its slow growth (in other words, limited opportunity for vegetative propagation). The species forms a thick and tough tangle of tiny oval pseudobulbs with tough thickened serrated foliage. The plant parades its showy pale pink flowers that never fully open, on a long, and often branched, wiry spike. The very durable flower is dominated by an underhung tubular lip with a fimbriated, frilly edge that somewhat resembles the genus *Cattleya* (hence the Latin name of the species). Cultivation is somewhat complicated, as the species loves light and suffers a lot in winter. It should therefore be kept in a temperate environment at that time. It blooms in late summer and in the fall, and comes from Cuba and other islands in the Caribbean.

Caularthron bicornutum

INTERMEDIATE-THERMOPHILIC

The representatives of this small genus (2 species) used to be considered members of the genus *Epidendrum*, but were excluded from it on the grounds of the different position of their flower lip. Their robust, prolonged cylindric pseudobulbs are hollow and, in the case of

Caularthron bicornutum

brick-red flowers with an almost invisible white lip are only 0.8 in/2 cm in diameter. They appear singly or in small groups in the axils of the leaves. Grow this plant epiphytically in a moderately damp semi-shade; as its roots are very tender, it needs to be mounted in a layer of moss. Flowerpot cultivation is not recommended because the roots have a tendency to mold. The flowers appear irregularly several times a year. The plant's natural habitat is in the Philippines.

Ceratostylis rubra

C. bilamellatum, they provide a dwelling for ants. The pseudobulbs of the better-known *C. bicornutum* reach lengths of up to 10 in/25 cm, and are covered with 3-4 leaves (up to 14 in/35 cm long) at the upper part. The clustered erect inflorescence grows out of the apex of the pseudobulb and bears up to 20 white, 2.4 in/6-cm-wide, showy flowers. This epiphytic species is a sought-after rarity. Grow it on a suspended support, or even better, in a permeable medium in a flowerpot. After fading in winter, it requires a drier period of rest. It comes from Brazil, Colombia, Guiana, Trinidad, Tobago and Venezuela (where the photograph was taken).

Ceratostylis rubra   □   ⊡   ☺   ☺

INTERMEDIATE-THERMOPHILIC

The small epiphytic orchids of the genus *Ceratostylis* form attractive clusters. Their popularity with collectors is enhanced by their small, gaudy-colored flowers that often appear in larger quantities on one spike. The species *C. rubra* has single or poorly branched stems covered with a brown membranous casing. The showy

Chiloschista sp.

Chiloschista sp., Thailand

Chiloschista sp.

Chiloschista

THERMOPHILIC

Their morphology and life style makes the orchids of the genus *Chiloschista* absolutely exceptional, and not only within the *Orchidaceae* family. And since, apart from being extraordinary, they are also very beautiful (and miniature-sized to top it all!), they are among the most widely sought-after and most highly coveted plants collected. The *Chiloschista* orchids have lost the ability to form leaves (which appear only rarely, and in a reduced form), and the function of assimilation has been fully overtaken by the flat roots. The stem is also shortened to an absolute minimum and adds only a few millimeters of growth each year. New greenish roots, typical of orchids, grow from underneath its growth apex. The leaves then spend many years increasing in length. The root tangles grow thickly over the support or stick out into space. Flower stalks bearing clustered inflorescences of fairly large and very showy flowers are formed at the same place as the new roots, colored mostly in various combinations of deep yellow, orange and coffee brown. Cultivation is not as complicated as it might seem at first sight. Mount the plants onto barren bark or a wooden support (sticks of elderberry branches are recommended, as its soft bark allows the orchid roots to grow in well). The small plants need a fairly humid air, frequent misting and a well-ventilated station with an excess of indirect sunlight. The first two years after mounting are critical for the plants; once they catch on well on the support, the risk

Chiloschista sp.

Christensonia vietnamica

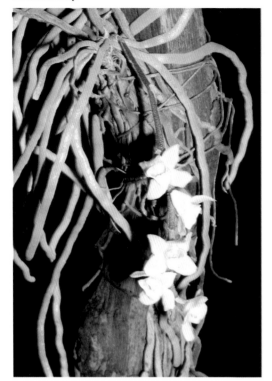

of any losses is considerably diminished. Be careful not to harm the roots while handling the plant or attaching it to a support! There are many uncertainties concerning the taxonomy of the genus *Chiloschista*, which numbers about ten species. The flowers appear toward the end of winter and in the spring. The plants come from the warm regions of Asia, including southern India, Thailand, Burma and Malayan Penninsula and Java.

Chiloschista sp.

Christensonia vietnamica

INTERMEDIATE-THERMOPHILIC

This species is living proof that an attractive orchid with showy flowers can be discovered even today. It resembles the genus *Vanda* in appearance: sparse inflorescences bearing large yellow-and-green flowers with a broad pure white lip grow out of the axils of the leaves that are arranged in two rows. This small light-loving epiphyte has the same requirements as the orchids of the genus *Vanda*. Cut down on watering a little in winter and decrease temperature; this is the only way the plant can cope with the lack of light. Flowers appear between December and July. The species was not described until 1993, when specimens were collected in southern Vietnam, despite the fact that it is quite widespread in that region!

Chysis bractescens

Cirrhopetalum pseudopicturatum

Cirrhopetalum   □ ⊡ ☺

INTERMEDIATE-THERMOPHILIC

The representatives of this genus were excluded from the extensive and diverse *Bulbophyllum* genus. The reasons that led to this were not so much scientific as related to gardening and cultivation. The only significant feature that the species of the genus *Cirrhopetalum* are

Cirrhopetalum pachybulbum

Chysis bractescens   ■ ☺ ☹

INTERMEDIATE-THERMOPHILIC

Orchids belonging to the small genus *Chysis* have a very singular morphology, an intriguing life cycle and pretty flowers. The species *C. bractescens* is characterized by long, spindle-shaped, partite pseudobulbs which overhang the plant and, at the time of growth, a covering of 5-7 leaves that later fall off. The lateral spikes grow simultaneously with the springing of new shoots and are fairly short. One inflorescence bears 10 yellow, fleshy flowers that are 2.8 in/7 cm in size and have a china-like apearance. The lip is yellow, with red embellishment. This attractive species is not difficult to cultivate: grow it epiphytically on slabs of bark, in warm semi-shade. After the pseudobulbs fully mature, treat the plant to a significantly cool and dry period of rest. *C. bractescenc* blooms between May and June and comes from Mexico and Guatemala.

Cirrhopetalum sikkimense

distinguished by is the appearance of their inflorescences: the tiny flowers are arranged in characteristic, usually overhanging heads or umbels. Over 60 species have already been described, most of which are among the attractive petite or miniature orchids that are popular with cultivators. Small, egg-shaped pseudobulbs grow at a certain distance from each other on a trailing rhizome and bear only one leaf each. The morphology of the flowers is very diverse: the tepals assume different sizes and shapes. The lip is sometimes curiously movable—thanks to a thin connection with the base of the flower. Cultivation has no special requirements, as these rather light-loving plants can thrive even in small cultivating equipment. Round-the-year moisture and warmth are a guarantee of a good development of the new pseudobulbs. The plants usually bloom between the fall and spring, but since they grow continuously, they can bloom at other times as well. The best-known and most often cultivated species is *C. medusae*. The genus has a large geographical range that includes eastern Africa, Madagascar, Asia, New Guinea and New Caledonia.

Cirrhopetalum curtisii var. *purpureum*

Cleisostoma simondii

Cleisostoma simondii □ ☺

INTERMEDIATE-THERMOPHILIC

A delicate representative of dwarf Asian epiphytic orchids with extended stems. *C. simondii* has green, scarcely lignifying and very rarely branched shoots that reach lengths of up to 12 in/30 cm. They bear two sparse rows of fleshy leaves that are 2-3.2 in/5-8 cm long and almost round in cross-section. Plenty of aerial roots grow out of the stems. The overhanging inflorescence bears up to 15 rather showy flowers that are almost 4 in/1.5 cm in diameter. The tepals are brown-and-yellow with dark lengthwise stripes, and the lip is

Cochleanthes discolor

purple with a blunt spur-like protuberance at the bottom. *Cleistosoma* orchids are among popular specimens of small botanical collections and are frequently offered by Thai orchid farms. Nobody needs to be afraid to cultivate them; mount the plants on a cork support, for example, and provide them with sufficient light and warmth, complemented with frequent watering during vegetation. Reduce temperature and watering intensity somewhat in the winter. *C. simondii* blooms between October and November and is native to Thailand and other countries in southeastern Asia.

Cochleanthes discolor ■ ☺

INTERMEDIATE

There are several uncertainties connected with the genus *Cochleanthes* that numbers fifteen species. For a long time, botanists were unable to agree on the exact classification of the plants. The pseudobulbs of *C. discolor* are fairly large and bear long leaves reaching lengths of up to 10 in/25 cm that are arranged to look like a fan. Single flowers grow on shortish spikes at the base of the pseudobulb; they are up to 3.2 in/8 cm in size and bear a slight resemblance in shape to orchids of the genus *Lycaste*. They are whitish to greenish, with a tinge of violet; the robust, tubular lip is deep purple on the inside and yellowish on the bottom. *C. discolor* is an epiphyte that requires semi-shade and a higher degree of air humidity. If you plant it in a moderately coarse epiphytic mix in a flowerpot, and allow for a brief period of rest, you may reap a greater amount of flowers that appear between May and June. The species was discovered in Cuba, Panama, Costa Rica and Honduras.

Coelogyne asperata

Coelogyne asperata   ▣ ■ ☺

INTERMEDIATE-THERMOPHILIC

C. asperata is a somewhat obscure representative of *Coelogyne* orchids—a genus that is highly significant with regard to cultivation (the total number of species that usually bear very showy flowers oscillates around 100, depending on the perspectives of individual authors). The pseudobulbs of this rather robust species are up to 6 in/15 cm long; the length of the leaves sometimes exceeds as many as 20 in/50 cm. The overhanging inflorescence reaches a length of up to 12 in/30 cm and consists of 10-15 showy, fragrant flowers. The tepals are white and the lip is waved in an attractive manner and decorated with a complex yellow-and-brown ornament. Grow it as you would the thermophilic species *C. dayana*. The plant blooms in the fall and winter, and comes from the Malayan Peninsula, Borneo and Sumatra.

Coelogyne cristata   ☺

CRYOPHILIC

"An orchid for cactus-fans". Its love of a cool environment and the need for winter rest used to make *C. cristata* a frequent and popular inhabitant of cactus greenhouses with mimimal heating. In the past decade, it has lost its significance for cultivation and become, paradoxically, quite rare. *C. cristata* forms sphere-shaped smooth pseudobulbs that reach a length of up to 2.4 in/6 cm. Each of them bears a couple of narrow, lanceolate, tough leaves. A raceme of 3-9 flowers with showy lips embellished with yellow protuberances grows out of the base of each pseudobulb in early spring. One negative quality of the flowers is their excessive flaccidity and a rumpled appearance. Grow the orchids in flowerpots filled with a permeable and always slightly moist medium; in the winter, they will do well in an environment that is only slightly heated. The species owes its cryophilia to its habitat—Himalayan altitudes of over 6,500 ft/2,000 m above sea level.

Coelogyne dayana

across and bearing a number of showy flowers. Sadly, their beauty is extremely transient: the whole show lasts no more than several days! The species has narrow, egg-shaped pseudobulbs bearing two narrow, lanceolate leaves with lengthwise waving. The lip is white with a chocolate-brown decoration and white crests, the other tepals are cream-white. The inflorescences grow from the top parts of the newly-forming shoots; unlike the case of *C. massangeana*, these shoots later develop into ordinary pseudobulbs (proterant inflorescences). This species is not very difficult to cultivate: the plants require medium warmth, semi-shade and are in permanent need of a slightly moist root environment. Do not transport or replant them unless you absolutely have to. The species does not have a clearly-defined rest period. If the plant begins to produce flowers, place or hang it in a way that will allow the inflorescence to grow undisturbed in a downward direction. The species is native to Thailand, Malayan Peninsula, Borneo, Java and Sumatra.

Coelogyne fimbriata   ▫ ☺

CRYOPHILIC-INTERMEDIATE

This orchid that represents a very notable genus—with regard to cultivation—is one of the smallest species. It is a popular plant, and frequently cultivated by amateurs. Its oval bifoliate pseudobulbs reach a maximum size of 1.2 in/ 3 cm and they grow in 1.2-2 in 3-5 cm distances from each other on a trailing rhizome. The leaves are narrow and lanceolate, the flower shoot grows out of their axils and bears 1-2 flowers. The color of the flowers is an unusual shade of creamy brown; they are a little transparent, with a russet embellishment on the lip. The plant is highly decorative, especially if allowed to grow into bigger bunches. Cultivation is manageable even by a novice orchid-grower, who must provide the plant with a somewhat cooler (thus also shadier) and moister environment; in the summer, you can place it in the crown of a tree in the garden. Cultivation in flowerpots is preferable to epiphytic culture. The plant bloom between August and November, and comes from a vast Asian area—China, northern India, Malaysia, Thailand, Vietnam and other countries.

Coelogyne fimbriata

Coelogyne dayana   ■ ☺

INTERMEDIATE

These robust plants are inconspicuous outside the flowering period. Everything changes as soon as a curious serrated stick springs from the clusters of robust pseudobulbs. In a matter of days, this curious shape turns into a rope-like overhanging inflorescence over 3 ft/1 meter

Coelogyne dayana

Coelogyne lactea ▣ ☺

INTERMEDIATE

An attractive representative of the genus *Coelogyne*. It grows in drier, sparse forests in the company of the deciduous *Dendrobium* orchids. Its egg-shaped pseudobulbs are 4.8. in/12 cm tall, bearing a couple of leaves with a typical *Coelogyne* grooving that reach lengths of 8 in/20 cm. The horizontally projected flower raceme consists of 5-10 attractive cream-white flowers that are 1.6. in/4 cm in diameter. The showy lip is embellished with a delicate, yellow-to-light-brown ornament. Grow the species as you would the more thermophilic representatives of the genus (e. g., *C. dayana*). You will facilitate the blooming process by slightly reducing the temperature and watering in the winter. The species blooms between February and April and comes from Burma, Laos, Thailand and Vietnam.

Coelogyne lactea

Coelogyne massangeana ■ ☺

INTERMEDIATE

This orchid resembles the species *C. dayana* in appearance. It has an approximately 32 in/80 cm-long, overhanging flower spike that bears 15-20 wide-open, yellowish white flowers with a fine brownish marking on the lip. At first glance, the inflorescence seems to be growing out of the base of a mature pseudobulb, but appearances are deceptive; the flower stalk is in fact formed at the apex of a peculiar leafless shoot with a tiny, dwarfed pseudobulb at the end (a heterant inflorescence). The leafless shoot ceases to develop after the flowers fade, but it remains a live for up to several years, cached in a cluster of ordinary vegetative pseudobulbs. Cultivation rules are the same as with *C. dayana*. *C. massangeana* originated in Thailand, Java, Sumatra and Borneo.

Coelogyne massangeana

Coelogyne nitida ▣ ☺

INTERMEDIATE

This species' "space-saving" dimensions, modest demands and beautiful flowers make it ideal for cultivation. However, its cultivation value has not yet been fully recognized, and it is rarely included in collections. This is a fact even though the species was first described as far back as 1822. The elliptic pseudobulbs of this epiphyte reach up to 3.2 in/8 cm in height, the apical leaves (1-2) are 6-10 in/15-25 cm long. The horizontally projected flower spike reaches a length of 8 in/20 cm and bears 3-6 showy white flowers that do not exceed 1.8 in/4.5 cm in diameter. The flat snow-white lip is decorated in the throat with an impressive orange-to-yellow marking. The species is ecologically very adaptive. Grow it as you would *C. lactea*. The plant is in bloom between February and April, and inhabits a large area including the Himalayas, Nepal, Burma, Laos and Thailand.

Coelogyne nitida

Coelogyne ovalis

Coelogyne speciosa

Coelogyne ovalis ⊡ ◼ ☺

CRYOPHILIC—INTERMEDIATE

This plant is enlarged version of *C. fimbriata*. Even the flowers look the same, except they are up to 50% larger and grow usually singly out of the apices of the pseudobulbs. Also the rules of cultivation of this lovely orchid are the same as those of its smaller "sister", except that *C. ovalis* is a little more cryophilic. It blooms in June and July. Its original habitat—lower to medium altitudes (up to 6.500 ft/2,000 m) of the Himalayas—corresponds with the fact that the species thrives in a cooler and well-ventilated environment.

Coelogyne speciosa ◼ ☺

INTERMEDIATE

This species, which is not yet commonly included in collections, has flowers of quite an unusual color and size. The pseudobulbs reach lengths of up to 3.2 in/8 cm and bear a 8-12 in/20-30cm long, narrow lanceolate leaf. The inflorescence consists of no more than 2-3 flowers of a very unusual size by *Coelogyne* standards—up to 4.8 in/12 cm. The lip has a russet decoration and a frilly surface; the color of other tepals is a cross between yellowish and brownish. An albinic form—var. *alba*—is also known to exist. The plant's life requirements resemble those of *C. dayana*, except that it is a little less demanding of warmth. The best way to grow it is in a flowerpot with a light, fine substrate, although it will withstand epiphytic cultivation. It blooms early in the year—between January and April. It comes from medium elevations (3,300-5,000 ft/1,000—1,500 m above sea level) of mainland Malaysia, from Borneo, Java and Sumatra.

Comparettia falcata ☐ ⊡ ☺

INTERMEDIATE

This species is—thanks to its small proportions, showy flowers and a very large geographical range—a frequent (and pretty!) guest in smaller collections of botanical or-

chids. It has reduced pseudobulbs that are 0.8-1 in/2-2.5 cm long and covered by membranous bracts. Its single apical leaf is tough, tongue-shaped and reaches 5.2 in/13 cm in length. The flower stalk can be as long as 16 in/40 cm and bears 5-15 pink-and-purple flowers with a conspicuous spur. The size of the flowers does not exceed 1.6 in/4 cm in diameter. Grow it epiphytically, in semi-shade. The plant blooms in the winter (that is why the flowers in cultivation are sometimes deformed or insufficiently colored) and it is known to grow all over Central America, West Indian Islands and in the northern part of South America.

Comparettia falcata

Comparettia speciosa

Comparettia speciosa   ▢ ▣ ☺

INTERMEDIATE-THERMOPHILIC

A truly magnificent orchid that is even endowed with many cultivation prerequisites, as are most of the 12 species of this small New-World genus that have so far been described. *C. speciosa* grows little reduced pseudobulbs bearing a single, belt-shaped, thick leaf that reaches a length of 7.2 in/18 cm. The inflorescence is formed at the base of the pseudobulbs; it reaches a length of 20 in/50 cm and bears 6-25 spectacular (hence the Latin generic name) flowers. Their shiny orange tepals are formed in the same way as those of all the other *Comparettia* orchids—they are dominated by an excessively broadened lip. The species is not very difficult to cultivate, just beware of frequent overwatering, which causes the fine roots to mold. The roots are also sensitive to excessive salting. It blooms in the fall (October and November) and was discovered in the lower elevations of Ecuador.

Coryanthes alborosa

Coryanthes alborosa   ▢ ▣ ☹

THERMOPHILIC

The small genus *Coryanthes* numbers about 20 species and is renowned for its unique specialization: in the wild, it grows exclusively in the tree nests of *Azteca* ants. This phenomenon is probably related not only to the protection, but also the nutrition of the plants, which in turn makes these orchids very difficult to cultivate. The egg-shaped pseudobulbs of the species *C. alborosa* bear a couple of rather slim leaves. The bizarre flowers on overhanging spikes have, in a similar manner to those of the related genus *Stanhopea*, a very complicated morphology and they are white, covered with delicate red dots. Epiphytic cultivation is recommended but blooming is sporadic and usually takes place in the summer months. The species comes from Central and South America; a more precise localization has not yet been completed.

Coryanthes macrantha   ▢ ▣ ☹

THERMOPHILIC

Pollination of the extremely complex flowers of the genus *Coryanthes* is a strikingly complicated process: first of all, special glands fill in the reversed lip with a liquid; subsequently, the pollinators (bees) are attracted by the peculiar fragrance of the flower and often end up immersed in the liquid. When trying to save themselves, they are unable to fly and are bound to crawl through a small tunnel at the top of the lip, sticking the pollen onto their bodies as they crawl. After they are set free, the whole process is repeated on the stigma of the next flower, where the bee delivers the pollen. Amazingly, each species has its own specific fragrance and thus attracts only "its own" particular species of bees—hybridization is therefore prevented! The species *C. macrantha* has yellow-and-white flowers with delicate red dots and a very complex morphology. Grow it as you would the preceding species. The plant comes from Peru, Venezuela, Trinidad and Guiana.

Coryanthes macrantha

Cryptoceras sp., Mexico

of the leaves. A notable feature of *Cryptoceras* orchids is the specific morphology of their flowers: the flowers cannot open too wide, as their tepals are coarctate at the ends. To date, over 20 species have been known to exist; however, Mother Nature in the New World certainly has not yet "emptied her cartridge" and may still have a lot of surprises in store. *C.* sp. Mexico flowers in the spring. The miniature—barely 3.2 in/8 cm-long—plant in the photo was found on the outskirts of a rain forest near Palenque in southern Mexico.

Cycnoches chlorochilon

INTERMEDIATE-THERMOPHILIC

The orchids of the genus *Cycnoches* are remarkable for their life style, and also their rather large, spectacular flowers. It does not differ very much from the genera *Catasetum* and *Mormodes* in appearance and ecological needs. The species *C. chlorochilon* is sometimes considered a subspecies of *C. ventricosum*. The pseudobulbs are up to 14 in/35 cm in size, the leaves are even longer. A short stalk numbers 3-10 green-and-yellow flowers that are 3.2-4 in/8-10 cm in diameter. As with the other *Cycnoches* orchids, the flowers are resupinate—their lip is pointing upward. The species blooms between June and August and comes from Panama, Colombia, Venezuela and Guiana.

Cycnoches chlorochilon

Cryptoceras □ ☺

THERMOPHILIC

The plants that belong to this insignificant genus resemble *Masdevalias*: small oval leaves grow out of a shortened trailing rhizome, huddled on shortish stems. Single flowers appear on the flower scapes formed at the base

Cycnoches chlorochilon

Cycnoches loddigesii □ ☺

THERMOPHILIC

The reversed flowers of the genus *Cycnoches* are characteristic by a long, thin and elegantly arched column in the shape of a swan's neck; hence the nickname—swan orchid. The species *C. loddigesii* has unique extended, spindle-shaped pseudobulbs that are 3.2-6 in/8-15 cm in diameter. The flowers are purple with a tinge of green, the reversed lip is whitish and covered with delicate purple spots. The showy and very decorative "swan-neck" column is deep red at the base, with green-and-red stripes at the end. The plant has no specific requirements; grow it in the same way as related plants (see *Catasetum macrocarpum*). The flowers appear in the summer. The plant is known to grow in Venezuela, Colombia and Brazil.

Cycnoches maculatum □ ☺

INTERMEDIATE-THERMOPHILIC

In the genus *Cycnoches*, synoeciousness (that is, an ability to form completely different male and female flowers on one plant at once) has gone so far that not only the flowers but also their arrangements are markedly different. In many cases, the female inflorescences are smaller, poor in flowers and more or less erect, whereas the male flowers are arranged in overhanging racemes bearing a large number of flowers. This type of orchid (belonging to the *Heteranthae* section) is represented by

C. maculatum. The photo shows a suspended male inflorescence; the female flowers are a little bigger, arranged in a rather poor semi-erect raceme and are also yellowish, with tiny brown spots. The pseudobulbs are only 6 in/15 cm long, which makes the species an interesting, but not very easily cultivated, curiosity among orchids. The flowers can be expected to appear between August and October. The plant is native to Venezuela.

Cycnoches maculatum

Cycnoches sp., Mexico

Cycnoches sp. ▪ ☺

INTERMEDIATE-THERMOPHILIC

Some species of the genus *Cycnoches* occur in regions where periods of rain and drought alternate more markedly. The plants are adapted to that and survive the drought with the help of massive, highly resistant, grooved pseudobulbs covered with a membranous casing. With the advent of the moister season, the seemingly dead organs come alive again; they produce new foliaged shoots with lateral flower spikes. Subsequently, the shoots give rise to a new generation of pseudobulbs that are usually a little bigger each time. The photo of an unspecified plant was taken on an intensively insolated tree trunk in southern Mexico, near the Aqua Azúl Cascades.

Cymbidium hybrid

Cymbidium hybrid

better in a temperate environment. Its pseudobulbs are intensely reduced and tough; the leaves are tough and belt-shaped and reach lengths of 16 in/40 cm. The overhanging inflorescence can be up to 20 in/50 cm long and bears sparse brown-and-red flowers with an interesting ornament on the lip. *C. aloifolium* is a semi-epiphyte (it grows, for instance, in the detritus of tree crotches in lower elevations). Cultivation is easy—the plant will settle for the same kind of care as is given to other intermediate orchids. It needs a brief period of rest in order to bloom profusely. It thrives better if mounted on a wooden slab—adding a little epiphytic substrate to the moss cloak of the roots is recommended. *C. aliofolium* flowers between May and October and is native to the rainforests on Ceylon, Sumatra, Burma, Vietnam, southern China and other countries.

Cymbidium aloifolium ▣ ■ ☺

INTERMEDIATE

Although the orchids of the genus *Cymbidium* have literally subjugated the commercial cut-flower greenhouses, you would search for the original botanical species in vain. Hybridization of this genus has almost reached the point of perfection, and the newly-formed plants are unbeatable as to their beauty, durability and richness of flowers, as well as for their strikingly low energy needs: in order to develop properly, they only need a temperature as low as 50-54°F/10-12°C in winter (see the chapter "Hybridization and Breeding of Orchids"). Even though the vast majority of botanical representatives of the genus (as in the case of their hybrid offspring) are notably cryophilic, *C. aloifolium* prospers

Cymbidium aloifolium

Cymbidium finlaysonianum ▣ ■ ☺

INTERMEDIATE-THERMOPHILIC

One of the exceptions that prove the rule: *C. finlaysonianum* is so thermophilic that it would definitely perish if exposed to the cool conditions used for the common *Cymbidium* hybrids. The species has strongly reduced pseudobulbs bearing multiple leaves that are up to 20 in/50 cm long, tough and shaped like a belt. The inflorescence is overhanging and consists of up to a few dozen flowers: they are 1.2-2 in/3-5 cm in diameter, colored in brownish yellow mixed with red, with the lip set off by a lighter shade. *C. finlaysonianum* grows epiphytically and comes from the warmer and moister elevations of southeastern Asia. Cultivation is similar to the case of the preceding species, but the temperature should not drop under 68°F/20°C, not even in the winter.

Cymbidium finlaysonianum

Cymbidium lowianum ■ ☺

CRYOPHILIC

This *Cymbidium* orchid is the most widespread of all the botanical species, although the situation is full of confusion and few people are able to distinguish "pure-bred" plants from the multitude of hybrids, for the creation of which the original orchid was once used. The bulky *C. lowianum* has oval pseudobulbs bearing up to 10 belt-shaped pointed leaves that reach a length of 30 in/75 cm. The flower spike reaches a length of 30 in/75 cm and bears up to 26 flowers that are very durable, up to 4 in/10 cm in diameter, with olive-green to yellowish tepals and a somewhat yellow lip with a red-edged middle lobe. The inflorescence is arched; if you want to use it for cut flowers, you'll need to straighten the stalk by tying it to a wooden stick. Otherwise, cultivation of this species is very easy. The only problem can arise from its need of a cool environment in the summer: you should therefore transfer it to a partly shaded place under an open sky, where *Cymbidia* can remain until the arrival of the first frost. The substrate should never go completely dry. The flowering period comes between January and April and the plant is native to Burma and the Himalayas.

Cymbidium lowianum

Cynorkis sp., Madagascar

Cynorkis ▣ ☺ ☺

INTERMEDIATE

These terrestrial orchids form root bulbs of a peculiar shape that gave the name to the whole genus: the organs happen to resemble canine testicles (the Greek word "*kynos*" means dog, and "*orchis*" means testicle). The sparse leaves grow near the ground; the erect flower stalk with glandular hairs bears one or more flowers arranged in an apical raceme. The multi-flowered stalk of the Madagascar-originated plant in the photo measures 14 in/35 cm. The tepals are green-colored, the showy white lip is extended into four lobes and has a purple spot on the narrowed base. As a cultivator of this species, you must respect two growing periods: at the time of development, the plant must be kept in a moist, shady, warm place, whereas in winter, a longish dry and cool break is advisable. 125 species of the genus *Cynorkis* are reported as growing in Madagascar, as opposed to 17 species in mainland Africa.

Cyrtopodium glutiniferum ■ ☺

INTERMEDIATE

Only the epiphytic members of the genus *Cyrtopodium* are suitable for cultivation, as the bulbs of the terrestrial species are too robust (longer than 20 in/50 cm!). The clustered inflorescences bear typical, conspicuously large, evergreen bracts, identical in color with the flowers. The

Dendrobium albo-sanguineum

INTERMEDIATE-THERMOPHILIC

A dwarf species with rich and beautiful flowers. Typically, it has "stem" pseudobulbs that are somewhat thick to resemble a club and up to 10 in/25 cm long. Sparse flower racemes grow out of the internodes between individual apical grooves. The snow-white flowers have two purple-and-red spots on the lip. Grow this species as you would the other deciduous and semi-deciduous representatives of the genus: in winter, support the good growth of new pseudobulbs by providing frequent watering, fertilization and a sufficient amount of light and fresh air. Rouse the plant to bloom by reducing temperature and watering in winter. Flowers can be expected between February and March. The plant was discovered in Thailand and Burma.

Dendrobium albo-sanguineum

terrestrial species *C. glutiferum* has smaller—"only" 8 in/20-cm-tall—deciduous, spindle-shaped pseudobulbs. The flower stalk is often branched out and reaches a height of 3.3 ft/1 m. It bears a large number of tiny (0.6 in/1.5 cm) flowers. Should anyone actually choose to grow this species, it is recommended to use a permeable mix with an addition of soil. In order to bloom and develop well, the plant needs moderately moist semi-shade in the summer and a period of rest in the winter. The plants bloom in the spring. The species grows in Venezuela and the neighboring South American countries.

Dendrobium aggregatum

INTERMEDIATE-THERMOPHILIC

This species belongs to a minority within the genus *Dendrobium*, as its egg-shaped, quadrangular and apparently aggregated (hence the Latin name), unifoliate pseudobulbs have atypically only one groove. That is one of the reasons why the species is sometimes classified as a member of a separate genus *Callista*. Up to 15 deep yellow flowers grow on a compact overhanging raceme on the side of the pseudobulb. At the time of vegetation, this epiphyte needs an abundance of warmth, sunshine and water, as opposed to the winter, when a cooler and drier environment is required. The plant blooms between March and May and comes from the Himalayas, Burma, Thailand and Laos.

Dendrobium amethystoglossum

Dendrobium antennatum

Dendrobium amethystoglossum ▣ ■ ☺

THERMOPHILIC

A typical representative of the genus, as regards morphology: it has long, grooved pseudobulbs, thickly foliaged, and up to 32 in/80 cm long. The overhanging raceme of white, purple-lipped flowers that are 1-2 in/3 cm in diameter, grows from the apex of the foliaged pseudobulbs; it follows that the plant most likely does not need an extensive period of rest. Grow it epiphytically—or, better still—in a light media in a wooden basket. Flowers appear on the mature pseudobulbs between November and March. The species is native to the Philippines.

Dendrobim anosmum ⊡ ▣ ☺

INTERMEDIATE-THERMOPHILIC

These rather large purple flowers with beautifully frilled lips grow in pairs from the internodes of the leafless pseudobulbs. Grow the species epiphytically like the other

Dendrobium anosmum

deciduous species (see *D. albo-sanguineum*). Flowers appear at the beginning of the rainy season, that is, in March and April. As with almost all "tree-dwellers" (a literal translation of the Latin term *Dendrobium*), the species grows epiphytically, in sparse semi-decidous forests at medium altitudes and in foothills. It has a very large geographical range—from Sri Lanka and India, to the Philippines and New Guinea.

Dendrobium antennatum ▣ ☺ ☺

INTERMEDIATE-THERMOPHILIC

An interesting evergreen *Dendrobium* orchid—its flowers have (as in the case of a similar species, *D. stratiotes*) an extraordinary morphology. The stem pseudobulbs are erect, up to 16 in/40 cm tall and thickly foliaged. The sparse inflorescence bearing 3-7 flowers is up to 12 in/30 cm tall. The flowers are whitish, 1.6 in/4 cm in diameter. The lateral sepals are extended in the rear part and form a blunt spur-like protuberance. However, what attracts attention are chiefly the erect, spindle-shaped, green-and-yellow petals reaching up to 1.8 in/4.5 cm in length. The lip is embellished with a delicate pinkish purple marking. The species requires the same conditions as *D. phalaenopsis*, it flowers between May and August and comes from New Guinea.

Dendrobium bellatulum □ ⊡ ☺ ☺

INTERMEDIATE-THERMOPHILIC

A miniature gem with large flowers—that is the only description worthy of this dwarf semi-deciduous orchid. The very thick spindle-shaped pseudobulbs are not bigger than 2.8 in/7 cm and the nodes of their grooves give rise to single white flowers with a stunning orange-to-yellow lip,

Dendrobium capillipes

Dendrobium capillipes

Dendrobium capillipes

INTERMEDIATE-THERMOPHILIC

that are up to 1.6 in/4 cm in diameter. Rules of cultivation go along the same lines as with the deciduous *Dendrobium* orchids. The plant blooms between the fall and spring, and is native to Thailand, southern China, Burma and India.

A beautiful miniature with pansy-shaped, sulfur-yellow flowers. The small and very thick pseudobulbs are up to 2 in/5 cm long and arranged in thick, compact racemes numbering many pseudobulbs. The flowers grow on thin spikes, 1-2 on each, from the apices of the completely barren pseudobulbs. If cultivated in the Temperate Zone, the plants find it hard to keep "in shape": they do not "get fat", as could be expected, but the lack of light causes them to extend, grow thinner, and makes them unwilling to bloom. With well-wintered plants, you can expect the flowers to appear between March and April. The species was discovered in northeastern India, Burma, Thailand, China and Vietnam.

Dendrobium capillipes

Dendrobium chittimae

INTERMEDIATE

A smaller species, interesting mainly for the collectors of dwarf orchid curiosities that have interesting flowers. The pseudobulbs are extended to resemble a stick, they are thin and thickly foliaged. Flowers appear in the individual internodes, always one in each. They are up to 1 in/2.5 cm in diameter, cream-white with a remarkably frilled end of the purple-yellow cone-shaped lip. This semi-deciduous to deciduous species has no special cultivation requirements. It blooms between February and March, and comes from Thailand and other countries of southeastern Asia.

Dendrobium chittimae

Dendrobium christyanum

INTERMEDIATE

A congenial species as far as size and appearance are concerned. It creates short thick spindle-shaped pseudobulbs with 2-3 grey-and-green leaves on the top. The flowers grow singly or in pairs and are quite large (1.6 in/4 cm) in proportion to the size of the plant. Their tepals are snow-white, each with a blunt protuberance jutting out backward and a lip extended forward; its gullet and axis are adorned with an impressive red spot that gradually turns orange and yellow. This species needs a fairly warm period of rest. Its late blooming in the year (June to August) complicates its cultivation, as new pseudobulbs often do not stop developing before winter and the lack of light causes them to be small or deformed. Thailand and Vietnam are the species' countries of origin.

Dendrobium chrysotoxum

INTERMEDIATE-THERMOPHILIC

The goldish, spindle-shaped pseudobulbs are grooved lengthwise. They are ended by two (or even three) extended oval tough leaves. The flower stalk grows out of the apex of the pseudobulb and is covered with up to 20 flowers. The flowers are yellow, the lip orange-and-yellow with a frilly edge. Its anatomic differences some-

Dendrobium chrysotoxum

Dendrobium crepidatum

INTERMEDIATE

A beautiful deciduous orchid with extended grooved pseudobulbs; their length does not exceed 8 in/20 cm, which makes *D. crepidatum* a highly space-saving plant for collections. Its waxy, tough flowers grow in twos out of individual joints. Their lips are embellished with a showy deep-yellow spot, the other tepals are pinkish. Flowering season stretches from April to June. The plant is known to grow over a vast area, including India, the Himalayas, Burma, Thailand and Laos.

Dendrobium cruentum

INTERMEDIATE-THERMOPHILIC

One of the world's rarest orchids that is hardly ever found in the wild—its habitats are all but extinct now. The species was native to the warm lowlands of the Malayan Peninsula, an area that has been subject to intensive farming for more than a millennium. The species *D. cruentum* is therefore listed in Appendix 1 of the CITES international convention. It is one of the indeciduous *Dendrobia*. Its stem pseudobulbs reach 12-16 in/30-40 cm in length, and produce on their apexes 1-2 showy flowers (1.4-2 in/3.5-5 cm in diameter) with yellow-and-green tepals. The lip is covered with brick-red verrucose protuberances. Grow the plants as you would the other thermophilic *Dendrobia*. The flowers appear irregularly throughout the year. *D. cruentum* comes from Malaysia and Thailand.

Dendrobium cruentum

times classify the species as a member of the genus *Callista*. This orchid is not hard to cultivate, just make sure to provide it with a rather long and warm resting period in the winter. The inflorescence appears sooner than with related species—as early as December. The geographical range is extensive and includes southern China, the Himalayas, Burma, Thailand and Laos.

Dendrobium crepidatum

Dendrobium cuthbertsonii

Dendrobium dearei

THERMOPHILIC

Within the genus *Dendrobium*, white flowers are not a very common occurrence; therefore, they are among the features that make *D. dearei* a valuable species (and not only for cultivators). The plant is very bulky—its pseudobulbs reach up to 32 in/80 cm in size. They are thickly covered with leathery, durable foliage. The flowers measure 2.8 in/7 cm in diameter and are snow-white with a greenish gullet; they are arranged in a sparse raceme. This species is one of the indeciduous *Dendrobium* orchids, and therefore has a greater demand for moisture and warmth throughout the year. *D. dearei* usually blooms between May and June. It comes from the Philippines.

Dendrobium densiflorum

INTERMEDIATE

A spectacular orchid that is unfortunately rather bulky. Its slim, club-shaped pseudobulbs bear 4-5 leaves and are up to 16 in/40 cm tall; after a period of rest, a robust overhanging compact raceme of yellow flowers grows out of their apex. The flowers are orange-and-yellow with a velvety lip. Grow the plant epiphytically or in flowerpots, as you would the other deciduous *Dendrobium* orchids. The inflorescence appears between

Dendrobium densiflorum

Dendrobium cuthbertsonii

CRYOPHILIC-INTERMEDIATE

A miniature orchid that stands out from the genus not only for its appearance, but also its manner of cultivation. A much sought-after rarity, its beautiful tubular flowers are up to 2 in/5 cm in diameter and dwarf the small (0.8-1.2 in/2-3 cm), stick-shaped pseudobulbs and the equally small, tough, rough-surfaced leaves. The color of the flowers varies— there are specimens colored in pastel shades of dark red, brick orange, yellow and purple. The plants do not require a period of rest and their roots should never be left to overdry; therefore, it is advisable to grow this species in flowerpots. Excessive summer heat may also be harmful. The flowers are durable and appear practically all year round, most often in the spring and summer. *D. cuthbertsonii* is native to the alpine altitudes (7,380-9,840 ft/2,250-3,000 m above sea level) of New Guinea.

Dendrobium dearei

March and May (or even August and September) and the species' habitat consists of the foothills and mountainous regions of the Himalayas, Burma and Thailand.

Dendrobium devonianum var. *album*

INTERMEDIATE

A species with thin stick-shaped overhanging pseudobulbs that are up to 16 in/40 cm long. After the pseudobulbs mature, 1-2 large flowers with frilly-edged, heart-

Dendrobium devonianum var. *album*

shaped lips grow out of their nodes. The surface of each lip is decorated with two orange-and-yellow spots. The edges of the lip and the other tepals of a typical representative of this species are pink-and-purple; in contrast, the plant introduced in the photo has pure white flowers— except for the indispensable yellow spots. The best way of growing them is epiphytic, much like the other deciduous species. *D. devonianum* blooms between spring and summer and is native to the northeast of India, Burma, the southwest of China and the north of Thailand.

Dendrobium exile

INTERMEDIATE

A small, somewhat obscure species suitable for the lovers of unconventional orchids. Its pseudobulbs have an unusual appearance: the species' thin, extended stems are thickly covered with two rows of unique fleshy leaves that are arranged in a reverse, tree-like manner. The length of the partly deciduous leaves that are almost round in cross-section does not exceed 2-2.4 in/5-6 cm. One or two flowers grow out of the nodes formed by the upper parts of the stems and are quite large. The white lip is embellished with an orange-and-yellow spot in the gullet. Grow the species in relatively moist conditions without a substantial period of rest. *D. exile* blooms in December and comes from Thailand, Burma, Laos and other countries.

87

Dendrobium farmeri

Dendrobium findlayanum

Dendrobium farmeri

INTERMEDIATE

This orchid species resembles *D. densiflorum* in appearance and cultivation requirements, but it is somewhat smaller. The shape of the raceme bearing up to 20 flowers and the shape of the flowers are also identical; however, the tepals are whitish, except for the orange-and-yellow base of the velvety lip. The flowers appear between February and May. The plant is native to the lower altitudes of the Himalayas, Burma and Thailand.

Dendrobium farmeri

Dendrobium findlayanum

INTERMEDIATE

This plant is a pleasure for the eye of many a lover of epiphytic curiosities, even when it is not in bloom. It has curiously-shaped, deciduous pseudobulbs that are 8-10 in/20-25 cm long and whose individual pear-shaped links—narrowed at the base and extended at the apex—overlap. Moreover, the species produces very pretty flowers that appear on the terminal joints, 1-2 on each. The wide lip on each flower has a noticeable orange-and-yellow spot in the middle. There is one drawback connected with the cultivation of this species: it requires a great deal of light. Insufficient light often causes the pseudobulbs to assume a traditional shape, which causes deformities, extensions etc. *D. findlayanum* blooms between February and April and it comes from Thailand, Laos and Burma.

Dendrobium formosum

CRYOPHILIC-THERMOPHILIC

A bulky species with large, aureate flowers. Its erect, thickly foliaged pseudobulbs are up to 18 in/45 cm long and typically covered with conspicuous black protuberances in the upper part. The snow-white flowers measure 3.8 in/8 cm in diameter. The lip has a 0.8-in/2-cm-long spur and is embellished with a yellow decoration

Dendrobium formosum

Dendrobium friedericksianum

inside. The species is indeciduous, yet it must be kept in warm and moist conditions in the summer, and temperate-to-cool conditions with reduced watering in the winter. It blooms between the fall and spring and is native to high elevations (up to 7,380 ft/2,250 m above sea level) of the Himalayas, Thailand and Burma.

Dendrobium friedericksianum

Dendrobium friedericksianum ☺

INTERMEDIATE

A semi-deciduous species with club-shaped, extended pseudobulbs bearing thick foliage at the time of growth. Large flowers appear on the upper parts of the mature and, by that time, usually barren pseudobulbs. The sulfur-yellow tepals are dominated by a brown-and-red gullet of the robust cone-shaped lip. The plant is propagated by dividing the bunches and mounting the separate clusters onto bare wooden slabs. As the pseudobulbs are very heavy, it is necessary to secure the plant against uprooting in the initial phase. It takes the plant between 1-2 years before it secures its stability with its own roots. The species blooms between February and May and comes from Thailand.

Dendrobium gratiosissimum

Dendrobium gregulus

Dendrobium gratiosissimum

INTERMEDIATE

If you manage to provide these specimens with the right cultivation conditions, they reward you with stunning flowers! Several whitish flowers with purple-edged tepals and orange-and-yellow, white-lined lip, grow from each of the individual joints. Ideally, two thirds of the surface of the thin, extended (up to 16 in/40 cm), overhanging pseudobulb can be covered with flowers! Cultivation is not complicated—during the vegetation period (spring to fall), the plant requires good nutrition, plenty of water and warmth, as opposed to a significantly drier and cooler winter break. After that, sit back and look forward to the early spring when the leafless pseudobulbs produce a large number of fantastic flowers. *D. gratiosissimum* comes from the southeast of India, southwest of China, Thailand, Burma and Laos.

Dendrobium gregulus

INTERMEDIATE

This slightly atypical representative of the genus will please its cultivators mainly with its ball-shaped, tiny (0.8-1.6 in/2-4 cm), radically reduced pseudobulbs. Its flowers are not very durable and attract less attention:

Dendrobium gregulus

they are 1.2 in/3 cm large, whitish, with a violet veining on the lip. They appear in great multitudes, 3-6 on each of the erect stalks that grow out of the apices of the new, usually bifoliate, pseudobulbs. This botanical curiosity's cultivation needs do not differ from those of other representatives of the genus. It blooms in early spring and comes from Thailand and the surrounding countries.

Dendrobium harveyanum

INTERMEDIATE

Although the world of orchids is immensely diverse, it would still be hard to find many plants whose flowers surpass in beauty those of *D. harveyanum*, whose yellow petal edge and round lip are lined with gorgeous long frilling. Moreover, the gullet of the lip boasts a deep yellow spot. It is just a shame the flowers do not last very long! The semi-deciduous and partly overhanging pseudobulbs are 12-16 in/30-40 cm tall, with

Dendrobium heterocarpum

INTERMEDIATE

This sizeable *Dendrobium* orchid has cylindrical, deciduous pseudobulbs that reach up to 16 in/40 cm in length. The pointed elliptic leaves are up to 6 in/15 cm long. The large flowers, at least 2.4 in/6 cm across, grow out of the apical parts of the mature, leafless pseudobulbs at the peak of the dry season. Their cream-colored tepals are extended and pointed in an unusual way, and their small, heart-shaped lip has a brown-and-yellow spot in the gullet. The plant grows over a vast geographical area—from Sri Lanka and India, through Burma and Thailand, to the Philippines.

Dendrobium heterocarpum

sparse overhanging racemes growing out of their apical joints. Grow them as you would the other *Dendrobium* orchids that require a considerably dry and cool vegetation break. The species blooms between April and June and comes from Thailand, Burma and Vietnam.

Dendrobium hercoglossum

INTERMEDIATE

A semi-deciduous species possessing long pseudobulbs, with an unusual color of flowers—by *Dendrobium* standards. The light purple (bluish in some instances), symmetrical flowers have a waxy appearance and a dark purple cap in the middle (part of reproduction organs known by its Latin name *anthera*). The lip is whitish, with a pointed purple tip. Grow it epiphytically on a bare slab of cork or in an epiphytic basket. The partly overhanging pseudobulbs require a substantial period of rest before blooming. The flowers appear between March and May. The species is known to grow in the southwest of China, Thailand, Indochina and Malaysia.

91

Dendrobium infundibulum ■ ☺ ☺

CRYOPHILIC-THERMOPHILIC

This orchid with a tongue-twisting Latin name closely resembles the species *D. formosum* both in appearance and cultivation requirements. The features that distinguish it are its slightly smaller (2.8 in/7 cm) flowers and lip shape. The subspecies ssp. *jamesianum* is grown more often and it has, in contrast to the typical representatives of the species, more robust straight-growing pseudobulbs and tomentose edges of the lip. Cultivation is the same as that of the species *D. formosum*. The flowers appear between March and June. The plant is native to India, Burma, Laos and Thailand.

Dendrobium infundibulum

Dendrobium jacobsonii ▣ ☺ ☺

INTERMEDIATE

Red color is not very common with the flowers of *Dendrobium* orchids, which makes every specimen endowed with red flowers a rare and cherished gem of orchid collections. The species *D. jacobsonii* has very long, thickly foliaged pseudobulbs that do not bloom before reaching complete maturity and shed nearly all their leaves. Individual brick-red flowers grow out of the internodes of the pseudobulbs, sometimes several seasons in a row. The flowers appear in early spring. The species comes from southeast Asia.

Dendrobium jacobsonii

Dendrobium jenkinsii

Dendrobium kingianum

CRYOPHILIC-INTERMEDIATE

Perhaps every amateur orchid grower must have owned a *D. kingianum* early in his cultivation career. It is a completely undemanding species. As it is also easy to propagate by division of bunches or by forming daughter pseudobulbs, it was passed among people until recently. An even greater popularity of this species was prevented by its unwillingness to bloom and the fact that the flowers are small and rather unsightly. The conic pseudobulbs are 6 in/15 cm tall and bear 4-5 leaves. An erect raceme of 3-8 tiny flowers grows from their apex, the color of the flowers ranges between purple and white with a tinge of pink. *D. kingianum* is a very cryophilic species that can be grown, for instance, along with *Cymbidium* orchids. The flowering season comes in the spring. The species is native to eastern Australia.

Dendrobium kingianum

Dendrobium jenkinsii

INTERMEDIATE-THERMOPHILIC

This small species is popular with amateur growers both for the shape of its tiny (1.2-1.6 in/3-4 cm) unifoliate pseudobulbs and for its large yellow-and-orange flowers. It has been slowly disappearing from orchid collections owing to its difficult cultivation. In order to develop well, the plant needs a barren slab of bark for support and full sunshine (sunburn can be avoided by placing it in the open air on a rainproof spot). Water moderately all year round, and reduce watering even more in the winter to avoid molding. The flowers appear between March and April. The plant is native to Thailand, Burma and Laos.

Dendrobium lamellatulum ▣ ☺ ☺

INTERMEDIATE-THERMOPHILIC

This species features extended pseudobulbs, significantly flattened from two sides. The tiny (0.6-0.8 in/1.5-2 cm) flowers are less attractive, although the remarkable spur on each flower, formed by tepals extended backward, certainly deserves credit. The flowers grow (sometimes repeatedly) in bunches on the apices of the pseudobulbs that have shed their leaves; they are white, greenish or yellow, with a honey brown spot in the gullet of each lip. Grow them in a similar manner as you would other deciduous species of this genus. The plant blooms in March and grows in the countryside of Thailand, Burma, Malaysia, Indonesia, the Philippines and elsewhere.

Dendrobium lanyiae ☐ ▫ ☺ ☺

INTERMEDIATE-THERMOPHILIC

A collector's treasure of the highest class! The flowers' proportions are almost gigantic compared to the small size of the plants. Furthermore, the species boasts a nearly unprecedented color of the tepals, by the standards of the genus. The deciduous, thick, cylindrical pseudobulbs are no more than 2-2.4 in/5-6 cm long and, in the flowering season, completely covered with spectacular orange-and-red flowers with white lips decorated with red venation. Two or three flowers grow from the knots on the leafless pseudobulbs at the peak of the dry season. When in bloom, the plant resembles another collector's hit—*D. unicum*. The flowers appear on *D. lanyiae* in early spring. The species is native to Thailand, Burma and Laos.

Dendrobium linguiforme ☐ ☺ ☺

INTERMEDIATE

A curiosity orchid species, popular chiefly for its peculiar appearance, thanks to which it was described as far back as 1800! A basic feature of this epiphytic or litho-

Dendrobium lanyiae

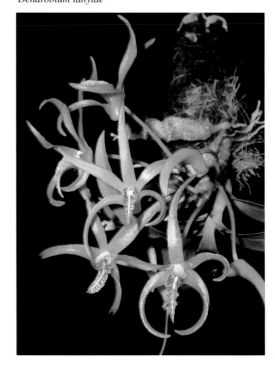

Dendrobium linguiforme

Dendrobium loddigesii

phytic orchid is a trailing, branching rhizome with very thick, tough, sideways-grooved leaves that reach lengths of up to 1.6 in/4 cm and are staggered on the rhizome with short gaps between one another. They resemble a tongue in appearance (hence the species name). The flowers grow in an erect raceme that numbers many flowers—and their position is reversed (i.e., their tiny lip is pointing upward). They are about 0.8 in/2 cm across, white or cream-colored, with reddish markings on the edges of the tepals. From a cultivator's perspective, *D. linguiforme* is a species of a quite unpredictable, almost "whimsical" character that requires plenty of patience on the part of the grower. Grow it epiphytically on a slab of hard bark; do not divide the clusters too often, and add a handful of *Sphagnum* moss underneath the newly mounted plants. The plant comes from the tropical areas of Australia.

Dendrobium lituiflorum   ■ ☺

INTERMEDIATE

An orchid with lovely flowers and thin, overhanging pseudobulbs that reach a length of up to 24 in/60 cm. The leaves measure 4 in/10 cm and the plant sheds every single one of them. One or two flowers are formed in the internodes between the individual joints and are quite bulky (up to 2 in/5 cm). The whitish, cone-shaped lip with a purple gullet is surrounded by other violet tepals. A well-grown specimen in full bloom is an unforgettable sight. Cultivation requirements are the same as those of other deciduous *Dendrobium* orchids. The species flowers in the spring (April to May) in semi-deciduous, insolated forests of India, Burma and Thailand.

Dendrobium loddigesii   ☺

CRYOPHILIC-INTERMEDIATE

A widely known and very popular small clustered orchid. Its stem-like, semi-deciduous, overhanging pseudobulbs are up to 8 in/20 cm long. The tiny leaves are partially deciduous. 1-2 spectacular purple flowers with orange-

and-yellow lips appear in the upper parts of "well-rested" pseudobulbs. In the past, it was *D. loddigesii* more than any other species that taught orchid growers interested in deciduous and semi-deciduous orchids the proper rules of cultivating them. Plants that were kept in warm glass cases all year round would grow wildly but never bloom; not until their growth was suspended by placing them in a cool, dry and light environment. This species does not produce flowers before the rest period is over (between February and April). The plant comes from medium elevations of southern China and Laos.

Dendrobium lituiflorum

Dendrobium macrophyllum

Dendrobium macrophyllum ◨ ☺ ☺

INTERMEDIATE-THERMOPHILIC

The pseudobulbs of this species are club-shaped, up to 12 in/30 cm long and they bear a pair of large (hence the Latin name), leathery, longish, oval leaves. The greenish-white-to-yellowish, bizarre looking flowers grow in a sparse raceme out of the apex of the foliaged pseudobulb. The outer parts of their sepals are very hairy and each of the robust lips is embellished with a beautiful brown marking. The plant comes from relatively warm and moist areas—the rules of epiphytic or pot cultivation need to be adapted to this. The flowers appear between May and June and the plant is native to the islands of Java, Sumatra and New Guinea.

Dendrobium nobile

Dendrobium nobile ◨ ■ ☺

CRYOPHILIC-INTERMEDIATE

One of the best-known species of the whole genus has been used to create a large number of decorative hybrids serving mainly to please the eye of amateur orchid growers. Nowadays, the original species is almost completely replaced with colorful hybrids that are livelier and more eager to bloom. The only disadvantage of this orchid is the large size of its thick, irregularly swollen, extended pseudobulbs. Two or three flowers ranging in color between light purple and pink appear on the individual joints of the upper parts of the pseudobulbs. The flower lip sports a dark purple spot in the gullet. The species is abundant in amateur collections, partly for its ability to create daughter plants on the apices of its old pseudobulbs. The flowers are induced to grow only in an environment that is sufficiently dry, light and cool. The species can be cultivated in a flowerpot or basket, as well as epiphytically. *D. nobile* blooms between March and May and is native to a vast Asian area that includes southern China, the Himalayas, Nepal, Thailand, Laos, Vietnam and Taiwan.

Dendrobium parishii ◨ ☺

INTERMEDIATE

A beautiful dwarf species, sold until recently in great numbers on black markets in Bangkok. Its pseudobulbs are irregularly swollen, very massive and only 6-8 in/15-20 cm long. The leaves reach a length of

Dendrobium peguanum

about 4 in/10 cm and are shed completely during the winter period. The individual deep purple flowers grow out of the upper parts of the pseudobulbs and reach very impressive proportions, sometimes over 2 in/5 cm across. The surface of the rather small, whitish lip is smooth and velvety and the throat is decorated with a dark purple spot. Newly mounted plants need to be well attached to an epiphytic support owing to the great weight of the pseudobulbs. As with the other deciduous species, *D. parishii* requires very different conditions during its vegetation period than during its rest period. It blooms between May and June and comes from northeastern India, Burma, Laos, Thailand, Vietnam and southern China.

Dendrobium peguanum □

INTERMEDIATE

A very pretty dwarf orchid, perfect for growers with limited cultivation space. The pseudobulbs of this species resemble a barrel; they are intensely swollen and only 1.2-1.6 in/3-4 cm long. During the vegetation period (between spring and fall), they are covered with 4-5 fresh green leaves that are subsequently shed. The whitish flowers with a brown-and-green lip and a purple spot in the center grow in sparse racemes out of the upper parts of the pseudobulbs between January and March. In their homeland (Thailand, Burma, Laos, etc.), the plants grow over thicker branches of semideciduous trees.

Dendrobium phalaenopsis

Dendrobium phalaenopsis ▣ ■ ☺

INTERMEDIATE-THERMOPHILIC

Undoubtedly the most important representative of the genus: the business of many (especially Asian) producers dealing in cut flowers depends on growing its perfectly thoroughbred colorful cultivars. Besides their beautiful looks, the inflorescences of the hybrids are distinguished by an exceptional durability and a firm spike. The biological species is sometimes labeled with the biological term *D. biggibum* ssp. *phalaenopsis*. The species name suggests a resemblance in the appearance of the beautiful flowers (or even the whole inflorescences) to an unrelated genus *Phalaenopsis*. It belongs in the group of indeciduous and thermophilic *Dendrobium* orchids—its extended, thick pseudobulbs, whose length does not exceed 24 in/60 cm, do not shed foliage after the tissues achieve maturity. The long (up to 20 in/50 cm) flower spike bears 6-15 flowers that reach sizes of up to 3.2 in/ 8 cm across. The flowers of the original species are purple, with a deep purple lip, but there are a lot of color exceptions (including a highly-valued snow-white form

Dendrobium phalaenopsis

Dendrobium phalaenopsis

Dendrobium phalaenopsis

Dendrobium phalaenopsis

termed var. *hololeucum*). Grow the plants in a well-ventilated and well-lighted, warm place in suspended baskets or flowerpots with a permeable, coarse substrate. Flowers appear on both the biological species and its hybrids during the commercially favorable winter period. The plant comes from northern Australia and New Guinea, where it grows mostly on rocks.

Dendrobium phalaenopsis

Dendrobium primulinum

Dendrobium pulchellum

Dendrobium primulinum

INTERMEDIATE-THERMOPHILIC

Another deciduous representative of the genus, with erect, medium-thick pseudobulbs that reach lengths of up to 14 in/35 cm. 1-3 flowers are formed in the knots of the upper joints of the pseudobulbs and are 2 in/5 cm across. Their color is purple with a tinge of pink; the lip is whitish-to-yellowish and has a velvety, felt-like surface. Cultivation is the same as in the case of other representatives of this ecological section of the genus. *D. primulinum* blooms between April and May and its habitat includes China, the Himalayas, Burma, Thailand, Laos, and Vietnam.

Dendrobium pulchellum

INTERMEDIATE-THERMOPHILIC

A very pretty orchid when in bloom; outside of the flowering period, it does not differ in appearance from other deciduous *Dendrobium* orchids with long and narrow pseudobulbs. Somewhat out of the ordinary, the flowers grow abundantly in an overhanging raceme at the ends of the pseudobulbs. They are white or cream-yellow, with a hairy, velvety lip embellished with two

impressive crimson spots. The plant blooms between February and April, both in cultivation and in the wild (India, Burma, Malaysia, Indochina).

Dendrobium sanderae

THERMOPHILIC

A species closely related to, and identical in appearance and cultivation with, the orchid *D. dearei*. It is one of the indeciduous representatives of the genus—large flowers

Dendrobium sanderae

appear on the apices of the pseudobulbs between vividly green leaves. The pseudobulbs are quite long—20-28 in/50-70 cm. The large white flowers reach lengths of up to 3.6 in/9 cm and are decorated with a largish spur and a wide, two-lobed lip embellished with a red marking. The species is not very suitable for amateur collections, as it is quite bulky. If you wish to grow this species, do so in somewhat moist, warm conditions, without a substantial period of rest. The flowers open in the fall—between November and December—and the plant comes from Luzon in the Philippines.

Dendrobium scabrilingue · ■ ☺ ☺

INTERMEDIATE-THERMOPHILIC

A species with pronouncedly jointed semi-deciduous pseudobulbs and flower lips that vary greatly in color. The pseudobulbs reach lengths of up to 10 in/25 cm and their apical parts give rise to sparse inflorescences with tiny flowers. The tepals are always pure white, while their lip color ranges from light yellow to shiny orange. Grow the plant epiphytically in somewhat moist conditions; the winter rest need not be overly substantial. The species blooms between December and March and comes from the medium altitudes of Thailand, Laos and Burma.

Dendrobium scabrilingue

Dendrobium scabrilingue

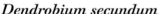

Dendrobium secundum ■ ☺

INTERMEDIATE-THERMOPHILIC

One of the best-known *Dendrobium* orchids, popular more with scientists and professional cultivators than with gardeners and exotic-plant lovers: the reasons being that the flowers are exceptionally tiny (about 0.4 in/1 cm)—so tiny that even their multitudes per raceme cannot compensate for their size. The pseudobulbs are deciduous, up to 20 in/50 cm long, and narrow at the ends. The flowers are pinkish purple with a minuscule yellow lip. The plant requires epiphytic cultivation, plenty of sunshine and air during the growth period, and only a slight reduction of temperature in winter. Several inflorescences can grow at once out of the apical knots of the pseudobulbs between the fall and spring. The plant is native to a large geographical area that includes Thailand, Vietnam and Malaysia, the Philippines and islands in the Pacific Ocean.

Dendrobium senile ⊡ ☹

INTERMEDIATE-THERMOPHILIC

A spectacular, highly-valued and highly sought-after curiosity—anyone who as much as looks at a specimen of *D. senile*, even outside the flowering period, will understand why. Both the fat, deciduous pseudobulbs and the vividly green belt-shaped leaves bear a thick layer of white hairs. Besides its "senility," the species prides itself on cultivation-friendly

proportions (the length of the pseudobulbs does not exceed 8 in/20 cm), as well as on its gorgeous yellow flowers with a red-and-green decoration on the lip. Unfortunately, the plants sometimes stagnate in collections, form dwarfed or deformed pseudobulbs, don't bloom and even mold. This is probably caused by a lack of light coupled with excessive

Dendrobium senile

Dendrobium sukhakulii

Dendrobium sukhakulii

INTERMEDIATE

A lovely small orchid, whose importance for cultivation and collections has not yet received its due recognition. The stem pseudobulbs are of medium thickness and up to 8 in/20 cm long, and their upper knots give rise to long overhanging racemes of deep yellow flowers with a huge flat lip on each. The center of the flower is highlighted with a pronounced yellow spot. Grow the species epi-phytically, the same as you would other deciduous repre-sentatives of the genus. Flowers can be expected between February and April. *D. sukhakulii* occurs in Thailand, Burma and Laos.

Dendrobium sulawesiense

INTERMEDIATE-THERMOPHILIC

An unfulfilled dream of many an orchid admirer, *D. su-lawesiense* is a very beautiful, but unfortunately rare, species. Its stem pseudobulbs are not very thick; they are up to 14 in/35 cm long and are usually shed after the growth period is over (although this is by no means a rule). Clusters of fabulous, largish flowers grow out of the internodes of the upper parts of the mature pseudob-ulbs. The belt-shaped flowers light up their surroundings with their pinkish-purple color. The tepals are extended backward in the lower part of the flower, thus forming a spur-like protuberance. The flowers appear in the spring and early summer. The species is native to the Sulawesi region in Indonesia.

moisture and poor ventilation. Mount the plant on a bare slab of pine bark and reduce watering but not temperature in win-ter. From early spring to the high spring season, 1-2 flowers grow out of the apices of the pseudobulbs. The species, sometimes classified as a *Callista* orchid, can still be found in the wild in Burma, Laos and Thailand.

Dendrobium sulawesiense

Dendrobium sulcatum

Dendrobium sulcatum

INTERMEDIATE-THERMOPHILIC

The pseudobulbs of this impressive species are intensely swollen with sideways grooves, they are flattened on the sides and bear 3-4 egg-shaped leaves in the apices that reach lengths of 6 in/15 cm. If the summer is particularly dry, the plant sheds all its foliage; if it is somewhat moist, overhanging inflorescences can appear between the surviving leaves. The flowers are 1.4 in/3.5 cm across, yellow, with a velvety, frilly lip embellished with red markings, and 10-20 of them populate a dense, compact raceme. Grow the plant epiphytically. While it is recommended to reduce watering in winter, do not "force" the plant to shed all its leaves by exposing it to excessive drought. The flowering season comes in the spring. The plant is native to Thailand.

Dendrobium thyrsiflorum

INTERMEDIATE

This species is sometimes classified as *D. densiflorum* var. *albo-lutea*. This pretty much sums it up about the relation, appearance and ecological requirements of this orchid. In contrast to the yellow-flowered *D. densiflorum*, this plant has sparser, overhanging inflorescences and tinier white flowers with an orange-and-yellow lip. It blooms in early spring and comes from the area between Nepal and Thailand.

Dendrobium tobaense

INTERMEDIATE-THERMOPHILIC

D. tobaense is a highly valued and very rarely cultivated species. It comes from warmer regions without a substantial drought period, which is why its intensely long and rather thin pseudobulbs usually keep their foliage. The highlights of the plant are its medium-sized star-shaped flowers that feature a color combination atypical of *Dendrobium* orchids. The yellow-and-white tepals are decorated with green venation and each is ended with a showy long, narrow tip. The lip is orange-and-red at the base and its tip is extended into a whitish, narrow, tongue-shaped protuberance. The cultivation requirements of the plant are similar to other thermophilic representatives of the genus. It blooms in early summer and grows in northern Sumatra.

Dendrobium thyrsiflorum

Dendrobium tobaense

Dendrobium unicum

INTERMEDIATE

If you order specimens of *D. unicum* by mail, what you receive may be quite a disappointment: its long, thin, reddish, dry, sticklike pseudobulbs might make you think that there is nothing remarkable about this orchid. How wrong you would be! After the resting period is over, the individual knots of the jointed pseudobulbs reaching lengths of 6 in/15 cm give rise to ravishing orange-and-

Dendrobium unicum

red flowers resembling the species *D. lanyiae*. The backward-twisted tepals are well counterbalanced by a whitish lip that is markedly protruding forward and is decorated with a delicate purple-and-red venation. In order to form new shoots, the plant needs a lot of sunshine, water and nutrients, and a substantial period of rest in winter. When offered by Asian orchid farms, the species tends to be listed as *D. arachnites* (which is a related but rarer species). The plant blooms between March and May and the species comes from Thailand and Laos.

Dendrobium victoriae-reginae

INTERMEDIATE-THERMOPHILIC

This orchid will immediately catch your eye with the color of its tepals that is rare and unique not only within the *Dendrobium* genus, but among orchids throughout the world. The semi-deciduous pseudobulbs reach a length of up to 20 in/50 cm, but in most cases they are much shorter. Sparse inflorescences bearing 1-3 flowers grow out of the knots of the upper parts of the mature pseudobulbs. The flowers are purplish-blue, with a slightly darker, lengthwise venation on the tepals and a whitish center. Grow the plant in a somewhat warm and moist environment and provide it with just a brief period of rest. Flowers appear irregularly, usually at the end of the summer. The species comes from the Philippines.

Dendrobium victoriae-reginae

Dendrobium virgineum

INTERMEDIATE-THERMOPHILIC

A semi-deciduous robust *Dendrobium* orchid with large flowers. The pseudobulbs are 14 in/35 cm long. The flowers are up to 3 in/7.5 cm across and appear from between the uppermost broad, leathery leaves. The white flower with a spur-shaped protuberance is dominated by a robust, wavy, lobed lip embellished with two orange-and-red spots. Grow the plants epiphytically in warm and moist conditions throughout the year, without a substantial rest period. The flowers appear only sporadically in cultivation. They bloom in the wilderness in Thailand, mostly between June and August.

Dendrobium williamsonii

Dendrobium williamsonii

INTERMEDIATE

The pseudobulbs of *D. williamsonii* are foliaged in the upper parts and are up to 12 in/30 cm long. After they reach maturity and shed their leaves, their upper knots give rise to 1-2 cream-white-to-yellow flowers, 1.8 in/4.5 cm across. The lip is wavy, with an orange-red spot and a showy frilling. Grow the plants as you would most of the other orchids that are deciduous, bloom in the spring and come from the medium elevations of Thailand, Laos, Burma and Vietnam.

Dendrochilum ianiariense

INTERMEDIATE

What makes the genus *Dendrochilum* special is the "architecture" of its inflorescences: multitudes of tiny flowers are crowded on arched, overhanging spikes. The species *D. ianiariense* has—as do other *Dendrochilum* orchids—intensely reduced, unifoliate pseudobulbs with color-interval streaking (1.6 in/4 cm long), each tipped with a long (over 8 in/20 cm), narrow and very tough leaf. The inflorescence consists of two opposite rows of peculiar green-and-yellow flowers; its appearance is somewhat unusual, resembling a chimneysweep's brush. It is an epiphytic, and occasionally terrestrial species, which means that it can be grown

Dendrochilum ianiariense

Dendrochilum weriselii

suspended (if you cultivate it in this way, add a little *Sphagnum* moss to its roots), or in a permeable fine-grain mix in a flowerpot. The inflorescence appears irregularly, most often between early spring and fall. The species comes from southeastern Asia.

Dendrochilum weriselii   ☺

INTERMEDIATE

Orchids of the genus *Dendrochilum* are of particular interest to admirers of orchid curiosities. Their flowers are not endowed with individual beauty, but stand out as a group. If you consider only large-flowered species to be "genuine orchids", you had better ignore the whole *Dendrochilum* genus. *D. weriselii* resembles the previously mentioned species (and all the other 130 representatives of the genus) in the morphology of its green parts. Its flowers are brick red, with the bottom parts colored in yellowish green. There are a total of 40 of them arranged in two opposite rows, and they bloom almost simultaneously, starting at the bottom. Cultivation rules are almost identical with those that apply to the previous species. If a specimen blooms in the fall, the tepals tend to get insufficient coloring. The plants bloom between the spring and fall and they are known to grow, among other places, in the Philippines.

Diaphananthe pelucida ▫ ◼ ☺

INTERMEDIATE-THERMOPHILIC

Orchid lovers are not overly familiar with the *Diaphananthe* genus, as it was excluded from the African genus of *Angraecum*. Since it is rather unattractive, it can be found only in the collections of specialized botanical gardens or those of the most avid amateur enthusiasts. *D. pelucida* forms a partly ascending, firm and gradually lignifying stem foliaged with two staggered rows of leathery, belt-shaped leaves with a two-lobed tip on each. The inflorescence is overhanging, growing from the axils of the leaves and consisting of 30-50 tiny (0.4 in/1 cm across) white flowers embellished with showy spurs. Cultivate the plants as you would *Angraecum* orchids. The species blooms in the fall and comes from the rainforests of western Africa.

Diaphananthe pelucida

Dimerandra emarginata

Dimerandra emarginata ◼ ◼ ☺

INTERMEDIATE

Dimerandra orchids (a total of 8 species) are largish clustered epiphytes of a reed-like appearance. The species *D. emarginata* has a high (up to 16 in/40 cm), fleshy shoot covered with two rows of rather firm, 4-in/10-cm-long leaves tapering off into a sharp tip. Short spikes bearing one flower appear in tufts on the ends of the shoots—they bloom one by one and produce showy pink-and-purple flowers. Each flower is embellished with a backward-turned, fan-shaped lip colored in a darker shade of purple. The center of the flower is highlighted with a white base of the lip. The species' proportions prevent it from becoming ideal for cultivation, but its beautiful flowers guarantee a certain degree of popularity. The plants can be kept both as epiphytes and in a permeable mix in flowerpots or baskets. In order to develop well, the plant needs semi-shade, high air humidity and a brief winter rest. Flowers appear irregularly, most often between the fall and spring. The plant inhabits a large geographical area between Mexico and Ecuador.

Dinema polybulbon ☐ ☺

INTERMEDIATE

A very pretty miniature orchid, closely related to the genus *Encyclia*. It's just a shame that the large and decorative flowers do not appear on the plant more often. The oval pseudobulbs of this orchid are truly "pocket-sized"—they reach a length of only 0.8 in/2 cm; they are sparsely distributed on a trailing rhizome and bear a pair of leaves reaching lengths of about 2 in/5 cm. The yellow-and-brown flowers with broadened whitish lip grow individually on short flower spikes. Its proportions and

vitality (up to several new generations of pseudobulbs are added every year) make the plant suitable for any amateur collection, and help it thrive even in glass cases. Cultivation is not difficult—the epiphytically grown plants will settle for a piece of pine bark for support, a semi-shady environment and occasional fertilization. The only problem is that the plant is sometimes unwilling to bloom; in order to induce blooming, you may provide the plant with a brief period of rest. The plant blooms in the winter months and comes from the central part of Central America—including Mexico and Guatemala and the adjacent islands in the Caribbean.

Diploprora championi ☺

INTERMEDIATE-THERMOPHILIC

A representative of a small genus (4 species) that is not of great significance for cultivation; it includes tiny epiphytic orchids with a short (up to 7.2 in/18 cm) and thin stem. The stem is covered with leaves that are somewhat falcate and about 4 in/10 cm long. The species *D. championi* forms short raceme inflorescences of 3-5 yellowish flowers that are 0.6 in/1.5 cm across and bear a small whitish lip embellished with russet markings. Grow it as a standard thermophilic epiphyte. The plant blooms between March and June and comes from a vast Asian area—the photograph was taken in Thailand.

Diploprora truncata ☺

INTERMEDIATE-THERMOPHILIC

This species is not very attractive esthetically or with regard to cultivation; however, it is appealing for collectors of rare botanical orchids. It does not differ much in appearance

from *D. championi*. The monopodial clusters of leaves consist of 3-6 leaves. The erect, sparse flower raceme consists of 5-7 whitish flowers that are 0.7 in/1.7 cm in diameter. Their only decoration is the arched lip that is "cut off" at the end. Its yellow inner part is embellished with a delicate purple marking. The proportions and ecological needs of the species make it suitable even for smaller indoor glass cases with poor ventilation. *D. truncata* blooms between March and May and inhabits green terminal branches of trees on the mountaintops in northern Thailand (4,600—5,900 ft/ 1,400—1,800 m above sea level).

Domingoa hymenodes □ ▫ ☺

THERMOPHILIC

This species with attractive and rather large flowers is popular mainly with lovers of miniature orchids. The plant forms tiny stem pseudobulbs bearing single fleshy, narrowly lanceolate leaves. Long flower spikes with 1-2 flowers grow out of the apices of the pseudobulbs; the total number of flowers produced on one spike can, nevertheless, be a lot higher because flowers may appear on it in many successive years. The flower spike is intensely elongated and crimson red, the other tepals are yellow-and-green with a red, embossed, lengthwise nervation. The flowering period is irregular—the flowers appear up to several times a year. Cultivation is not very complicated: grow the plant epiphytically, in semi-shade, on a bare slab of bark. The old and seemingly dry flower spikes should never be removed after the end of the flowering period. Besides Cuba, the plant appears in Haiti and other islands in the Caribbean.

Doritis pulcherrima ▫ ◼ ☺

INTERMEDIATE-THERMOPHILIC

Even though the genus *Doritis* includes only one species, it is still quite confusing. The problem is that the plant is highly variable in appearance and that it has been used for breeding for many years now. It gets hybridized with the genus *Phalaenopsis* and endows the resulting hybrids—termed *Doritaenopsis*—with an overall resilience, resistance to lower temperature, as well as pink-to-purple shades of the flowers. It is often unclear whether a specimen you come across in someone's collection is a "pedigree" *Doritis* or its hybrid. In

contrast to *Phalaenopsis* orchids, the stem of *D. pulcherrima* is partly extended to resemble a tiny tree trunk, which makes it impossible for the dark green, fleshy, elliptic and somewhat purplish leaves to overlap each other. The inflorescence is erect and numbers 10-15 pinkish purple flowers with the lip colored in a darker shade of purple. With some specimens, the flower spike grows back after the flowers fade and it is therefore not recommended to remove it immediately. In the wild, *D. pulcherrima* is an epiphyte, and should therefore be cultivated by being mounted in a thick layer of moss on a wooden support, or planted in a very light bark mixture in a flowerpot. The species blooms in the fall and winter and comes from the vast area of southeastern Asia (Burma, Thailand, Malaysia, Vietnam, Sumatra).

Dracula sodiroea

Dracula bella

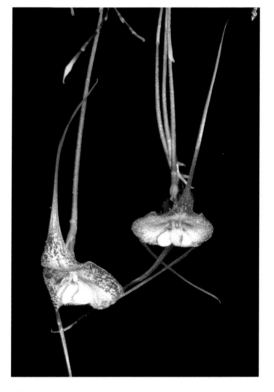

Dracula chimaera

Dracula   ▫ ☹ ☺

CRYOPHILIC-INTERMEDIATE

The genus *Dracula* is fairly "young"—it was not created until 1978 through the division of the large genus *Masdevalia*. The enigmatic name of the genus (the Latin word "*dracula*" means "little dragon") suggests the picturesque and mysterious appearance of the flowers of some species. The generic name, as well as some of the species names, (such as *D. vampira*, *D. chimaera*), aroused a huge interest on the part of orchid growers, resulting in the fact that many species are currently cultivated in sufficient numbers. At present, the genus *Drac-*

Dracula benedictii

ula includes approximately 80 epiphytic or terrestrial species. They bear an uncanny resemblance to one another in morphology and look like orchids from the "maternal" genus *Masdevalia*. The plants do not form pseudobulbs and their fundamental part is a shortened rhizome bearing a crowded cluster of thin, dwarfed stems—each one bearing one elongated leaf. Sometimes the leaves are succulent, thus assuming the function of storage organs. The flower spikes are usually erect or partially overhanging; in the case of several epiphytic species, they are even able to grow through the roots—the flowers then appear suspended under the plants. On the top of the spikes, there appears usually only one flower. If there are more, they open gradually one by one in very long intervals from each other. The flowers are ephemeral, and bizarre in appearance, dominated by a symmetrically arranged trio of sepals, whose tips extend to extreme lengths. The lip is small and inconspicuous. The edges of the tepals are often frilled. An overwhelming majority of *Dracula* orchids come from higher elevations of the South American Andes. The plants prefer well-ventilated shady environments with stable cool temperatures. The roots must never be left to overdry; it is therefore recommended to avoid epiphytic culture. Observe the cultivation rules that apply to growing cryophilic orchids of the genus *Masdevalia*. With most *Dracula* orchids, flowers appear in the spring, or irregularly. The plants are known to grow in the higher altitudes of Central, and especially South, America.

Drymoda siamensis

their tiny lineated leaves. Flowers appear before the on-set of the wet season. They grow individually on short spikes, have a pronounced lip and are light green with a russet marking. Grow them as you would deciduous *Dendrobium* orchids—provide them with a well-venti-lated, semi-shady environment with sufficient watering and fertilization in the summer, and a longish cool and dry dormancy in the winter. *D. siamensis* blooms be-tween February and March and is known to grow in Burma, Laos and Thailand.

Drymoda siamensis □ ☺

INTERMEDIATE

One of the tiniest orchids of the world—although its pro-portions are not the only feature that makes it attractive for cultivation: its flowers also assume unusual shapes. In the wild, the species grows in the company of deciduous *Dendrobium* orchids and its development during the year also resembles that of deciduous *Dendrobia*. Its small, flat, rounded pseudobulbs reach the size of 0.4 in/1 cm and, after the end of the vegetation period, shed all of

Elleanthus   ☺

INTERMEDIATE

When not in bloom, orchids of the genus *Elleanthus* slightly resemble *Sobralia* orchids—they have thin and stiff, reed-like stems covered with two rows of length-wise-grooved, pergameneous leaves. In contrast, the flowers are tiny and form more or less crowded inflores-cences with many flowers. 70 species of terrestrial and epiphytic orchids of this genus occur in the tropical areas of America. Most species (50) are reported to grow in Colombia. The plants are not very attractive for culture; those interested in growing *Elleanthus* orchids should use

Elleanthus sp., Ecuador

flowerpots with light humic substrate. The species in the photo (possibly *E. sphaerocephalus*) measures 24 in/ 60 cm across and has showy umbellate inflorescences colored in shiny purple. It blooms irregularly (most often in the winter). It was discovered in the Pululahua Crater in Ecuador.

Encyclia alata ■ ☺

THERMOPHILIC

The genus *Encyclia* is considered a "classic" among orchids—after all, it has been known by this name for almost 180 years. The plants are popular with cultivators because they usually have very showy and fragrant flowers and tolerate various cultivation errors. *E. alata* is not among the most frequently cultivated species, as it is too bulky to fit into standard amateur collections. The species forms conic pseudobulbs (up to 4 in/10 cm across) topped with 2-3 tough leaves that reach lengths of up to 16 in/40 cm. The inflorescence is branched and it can reach a length of over 40 in/1 meter and bear 15-20 flowers. The color of the flowers varies greatly; usually they are yellow-and-green with brownish edges of the tepals and a white lip with rufous venation. In the wild, the species often inhabits extreme locations, such as semi-deciduous (in other words, heavily insolated) trees right on the seacoast. It therefore requires plenty of light. Grow it epiphytically, but water it rather sparingly, especially when the orchid is not in growth. Flowers appear between May and October and the species is known to grow in Central America, in the area between Mexico and Nicaragua.

Encyclia alata

Encyclia aromatica

Encyclia aromatica ■ ☺

INTERMEDIATE-THERMOPHILIC

E. aromatica is perfect for amateur collections, although its inflorescence tends to be quite long. But who would object to an abundance of colorful, fragrant flowers? The pseudobulbs are almost ball-shaped, very stiff and equipped with two tough belt-shaped leaves. The proportions are very pleasant: the pseudobulbs reach lengths of up to 1.6 in/4 cm, the leaves 12 in/30 cm. The inflorescence—a panicle—is up to 40 in/1 m long, overhanging, branched and bearing many flowers. The flowers are quite large (up to 1.6 in/ 4 cm), pale yellow, with a purple marking on the lip. Cultivation is the same as in the case of *E. alata*, except for the heating requirements that are somewhat higher with *E. aromatica*. The plant blooms between July and August and comes from Mexico and Guatemala.

Encyclia fucata □ ■ ☺

INTERMEDIATE-THERMOPHILIC

A very pretty, smallish and rather undemanding species. Great numbers of it used to be collected in Cuba. Its bifoliate pseudobulbs are 1.2-2.4 in/3-6 cm long, the elongated leaves are firm, tough and they signal the plant's higher lighting demands. Some 15-30 pretty,

Encyclia garciana

small (1 in/2.5 cm across) flowers appear on a panicle inflorescence that reaches a length of 20 in/50 cm. The tepals are yellow and the lip is whitish, embellished with red venation. This plant is suitable for cultivation and comes from fairly dry and sunny regions. Grow it epiphytically and counterbalance the lack of light in winter by reducing the temperature. *E. fucata* flowers in late spring and summer and is native to the Caribbean islands.

Encyclia garciana □ ☺

INTERMEDIATE-THERMOPHILIC

A pretty, small species with rather large and nicely colored flowers. Its moisture requirements are a little above average, which makes *E. garciana* attractive for owners of small, poorly ventilated cultivation equipment. The elongated pseudobulbs bear 1-2 gray-and-green, 4-in/10-cm-long leaves with lengthwise grooves. The flowers are quite showy and there are 1-3 of them to each short spike; they are 1.6 in/4 cm in diameter, with a triangular profile. The whitish tepals are covered with delicate purple spots and the lip is colored in green-and-white. Grow it either epiphytically (make sure to provide more frequent misting), or, better still, in an epiphytic substrate in a flowerpot. The plant blooms in the fall and comes from Venezuela.

Encyclia gracilis

INTERMEDIATE-THERMOPHILIC

Another very pretty collection orchid of the genus *Ency-clia*. Its showy flowers open in the winter. The 2-in/5-cm tall pseudobulbs of *E. gracilis* are of an onion-like appearance and bear a couple of tough leaves that reach lengths of 8 in/20 cm. Some 7-15 flowers grow in a usually unbranched inflorescence and are about 1 in/2.5 cm in diameter. Their basic color ranges between green-and-yellow and green-and-brown, the lip is whitish, with pinkish venation. The plant is fairly undemanding in culture and should be grown in the same way as the other epiphytic *Encyclia* orchids (see *E. alata*), except that the

Encyclia gracilis

temperature requirements of *E. gracilis* are lower. The species blooms between September and December and comes from the Bahamas.

Encyclia phoenicea

INTERMEDIATE-THERMOPHILIC

The decorative appearance of the flowers of this beautiful orchid is complemented by their intoxicating chocolate fragrance; ergo, in some countries it bears the nickname of "the chocolate doll". The species is also attractive for its relatively collection-friendly dimensions and its resistance to drought and cultivation blunders. *E. phoenicea* has conically narrowed pseudobulbs (in contrast to a similar orchid, *E. atropurpurea*), each bearing a couple of narrow, tough leaves. The sparse inflorescence on a stiff, wiry spike consists of 5-20 large flowers whose colors vary a great deal. Their lips are white with red venation, the color of the tepals oscillates between green and deep purple. The flowers last for up to six weeks. *E. phoenicea* is an epiphyte with above-average light demands. This orchid has one disadvantage regarding its cultivation: its clusters are slow to proliferate and impossible to propagate—which is why they are relatively rare in collections today. It blooms in late summer and in the fall and comes from Mexico, Cuba and other islands in the Caribbean.

Encyclia phoenicea

Encyclia vespa
(Hormidium crassilabium)   ▣ ■ ☺

INTERMEDIATE

A highly variable plant that is very hard to classify. Its bifoliate, bare pseudobulbs are 2-16 in/5-40 cm tall and consist of a number of joints, a feature which might possibly place it among *Epidendrum*, or rather *Hormidium*, orchids. It is a fairly plain orchid: its resupinated greenish flowers are arranged in an erect inflorescence bearing 3-7 flowers and their tepals are decorated with purple spots. *E. vespa* is a completely undemanding species, well-suited even for amateur collections. It can be grown in semi-shade, either epiphytically (which will keep it smaller in proportions) or in an epiphytic substrate in a flowerpot (in which case you have to be prepared for much bulkier products). The plant blooms between the fall and late winter and is known to grow in the tropical regions of the American continent.

Epidendrum ciliare   ▣ ☺

INTERMEDIATE

The genus *Epidendrum* includes a huge number of different species, whose affiliation with the genus is often highly uncertain. The cultivation value of the plants that tend to be quite robust is not very high—the flowers are long-lived but usually small. The typically umbellate inflorescences of the small-flowered species are quite impressive. *E. ciliare* is classified as a *Hormidium* or *Auliza* orchid, while its flat pseudobulbs resemble those of *Cattleya* orchids. The inflorescence consists of 3-7 "spider" flowers that sometimes reach lengths of 4 in/10 cm. The highlights of the yellow-and-white flowers with a tinge of green are their three-lobed lips; the middle part of each lip is extended to resemble a tongue and the lateral protuberances are impressively fimbriated. The plant blooms between November and February and its habitat includes the entire tropical area of Latin America, including Mexico and Brazil.

Epidendrum coriifolium   ▣ ■ ☺

INTERMEDIATE

A very showy orchid with bifoliate pseudobulb stems and impressively shaped flowers. It will draw your attention also to the color of its flowers that ranges between green and green-and-yellow. The flowers reach lengths of 2 in/5 cm and are arranged in a dense inflorescence that bears a total of 4-8 flowers. Each flower is dominated by a broad, circular lip, slightly "folded" along the central nerve. This species is quite easy to grow—either epiphytically, or in a coarse mix in flowerpots. Flowers appear in the spring or fall. The plant was discovered in Venezuela.

Epidendrum diffusum ■ ☺

INTERMEDIATE

The species *E. diffusum* hardly ranks among the most beautiful orchids of the world, but it is a typical representative of the type of *Epidendrum* orchids that create pseudobulbs (the other species form tall, "reed-like," densely-foliated stems). The pseudobulbs reach lengths of up to 8 in/20 cm, they bear 2-5 leaves and their apices give rise to huge overhanging panicles numbering many inconspicuous brown-and-green flowers. The cultivation requirements of this orchid are the same as those of any common epiphyte: it requires semi-shade and sufficient air movement. *E. diffusum* blooms between October and November and comes from Mexico, Guatemala and Cuba.

Epidendrum falcatum ▣ ☺

THERMOPHILIC

This epiphyte is very interesting, and not only when in bloom: its unusual-looking overhanging tufts of long leaves will undoubtedly spruce up any collection. And any orchid lover is bound to fall for them when they are accompanied by the snow-white flowers with their strangely positioned lips! The species *E. falcatum* used to be known under the name *Auliza parkinsoniana*. Narrow lanceolate fleshy leaves reaching lengths of up to 12 in/30 cm grow out of the rudiments of the intensely reduced pseudobulbs. No more than 3 large white flowers can be admired on the shorter flower spike. The lip turns somewhat yellow in time. It is three-lobed—the two lateral lobes are oval, the middle one is slim and pointed. Cultivation is easy; it is more of a problem to acquire this fairly rare and highly valued species with low propagation ability in the first place. Grow the plant as you would other thermophilic orchids, that is, epiphytically on a slab of bark (cork oak is recommended) in semi-shade. The plant easily tolerates being placed in small, poorly ventilated epiphytic cases. It blooms in high summer and was discovered in Mexico, Guatemala, Honduras, Costa Rica and Panama.

Epidendrum coriifolium

Epidendrum diffusum

Epidendrum falcatum

Epidendrum oerstedii

INTERMEDIATE

This species is closely related to *E. ciliare* or *E. falca-tum*—all three of them are, because of their unique-shaped white flowers, sometimes classified as members of an independent genus *Auliza*. *E. oerstedii* has an erect stem whose highest two internodes are transformed into an elongated pseudobulb. An apical inflorescence grows out of the shortened spike and bears 2-3 flowers. The flowers are up to 4.4 in/11 cm across, their tepals are narrow and pointed, and the lips are three-lobed. The middle lobe on the lip is thin, pointed and very intensively elongated—a characteristic feature of the species. The plant is suitable even for novice cultivators. Grow it epiphytically in semi-shade and with year-round watering. The flowers appear in the spring. The species was discovered in Costa Rica and Panama.

Epidendrum pseudepidendrum

INTERMEDIATE-THERMOPHILIC

A truly spectacular orchid with regard to the appearance of its flowers; unfortunately it is too bulky—its tree-trunkish stems with two rows of leaves that reach lengths of 6.4 in/16 cm easily surpass a length 32 in/80 cm! Some 3-5 green flowers appear between June and July, they are unusually large and sport an orange-and-red lip. The species is not hard to cultivate; as with all the other representatives of the genus *Epidendrum*, it requires a substantial amount of light (otherwise the shoots extend excessively and do not produce flowers), regular watering and a period of rest in the winter. The orchid was discovered in Panama and Costa Rica.

Epidendrum radicans

INTERMEDIATE

A true symbol of the entire genus: it would be hard to find an orchid lover who would not recognize its typical orange-to-dark-red umbels of flowers! They do not change their shape much in the course of time, even though the flowers open one by one in long intervals. The inflorescence remains on the plant for up to several months, which is why the plants are sometimes grown for cut flowers. *E. radicans* tends to be mistaken for (or associated with) a very similar and hardly distinguishable species *E. ibaguense*. Its reed-like, ascending shoots reach lengths of up to 6.5 in/2 m and their entire surface is gradually covered with a multitude of aerial roots (hence the Latin name *radicans* = rooting). The species has an exceptionally high ability to regenerate and, in the tropics, it even thrives on regularly mowed urban lawns! Cultivation is the same as that of *E. pseudepidendrum*. *E. radicans* blooms irregularly in the course of the whole year and grows in many forms all over of tropical America.

Eria sp., Thailand—a lithophytic species

apex. Most *Eria* orchids are epiphytes or lithophytes of the warmest localities—in a culture they should therefore be mounted on bare suspended wooden supports. The plants need as much light as possible and a slight reduction of temperature in winter. The photographs of the species presented here were taken in Vietnam and Thailand; the genus is widespread all over the tropical Asia, in Polynesia and northern Australia.

Eria panea

Eria sp., Thailand

Erycina echinata

Erycina echinata   □ ☹

CRYOPHILIC

A representative of a tiny, delicate species that any orchid lover would certainly like to possess. However, there is one important catch—both of the known *Erycina* species are very hard to cultivate. The tiny, almost ball-shaped, bifoliate pseudobulbs are transparent and protected from sunshine by dry cases. The plants bloom after shedding all foliage during the peak dry season. The sulfur-yellow flowers with complex morphology and a big lip suggest the plants' relation to the genus *Oncidium* and are visible from a distance, in spite of their small proportions (only 0.8 in/2 cm across); they grow in small racemes out of the bases of the pseudobulbs. Their high cultivation requirements are caused

by their habitat—cool regions of the Mexican mountains. In order to develop well in culture, *Erycina* orchids have demands that are hard to meet: intensive sunshine, fresh air and cool temperatures throughout the year. Cultivation rules are the same as those of *E. citrinum*, except that, owing to its minute proportions, *E. echinata* is more sensitive to cultivation errors. It blooms between March and May and was discovered in Oaxaca, Mexico.

Euchile citrinum   ■ ☹

CRYOPHILIC

A large-flowered rarity that is perhaps the secret dream of every orchid grower. Sadly, it is very rare and difficult to cultivate. The local people of Oaxaca, Mexico (where the photo was taken) collect specimens of *E. citrinum* in bloom (unfortunately, along with the pseudobulbs) in light oak forests before Easter and hang them on fences and houses as decorations. *E. citrinum* forms egg-shaped pseudobulbs that reach lengths of up to 2 in/5 cm, grow only in an overhanging position and bear 2-4 leathery leaves. Flower spikes bearing 1-3 flowers each grow out of their apices. The flowers are beautiful, 2.4-3.2 in/6-8 cm across, partly open, and lemon-yellow (they also give off an intense lemony fragrance). Unfortunately they are not very durable. Cultivation is very difficult and is considered to be something like a cultivator's graduation exam: the species grows in altitudes above 9,800 ft/3,000 m above sea level and therefore requires cool temperatures, plenty of sunshine unfiltered by the atmosphere, and fresh air.

Euchile citrinum

Grow it epiphytically and, in winter, reduce temperature to 59 °F/15 °C and water only very modestly, because of the developmental stagnation caused by insufficient light. *E. citrinum* blooms between March and April and is known to grow only in Mexico.

Euchile mariae ▫ ◪ ☺

CRYOPHILIC-INTERMEDIATE

The only close relative of the previous species, with equally exotic, white flowers. In contrast to *E. citrinum*, its unifoliate, pear-shaped pseudobulbs grow in an erect position. Two to three longish leaves form on the apex

Eunanthe sanderiana

of each pseudobulb. The greenish flowers are dominated by a frilled, snow-white lip with green venation and a yellowish center. Grow this orchid in a similar manner as you would its yellow-flowered relative, except that *E. mariae's* demands of cool temperature and perfect ventilation are somewhat lower. The species was not discovered until 1937 and is used today for breeding green-flowered hybrids. It blooms in the spring and comes from higher elevations in Mexico.

Eunanthe sanderiana ◪ ■ ☹ ☺

THERMOPHILIC

This species has so far been classified as a *Vanda* orchid and, along with the blue-flowered species of *Vanda coerulea*, it is considered to be the beauty queen of Asian monopodial orchids. Its ascending, tough stem reaches a length of up to 24 in/60 cm and bears a number of 18-in/45-cm-long, belt-shaped leaves, arranged in two opposite rows. The flower spikes grow out of the axils of the leaves, and strong specimens bear more than one spike. The flower raceme consists of a maximum of 10 pink flowers with impressive crimson venation on the lower tepals. In Europe, *E. sanderiana* blooms only very rarely and grows extremely slowly. If it blooms at all, it does so in the fall. The species was discovered in the Philippines under the dramatic circumstances of the 1880 earthquake.

Galeandra sp., Mexico

Gastrochilus monticola

Galeandra ▫ ◼ ☹ ☺

CRYOPHILIC-INTERMEDIATE

A small genus of orchids from the New World includes dazzling species with very showy flowers. The
plants will also draw attention with their spindle-
shaped slim pseudobulbs covered with thin, semi-deciduous foliage. Yet their most prominent feature is
the bizarre-shaped, funneled flower lip with a back-
ward-extended spur. Most *Galeandra* orchids are epiphytes, but the genus also includes some terrestrial
species, which ought to be cultivated in a heavier
medium and a temperate environment. The epiphytic
species are not very easy to grow and they are rare in
collections. A necessary condition for the successful
development of the plants is perfect ventilation,
a maximum amount of light and lower temperatures in
the summer. New pseudobulbs are formed on the
plants even in the winter. Orchids of the genus *Galeandra* usually bloom in early spring and only grow in
the American tropics; about 20 species are known to
grow in a vast area between Florida and Brazil. The
orchid in the photo—*Galeandra* sp.—from Arriaga,
Mexico looks a little like *G. baueri* and represents an
undefined specimen of a fairly small, peculiar species
that lives epiphyticaly in the tops of pines at an altitude of 4,900 ft/1,500 m above sea level in the Chia-
pas, Mexico.

Galeandra batemanii

Gastrochilus monticola ▫ ◼ ☺ ☺

THERMOPHILIC

Representatives of the genus *Gastrochilus* do not form
pseudobulbs—their morphology somewhat resembles
orchids of the genus *Vanda*. The stiff and sometimes lignifying stem is shortened in some species, or intensely
elongated in other species. The inflorescence is always
shorter than the tough leaves arranged in two rows, and
it grows from their armpits. The spike of *G. monticola*
reaches a length of 8 in/20 cm and bears purplish brown,
0.6-in/1.5-cm-large flowers with a decorative white lip.
Some 3-5 flowers form a shortened inflorescence. The
plant needs plenty of diffused light and good ventilation.
The best way of growing it is epiphytically on a bare
wooden support. During the vegetation period, it requires plentiful watering that should be slightly reduced
in the winter time. The species does not bloom regularly
in culture—if it does, it blooms in the fall. It comes from
Burma, Thailand, Laos and other countries in southeastern Asia.

Gastrochilus obliquus ▫ ◼ ☺ ☺

INTERMEDIATE-THERMOPHILIC

An abundantly flowering representative of the *Gastrochilus* genus. In contrast to the previous species, its stem

Gastrochilus obliquus

is shortened, and the leaves are larger and fleshier. The flowers are 1 in/2.7 cm across and there are up to 25 of them on a short spike, forming a very dense raceme. Their tepals are deep yellow and covered with delicate red dots, the lip is white, dotted, with a showy red spot on the base. Grow *G. obliquus* much like the previous species. The flowers appear between November and December. The presented plant was photographed in Thailand.

Gastrochilus sp.   ◨ ☺

THERMOPHILIC

Orchids of this genus are considerable rarities and strangers to collections and they tend to puzzle botanical systematists. The shape of the flower in of the specimen the photo is, as with other *Gastrochilus* orchids, typical of the whole genus—their unusual brown-braided tepals are fleshy, arched like a spoon, and their lip consists of a sacciform *hypochilus* and a fimbriated

Gastrochilus sp.

epichilus. The flower spike is rather unusually elongated. The main cultivation rules do not differ from those applied to the previous species. In the winter, the plant requires (as do other *Gastrochilus* orchids) a fairly short dormancy that can be induced by a careful reduction of temperature and cessation of watering. The plant in the picture blooms in the fall and comes from Thailand.

Gomesa crispa   ◨ ☺

INTERMEDIATE

The small *Gomesa* genus that includes only about 20 species is quite showy in appearance, be it the form of the vegetative organs or the shape and proportions of the overhanging inflorescences. Unfortunately, the crispate flowers that are about 0.8 in/2 cm in diameter are extremely short-lived. *Gomesa* orchids used to be included in the genus *Rodriguezia*. The species *G. crispa* has 2.3-3.6-in/6-9-cm tall pseudobulbs bearing 2-3 pointed leaves that reach lengths of 10 in/25 cm. The overhanging, numerous, dense racemes of yellowish-to-greenish flowers grow out of the base of the pseudobulbs and are up to 8 in/20 cm long. In culture, it is an epiphyte with average requirements for watering and light. It blooms in the spring—May to June, and its habitat is in Brazil.

Gomesa divaricata ▫ ◼ ☺

INTERMEDIATE

This species, quite attractive when in bloom, does not differ much in appearance from other *Gomesa* orchids. Its pseudobulbs are up to 2.4 in/6 cm tall, round and flattened, with sharp edges, and ended with three long leaves. The shape and length of the inflorescence is reminiscent of the previous species. The whitish tepals are wavy, the markedly arched lip has two comb-like shapes at the base. The plant's cultivation demands are not very high; grow it epiphytically, providing the usual amount of water, good ventilation and the maximum amount of diffused light. The species usually blooms in the early months of spring and has been discovered in the Brazilian rainforests.

Gomesa divaricata

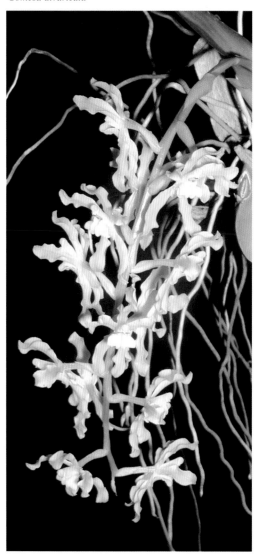

Gongora purpurea

Gongora ◼ ☺

INTERMEDIATE

All species included in the bizarre-flowering genus *Gongora* that play a significant role in cultivation look very much alike outside the flowering period, which is why they are introduced all at once. The orchids form grooved, conic and fresh-looking pseudobulbs that are usually ended with a pair of slim, oval leaves adorned with showy, solid venation. The pseudobulbs reach heights of 3.2 in/8 cm, while the leaves tend to be about four times longer. The roots are also worth mentioning: they are very fine and snow-white, forming a dense net in the air. Some of the roots are capable of reverse geotropic growth, that is, vertically upward. This specialization has been described in some other epiphytes as well (for instance, in *Anthuria* from the family *Aracae*) and serves to form something resembling aerial root-balls or nests; gradually, descending organic material gets caught in the roots and the plants subsequently use it for nutrition. The genus *Gongora* also boasts other attractions—above all its remarkable flowers. Multi-blossom flower axes grow out of the bases of the pseudobulbs, at first vertically upward, and later perpendicularly downward to the ground. The individual flowers are backward-oriented, i.e., their lip points upward, and they hang in space on almost circular-arched peduncles that are unique to the genus and impossible to overlook. The plants' ecological requirements,

Gongora sp.

Gongora sp., Ecuador

Gongora galeata

and hence also cultivation rules, are the same for all species of the genus *Gongora*. They all have average light needs. Grow them either epiphytically on a largish support (a slab of pine bark, a "head" of grapevine), or in a highly permeable substrate in an epiphytic basket or even a flowerpot—a disadvantage of this cultivation style is that the aerial roots do not get a chance to shine. As the inflorescences are overhanging, it is necessary to use suspended containers. As soon as the plants begin to show very delicate foundations of future inflorescences, watering should be reduced a little to avoid the danger of molding. After the flowers fade, the plants are in need of a brief rest. The genus numbers a total of about 25 species known to grow in tropical America, including Mexico, Caribbean islands and Brazil, with the most dense occurrence in Central America.

Gongora cassidea

Grammatophyllum scriptum var. *citrinum*

Haraella odorata

Grammatophyllum scriptum var. citrinum

INTERMEDIATE

The genus *Grammatophyllum* includes one of the largest orchids of the world—the gigantic *G. speciosum*, whose pseudobulbs reach lengths of up to 8.2 ft/2.5 m! Admittedly, the species *G. scriptum* is much smaller in proportions, but it is still robust enough never to become part of amateur collections. Its pseudobulbs reach lengths of up to 8 in/20 cm and bear 3 or 4 massive leaves that are up to 40 in/1 m long. The inflorescence is a spike of copious symmetrical, star-shaped greenish flowers. The flowers of a typical specimen are adorned with brown dots (hence the Latin name "*scriptum*") that are missing from a rarer variety, *G. citrinum*. Growing this terrestrial species is not complicated: it is quite happy in semi-shade, in a permeable medium with an addition of standard soil and modest watering. It blooms in late summer and comes from southeastern Asia.

Haraella odorata

THERMOPHILIC

A spectacular miniature orchid that is quite common in collections. The stem of these inconspicuous little plants reaches a length of up to 0.4 in/1 cm and is covered with elongated fleshy leaves that are up to 1.6 in/ 4 cm long. The lower part of the stem gives rise to short flower scapes bearing a single flower that is 0.8-1.2 in/ 2-3 cm across and sports a remarkably elongated lip. The edges of this russet lip are typically fimbriated. Growing this orchid is not hard—but bear in mind that as a tiny species, *H. odorata* is more sensitive to overdrying or other cultivation errors. It thrives in semi-shady conditions that are warm round the year. It blooms between July and November and comes from Taiwan.

Helcia sanquinolenta

CRYOPHILIC-INTERMEDIATE

The miniature genus *Helcia* includes only two species that resemble *Trichopilia* orchids. A difference can be found in the flat flower lip with an unfolded base. *H. sanquinolenta* is better-known and cultivated more often. It is a fairly small plant with large flowers. Its pseudobulbs are elongated and egg-shaped, they reach lengths of no more than 1.6 in/4 cm and they are ended with a single small egg-shaped leaf. The flower spikes bear single yellow-and-green flowers that are up to 2.8 in/7 cm across and have a whitish lip adorned with a crimson marking. The epiphytic species *H. sanquinolenta* comes from higher elevations of the Andes and should therefore be grown in the same way as the cryophilic *Odontoglossum* orchids. It blooms in January and February and was found in Colombia and Ecuador.

Helcia sanquinolenta

Hexisea bidentata

INTERMEDIATE-THERMOPHILIC

The flowers of the small genus *Hexisea* resemble *Epidendrum* orchids. Their slim, spindle-shaped pseudobulbs are characterized by one idiosyncrasy—sometimes they grow "daughter" pseudobulbs on the apex. The bifoliate pseudobulbs of *H. bidentata* reach lengths of up to 2.4 in/6 cm and are covered with dry sheaths. Their apices give rise to the above-mentioned new storage organs or a sparse spike of 3-5 shiny yellow flowers, 1.2 in/3 cm across. This epiphytic species thrives in the semi-shade of a well-ventilated orchid greenhouse. It blooms in the summer and its habitat includes the area between Costa Rica and Colombia.

Hexisea bidentata

Holcoglossum amesianum

INTERMEDIATE

Species of this genus are often included among *Vanda* orchids. But while they are closely related to *Vandas*, they differ in details of the flower anatomy—such as a longer spur, or a differently shaped lip. There are differences also in the overall appearance of the plants and the way they grow their foliage. *H. amesianum* does not stand out from the genus as far as appearance is concerned: its leafless, stiff stem gradually lignifies and never stops adding in growth, and it bears two rows of tough, thin leaves that are semicircular in cross-section and reach lengths of up to 8 in/20 cm. The erect inflorescence is formed in the armpits of the upper leaves and bears 15-30 blunt-spurred flowers with oval white tepals and a forward-protruding pinkish red lip with decorative edges. Grow the species as you would other *Holcoglossum* orchids (see *H. kimballianum*). The plant blooms in the winter and comes from southern China, Burma, Vietnam, Laos, Cambodia and Thailand.

Holcoglossum kimballianum

INTERMEDIATE

Outside of the flowering period, these plants closely resemble specimens of *H. amesianum*, except that their leaves are thinner and narrower. The tepals of the beautiful flowers are radically narrowed at the bases, and the broad, red-and-purple lip is interwoven with crimson venation. Despite being an epiphytic orchid, *H. kimballianum* ought to be grown in containers with a durable, fragmented substrate. Frequent is also a "naked" style of cultivation—in suspended wooden baskets, with the numerous long roots of the plants hanging down from them. Orchids of this genus need plenty of light and more warmth than *Vanda* orchids (it is a generally accepted rule that the rounder and narrower the foliage is of an orchid of either of the related genera, the more thermophilic and photophilic it is). In the winter, always reduce temperature and watering intensity, as the plants suffer from insufficient light that causes them to stagnate. *H. kimballianum* blooms between September and October and comes from southern China, Burma and Thailand.

Holcoglossum subulifolium

THERMOPHILIC

A very showy orchid when in bloom; outside of the flowering period, it is an inconspicuous and hard-to-maintain plant. It resembles both of the previous species in appearance, the sticklike leaves range in color between green and dark red, depending on the intensity of light. Between 2-5 white flowers appear on a spike that is shorter than the leaves, they reach lengths of up to 2.4 in/6 cm and attract attention mainly by their wide, tongue-shaped lip with a fimbriated edge. The base of

Holcoglossum kimballianum

Hormidium boothianum

the lip is decorated with a tawny marking. Cultivation failures (slow growth, unwillingness to bloom and molding of the plants) are caused by the enormous photophilia of this orchid. *H. subulifolium* flowers in late spring and comes from southern China.

Hormidium boothianum   ☺

INTERMEDIATE

This species differs slightly from the other orchids of the genus—its flowers are not turned by 180 degrees (that is, with their lips pointing upward, see the following species). The plant has decorative, circular, vividly green pseudobulbs, each bearing a pair of thin leaves. The flower spike grows out of the bases of mature pseudobulbs and bears 5-8 yellow-and-green, brown-speckled flowers. This undemanding orchid should be grown epiphytically in semi-shade, on a piece of bark or a chock of elderberry, and after the new pseudobulbs mature, it should be treated to a brief period of rest. It blooms between May and July and, besides Cuba, it is known to grow on the other islands of the West Indies, in South Florida and Mexico.

Hormidium cochleatum

Hormidium cochleatum ▣ ☺

INTERMEDIATE

An orchid attractive for cultivation that has been grown abundantly for many years, with a showy purple shell-shaped, reversed lip (see also the following species). Its slim, oval pseudobulbs are 2.4-4 in/6-10 cm long and bear two lanceolate leaves that reach lengths of up to 8 in/20 cm. The inflorescence is rather short and erect and consists of 5-8 flowers that open gradually one by one. The lip is complemented with lineated yellow-and-green tepals. It is a highly variable and very adaptable epiphyte. It can be grown either on a support or in an epiphtyic medium in a flowerpot. Flowers appear

Hormidium fragrans

in the fall and winter and the plant is known to grow in a vast area of Central America including the West Indies.

Hormidium fragrans ▣ ☺

INTERMEDIATE

The validity of the genus *Hormidium* is questionable —botanists have alternately included its representatives among *Epidendrum* and *Encyclia* orchids. As with other species of this genus, the flowers of *H. fragrans* are reversed (by 180 degrees)—the lip is thus positioned in the upper part of the flower. The slim pseudobulbs are up to 2 in/5 cm tall and bear one belt-shaped leaf that is twice as long. The inflorescence with 2-5 whitish flowers is erect; the flower lip is shell-shaped and decorated with purple stripes. This orchid is very easy to cultivate. As a commonplace species, it is now threatened with falling into obscurity. Flowers appear on the plant in late winter and in the spring. Specimens are reported to grow in the vast area of Central and South America.

Hormidium prismatocarpum

Hormidium prismatocarpum ▣ ☺

INTERMEDIATE-THERMOPHILIC

This species' narrow, egg-shaped pseudobulbs reaching lengths of up to 5.2 in/13 cm bear a couple of belt-shaped leaves. The flower raceme is approximately 12 in/30 cm tall and consists of many 2.4 in/6-cm-large flowers. The yellowish green tepals are covered with a showy pattern of brown spots, the lip is extended into a mauve tip. This species is not difficult to grow even for amateurs; you can either mount it on a wooden slab or cultivate the plants in a highly permeable substrate in flowerpots. It blooms between May and July and comes from Costa Rica.

Hormidium vitellinum

Hormidium vitellinum ⊡ ▣ ☺

CRYOPHILIC-INTERMEDIATE

In contrast to other species of the genus *Hormidium*, *H. vitellinum* is considerably more cryophilic; thanks to this quality, as well as for its showy flowers, it used to be grown for cut flowers at the dawn of production gardening. Its pseudobulbs are egg-shaped, up to 3.6 in/9 cm long and equipped with two tough thin leaves on the apex. The erect, 12-in/30-cm-tall inflorescence bears up to 20 shiny orange flowers, 1.2-2 in/3-5 cm in diameter. The plants thrive in a light and well-ventilated environment. In the winter, it is necessary to provide the plant with conditions for a substantial dormancy period. Based on the time when the plants are in bloom, scientists distinguish between two varieties: the plants of the variety *autumnalis* flower in the fall, whereas spring flowering is guaranteed by the var. *majus*. The species is native to Mexico and Guatemala.

Hygrochilus parishii var. *marriottiana* ▣ ☹ ☺

INTERMEDIATE-THERMOPHILIC

The name of the genus hints at the nectar-moistened flower lip (the Greek word "*hygros*" means moist, while "*chilos*" stands for lip) of this orchid. It is an epiphytic species, whose single thick stem reaches a length of up to 8 in/20 cm and is covered with two rows of elongated elliptic leaves that are 8-10 in/20-25 cm long. The robust flower spike measures up to 16 in/40 cm and bears 5-10 flowers that are up to 2 in/5 cm in diameter. A typical specimen of this species has yellow tepals covered with reddish brown spots, while the flowers of the var. *marriottiana* in the photo are pure brown. In both cases, the lip is purple and the flower column is white. Cultivation is similar to that of the thermophilic species of the genus *Vanda*, flowers appear between March and May. The species is known to grow in northern India, southern China, Laos and Vietnam; the var. *marriottiana* in the photo comes from the north of Thailand.

Hygrochilus parishii var. *marriottiana*

Isochilus linearis   ▫ ◼ ☺ ☺

INTERMEDIATE

The plants of this two-member genus are not grown very often by orchid lovers; this is partly owing to the higher requirements of the plants, and partly due to their plain looks. These terrestrial and epiphytic orchids form stiff, erect-to-overhanging stems, densely covered with two rows of soft leaves arranged to resemble a feather. The apical inflorescences bear a small number of bell-shaped

Laelia anceps var. *alba*

flowers crowded on the spike. The stems of *I. linearis* reach lengths of up to 20 in/50 cm, the leaves measure up to 2.4 in/6 cm each. The small flowers arranged in two rows are either white, orange or red. Because of the low resistance of the roots to overdrying, it is recommended to grow the plants in flowerpots, using a classic epiphytic substrate. The species blooms irregularly, usually in the spring, and it grows all over tropical America.

Laelia anceps var. *alba*   ◼ ☺

CRYOPHILIC

The genus *Laelia* is one of the most prominent genera within the entire orchid family, thanks to its lovely flowers, easy culture and a high number of genetic dispositions that are extensively used in breeding. In some cases, it can only be distinguished from the closely related genus *Cattleya* by minute details in the morphology of the flowers. *L. anceps* is a classic orchid, the cultivation of which goes far back into history. The apex of the unifoliate, slim, egg-shaped pseudobulb gives rise to a flower spike that reaches a length of 28 in/70 cm and bears 3-5 large, vividly purple flowers. Besides these typically colored plants, there exists an albinic variety that is a highly valuable collector's item and whose flowers are white with a tinge of yellow (see photo), and other color variations. Cultivation is relatively easy, the same as in the case of *L. autumnalis*. *L. anceps* blooms between December and January—a very favorable period for cultivators—and comes from Mexico.

134

Laelia autumnalis

Laelia autumnalis

CRYOPHILIC-INTERMEDIATE

This orchid is closely related to the previous species. It has spindle-shaped bifoliate pseudobulbs that reach lengths of up to 3.2 in/8 cm, and 4.8-6-in/12-15-cm-long, leathery leaves. The inflorescence is up to 20 in/50 cm tall and consists of 3-5 shiny purple flowers. *L. autumnalis*, too, has a very rare white variety. Grow the plants in a coarse, permeable mix in suspended flowerpots. Epiphytic culture is also possible—on largish branches or

Laelia dayana

slabs of bark. The plants require cool conditions in the winter and a rest of several weeks after the flowers fade. It is necessary to ensure sufficient light throughout the whole year, but make sure to protect the plant form getting burned by direct sunshine. The species blooms in the winter and its habitat is in Mexico.

Laelia dayana

INTERMEDIATE

L. dayana is considered by some botanists to be a subspecies of a very similar species *L. pumila*. It belongs among dwarfed and very beautiful orchids. Its pseudobulbs are barely 1.2-1.6in/3-4 cm long, ended with a single succulent, firm leaf that reaches a length of up to 4 in/10 cm. The mature flower sheath gives rise to a flower spike that bears 1-2 flowers and is a little shorter than the leaves. In comparison with the other body parts, the flower is literally gigantic—its width exceeds 4 in/10 cm. The tepals are mauve, the tubular lip is whitish in the gullet and crimson with dark lengthwise venation on the edge (*L. pumila* has bigger and paler-colored flowers with a longer and thinner lip). Grow the species in a standard epiphytic style on a piece of bark or branch. The plant blooms between May and October and grows in the crowns of tall trees in Brazil.

135

Laelia fidelensis ☺

INTERMEDIATE-THERMOPHILIC

A species that is easy to grow even in an apartment, but unfortunately quite rare and threatened with extinction in the wild. Sadly and paradoxically, this is not due to the fact that it does not grow in reservations and its habitats are therefore little known… In addition, the plant was not listed among the most endangered species of the world (even though it undoubtedly belongs on that list), which

Laelia flava

would have increased its attractiveness. The plant is rather decumbent and eager to branch out fast. Its unifoliate, barrel-shaped, yellowish pseudobulbs are only 10-4-6 in/ 15 cm long. 1-2 pale purple flowers, 0.4-0.8 in/1-2 cm across, grow on a slightly overhanging spike. The lip is a shade darker and broadened at the base to assume the shape of a heart. Grow it without a substantial period of rest in an environment that is warm and light throughout the year. The plant blooms in the spring (sometimes also in the fall) and comes from Rio de Janeiro, Brazil.

Laelia flava   ☺

INTERMEDIATE

The yellow-flowered representatives of the genus *Laelia* are not firmly placed in the minds of orchid growers, in spite of the high number of *Lealia* orchids with flowers colored in precisely this way. There are some uncertainties as to their taxonomy because many species considered "pure" until recently are today considered mere subspecies or varieties of *L. flava*. The plant in the photo could, using this logic, be labeled *L. itambana*. The pseudobulbs of this medium-sized orchid are 6 in/15 cm tall and ended with a leaf about 6 in/15 cm long. The deep yellow flowers are very showy, 3.2 in/8 cm across, growing sparsely on longish spikes. Grow them in the same way as *L. jongheana*. The plants bloom between winter and spring and come from Minas Gerais, Brazil.

Laelia furfuracea

Laelia fournierii   □   ⊡   ☹   ☺

INTERMEDIATE

This dwarf species is a good example of the remarkable adaptability of orchids—for it is occasionally found growing on completely barren, sun-drenched rock plates! If growing on rocks, the plant reduces its proportion to the smallest size possible: its unifoliate, barrel-shaped pseudobulbs are barely 1.6 in/4 cm long, its fleshy, tough

Laelia fournierii

leaf is even shorter. The flowers are whitish-to-pale-yellow, with a yellowish-to-orange lip. In epiphytic stations, the plants are somewhat bigger. Cultivation of this highly extreme species is quite problematic, as the plants are deprived of a sufficient amount of light in a greenhouse environment of the Temperate Zone. There have been attempts to cultivate it on stone slabs, and it is also possible to use cork bark. *L. fournierii* blooms in the summer and fall and comes from Brazil.

Laelia furfuracea   ⊡   ☺

CRYOPHILIC

This orchid is ecologically very similar to the previous two species. Its bodily proportions are more than likeable—2.4-in/6-cm-long pseudobulbs, tough, erect leaves that reach lengths of up to 4.8 in/12 cm. The flowers resemble *L. autumnalis* in color and shape, only they are sometimes a shade lighter. They bloom on a 12-in/30-cm-long flower spike that bears 2-5 flowers giving off pleasant fragrance. *L. furfuracea* produces flowers in the winter and grows epiphytically in the nature of Mexico (in the mountainous region of Oaxaca in altitudes up to 8,850 ft/2,700 m above sea level).

Laelia gouldiana

CRYOPHILIC

This plant is so close to *L. autumnalis* in appearance that, for a while, scientists considered it a natural hybrid of *L. anceps*. It has vividly purple star-shaped flowers, with a beautiful golden-yellow lip with purple venation—the nicest flowers of the entire group of long-stemmed Mexican species. Its cultivation requirements are not different from those of its closest relatives. It blooms in the winter and also comes from Mexico.

Laelia gouldiana

Laelia grandis

INTERMEDIATE

A unifoliate, largish species whose pseudobulbs reach lengths of up to 6 in/15 cm. The narrow leaves are a bit longer—up to 10 in/25 cm. Wavy, tawny tepals complement the pink, cornet-shaped lip with dark venation. The size of the flowers is very conspicuous and it is a feature that gave the species its name. The best way to grow it is in a coarse substrate in a flowerpot exposed to sufficient diffused light. The winter break must not be very long. The plant lives either as an epiphyte in forests on the coast of the Atlantic, or terrestrially in impenetrable inland growths in almost semi-desert type of locations. It is also often found in secondary localities—such as cacao plantations. This orchid blooms in the spring and is native to Brazil.

Laelia jongheana

INTERMEDIATE

Another miniature representative of the genus from Brazil. It is very rare and all but extinct in the wild—that is why it was included in Appendix 1 of the CITES international convention. The plant's pseudob-

138

Laelia jongheana

ulbs are barely 2.4 in/6 cm long and form dense clusters, and are ended with a single, though leaf that reaches a length of up to 4.8 in/12 cm. The flowers grow on short spikes bearing one flower each and are very large—up to 10 cm. The tepals are pale mauve, the white, tubular lip is frilled on the end, with purple spots and a yellow gullet. In the wild, the species grows mostly epiphytically on lighter stations, in culture it thrives on a slab of cork oak bark. The flowers appear in the winter. The plant has been discovered in Minas Gerais, Brazil.

Laelia pumila var. *semi-alba*

INTERMEDIATE-THERMOPHILIC

A beautiful, highly popular and sought-after miniature representative of the genus. Its pseudobulbs are never longer than 1.2 in/3 cm and bear a single, rather tough leaf that reaches a maximum length of 4.8 in/12 cm.

Laelia pumila var. *semi-alba*

The flowers grow one by one (rarely in pairs) on a short flower spike and are highly variable in color. The flowers of typical specimens are mauve, with an elongated, tubular lip that has a dark-edged inner part. The var. *semi-alba* in the photo has flowers whose coloring is visibly less intensive—the mauve shade is present only on the edge of the lip. Grow the plant epiphytically (it grows more slowly) or, better still, potted in a coarse epiphytic substrate. It requires quite a lot of light but should be protected from getting burned by direct sunlight through the greenhouse windows. *L. pumila* blooms in early summer and comes from Bahia, Brazil.

Laelia purpurata

INTERMEDIATE

A giant among *Laelia* orchids—its unifoliate, slim, egg-shaped pseudobulbs are up to 8in/20 cm long, and the leaves are even twice as long! The short flower spike bears 3-5 very large (up to 6 in/15 cm), mauve flowers. The lip is long and tubular, with a wavy edge, it is yellow on the inside and crimson with dark venation on the edges. The color of *L. purpurata* is highly variable; so far, approximately 50 varieties have been described. The orchid is very breeding- and cultivation-friendly, if only it did not possess such monstrous proportions! Cultivation is easier than that of the previous species. A cool winter break is unnecessary, and the plant's light needs are also slightly lower. *L. purpurata* blooms between May and October and its habitat is in Brazil.

Laelia purpurata

Laelia rubescens

Laelia rubescens

CRYOPHILIC-INTERMEDIATE

Systemically, this species belongs with cryophilic Mexican species represented, for instance, by *L. autumnalis*; however, it is the only one of them that also grows in another Central American country. Moreover, it differs from the rest in its smaller proportions and the shape of its flattened, oval, glossy psudobulbs that each bears a single elongated oval leaf. The thin and firm flower spike reaches a length of up to 20 in/50 cm and bears 3-7 flowers. The 2-2.4-in/5-6-cm-large flowers are either pure white or pinkish purple. The color of the three-lobed lip is reminiscent of *Dendrobium* orchids: it has a deep

Laelia sincorana

purple throat, providing a stark contrast with the yellow decoration on the middle lobe. Cultivate it in a similar manner as *L. autumnalis*. The flowers appear in the winter, both in culture and in the natural habitat of Mexico and Guatemala.

Laelia sincorana

INTERMEDIATE-THERMOPHILIC

A species closely related to *L. pumila*. Compared to *L. pumila*, its unifoliate pseudobulbs are even smaller and barrel-shaped and reach lengths of 0.8-1.2 in/2-3 cm. The leaves are also wider and shorter (up to 4 in/10 cm). Usually a single flower grows on each short spike. The flowers are literally outstanding—not only for their intensive carmine color but also their giant proportions (they reach a size of over 4 in/10 cm!). Since their habitat is not characterized by a very high level of air moisture, they can be quite successfully grown even on a windowsill. If cultivated in an apartment, they should be planted in a medium-coarse substrate in a flowerpot; in greenhouses, the plants also prosper if grown epiphytically. In any case, their development is extremely slow. Flowers appear in the spring and early summer. The plant comes from the Serra Sincorá mountains (hence its name) in Bahia, Brazil.

Lemboglossum bictoniense

INTERMEDIATE

Many orchid lovers know the representatives of the genus *Lemboglossum* by their old name of *Odontoglossum*, even though this "classic" genus was divided as far back as 1984. One way or another, if an orchid fan comes across a collection including a *Lemboglossum* specimen in bloom, he or she will speak with great respect not only for the plants of this species, but also for their successful growers. Little wonder, since the singularly beautiful *Lemboglossum* orchids are unfortunately also difficult to cultivate. *L. bictoniense* is the least demanding of the lot and is sometimes grown for cut flowers. The apex of its

Lemboglossum bictoniense

Lemboglossum cervantesii

derful backdrop for crosswise brown spots surrounding the center of the flower. Grow it in cool conditions throughout the year. The plants need a maximum possible amount of light, which renders them "difficult" collection species. Flowers can be expected between November and March. The plant comes from Mexico and Guatemala.

Lemboglossum cordatum

CRYOPHILIC-INTERMEDIATE

In the 1980s, the original genus of *Odontoglossum* was split up into many genera, such as *Lemboglossum*, *Miltonioides*, *Osmoglossum*, *Rossioglossum*, or *Ticoglossum*. To this day, however, many species that were then transferred to one of these new genera are still listed in orchid literature under their old generic name *Odontoglossum*, which may cause some confusion. The species *L. cordatum* has egg-shaped, 2.4-in/6-cm-long pseudobulbs ended with a single narrow leaf reaching a length of 8 in/20 cm. The sparse flower raceme consists of 5-8 flowers with a variable length of their pointed tepals. Their yellow color is complemented with brown spots. The lip is heart-shaped (hence the Latin name of the species), white, with sparse brown spots. Grow it in the same way as *Ticoglossum krameri* (see p. 250). The plants bloom between June and August in foggy alpine forests of Mexico, Guatemala, Honduras and Costa Rica.

Lemboglossum cordatum

egg-shaped pseudobulbs that reach lengths of up to 4.8 in/12 cm gives rise to a couple of narrow leaves that are up to 16 in/40 cm long. The flower spike is formed at the base of the pseudobulb and is sparsely covered with numerous flowers. The flowers are fairly small (1.2-1.6 in/3-4 cm); their narrow and long tepals are yellowish green and covered with dark spots. The lip is mauve. The flowers appear between December and May. The plant has been discovered in Mexico, Guatemala and Salvador.

Lemboglossum cervantesii

CRYOPHILIC-INTERMEDIATE

This species is a highly valued, beautiful, "pedigree" representative of the genus. Its small proportions make it cultivation-friendly; the egg-shaped unifoliate pseudobulbs are 1.2-2 in/3-5 cm long, the single narrow leaves reach lengths of 6 in/15 cm. The flowers growing on a sparse, short flower raceme are characterized by a regular roundness. Their shiny white tepals provide a won-

Lemboglossum rossii

Lemboglossum wyattianum

Lemboglossum rossii   □ ⊡ ☹ ☺

CRYOPHILIC-INTERMEDIATE

Its miniature proportions and showy flowers make *L. rossii* a very popular orchid—sadly, attempts at cultivation often face the problem of the cryophilia typical of the whole genus. The pseudobulbs are oval and only 0.8-1.2 in/2-3 cm long, the leaves reach lengths of up to 4.8 in/12 cm. The flower spikes usually bear only one flower (rarely 2-3). The flowers are up to 2.4 in/6 cm across, their sepals are yellowish, with brown spots; the wider petals have similar spots only at the base. The lip is wide, wavy and pink with a tinge of white. The plant blooms in a period favorable for cultivators—between February and April—and it has been reported to grow in Central American states between Mexico and Nicaragua.

Lemboglossum wyattianum   ⊡ ◼ ☹ ☺

CRYOPHILIC–INTERMEDIATE

The flowers of this species seem to be trying to prove that almighty Mother Nature is able to conjure up any color combination and that She possesses endless esthetic capacities and imagination! Some 2-4 flowers, reaching sizes of 2.8 in/7 cm, grow on a 6-in/15-cm-long flower spike and their beauty is absolutely indescribable—one look at their whitish, widened lip frilled on the sides and embellished with a complex purplish blue pattern will prove the truth of this claim. Moreover, the plant is rather small in proportions. It forms medium-flattened, elongated egg-shaped bifoliate pseudobulbs with lengthwise grooves, reaching lengths of 3.2 in/8 cm. The thin leaves are 8 in/20 cm long at the most. The species is attractive but, unfortunately, difficult to cultivate. It requires conditions recommended for the cryophilic representatives of the genus, it blooms between the fall and spring and comes from Ecuador and Peru.

Leochilus sp.   □ ⊡ ☺

INTERMEDIATE-THERMOPHILIC

The genus *Leochilus* includes about 15 mostly small and undemanding species, suitable for little amateur collections. The plant in the photo (*L. oncidioides*?) is, besides being undemanding in cultivation, attractive for its abundance of tiny, sometimes partly transparent, white flowers with a delicate reddish marking. The unifoliate pseudobulbs are ball-shaped and very minute (0.4-1.6 in/ 1-4 cm); the soft, lineated leaves are 4-6 in/10-15 cm long. Two or three overhanging inflorescences grow out of the bases of the pseudobulbs, each of them bearing 1-8 little flowers. The plant will even tolerate a less-ventilated, somewhat moist environment and semi-shade, which also makes it suitable for growing in indoor glass

Leochilus sp., Mexico

cases. Grow it epiphytically. It usually blooms between March and April. Its habitat is in the warm and moist area surrounding Orizaba, Mexico, but *Leochilus* orchids are even known to grow in lower altitudes all over Central America: between Mexico and Panama and also in Cuba.

Leptotes unicolor   □   ☺

INTERMEDIATE

All three representatives of this epiphytic genus are beautiful, miniature orchids, very popular with orchid collectors. The plants form sticklike pseudobulbs, each bearing a single thickened, reddish leaf that is almost circular at its cross-section. The leaves and pseudobulbs together are up to 2.4 in/6 cm long. The short flower spike bears two or three flowers that are 3-4 cm across. Compared to the even more popular *L. bicolor*, *L. unicolor* has monochromatic flowers—the color of the tepals can be either purple or white. Clusters of this plant mounted on wooden or bark supports are not very demanding in cultivation: they thrive in a place with partial shade and good ventilation. In excessive shade, the plants extend too much and are prone to molding. Reduce watering and lower the temperature in the winter. The plant blooms between January and April and is native to Brazil.

Leptotes unicolor

Liparis sp., Malaysia

Liparis sp.

Liparis nutans

Liparis   ☺

INTERMEDIATE

As far as cultivation is concerned, the tropical representatives of the genus *Liparis* are not really attractive—the plants are rather large and their flowers are usually unremarkable, growing in erect racemes. The flower spike is 14 in/35 cm tall and grows out of the apex of a usually bifoliate, cone-shaped pseudobulb that is not very firm. *L. nutans* is one of the few exceptions within the genus *Liparis* with showier flowers; their shiny orange color stands out especially well from the broad lip. Grow these orchids in a permanently slightly moist peat substrate in flowerpots. They are suitable as additional species of lower darker sections of indoor glass cases and greenhouses because they can grow in heavier shade. Caution: direct sunshine is sure to cause damage or completely destroy them. In the winter, you can reduce temperature somewhat in shadier growing environments. *Liparis* orchids are widespread not only in the tropics but also in Temperate and Cool Zones all over the world.

Ludisia discolor

Ludisia discolor

Ludisia discolor ▫ ☺

INTERMEDIATE-THERMOPHILIC

The name of the genus was a subject of dispute for some time; in the end, the name *Ludisia* was recognized as valid. Nevertheless, most cultivators know the representatives of the genus by their old name of "*Haemaria*". The genus includes only one species that is, however, highly variable in the color of its oval leaves. A fundamental part of the flower is a thickened, soft, succulent, decumbent stem ended with an ascending apex that keeps growing. The terminal dense raceme of tiny white flowers contrasts nicely the dark color of the velvety leaves with the color ranging between brown-and-green and brown-and-red. But be careful: their color also depends on the intensity of light they are exposed to; in excessive shade the plants assume an almost pure green color! For many years now, *L. discolor* has been a highly popular collection species (partly thanks to its capacity for rapid vegetative propagation). It requires a constantly moist peat substrate, rain water and deeper shade. It blooms between the fall and spring and comes from the southwest of Asia.

145

Lycaste aromatica

grance. Cultivation is not difficult: provide the plants with a temperate environment with a medium-high intensity of diffused light. If you want them to flower abundantly, plant them in flowerpots filled with a standard orchid substrate. Mounting them on epiphytic supports is also possible, but in such case the specimens require more frequent misting and fertilization. In the winter, after the leaves fall off, reduce watering and temperature, inducing thus a period of rest; this is also necessary for proper development of the next season's lot of flowers. *L. aromatica* blooms in early spring—both in artificial culture and in the wild, i.e., in Mexico, Guatemala and Honduras.

Lycaste cruenta

INTERMEDIATE-THERMOPHILIC

A somewhat robust species whose flowers are up to 3.2 in/8 cm in diameter. It is quite rare in cultivation—specimens of it are therefore well-guarded gems of every orchid collection. It should be grown in the same manner as *L. aromatica*. The species blooms between March and April and is known to grow in Mexico, Guatemala and Salvador.

Lycaste cruenta

Lycaste aromatica ▣ ☺

INTERMEDIATE

All the representatives of the genus *Lycaste* (a total of about 35 species) are very alike when not in bloom, and quite attractive, too: they form large, glossy green egg-shaped pseudobulbs decorated on their apices with two or three pointed elliptic leaves with pronounced lengthwise venation. The leaves usually last for one season only, and subsequently fall off. The typical flowers, whose inner tepals are shaped to resemble a little roof, grow one by one on thin spikes from the base of the pseudobulbs and there can be several dozens of them growing at once on well-developed specimens of some species! *L. aromatica* is the best-known species of the whole genus. Its orange-and-yellow flowers give off a strong, lovely fra-

Lycaste macrophyllum

not differ much from those of *L. aromatica*. Flower buds appear at the bases of the pseudobulbs between March and July. When exactly they appear depends on the climate of the habitats—for the plants grow over a vast area of Central and South America (between Costa Rica and Bolivia).

Lycaste virginalis   ◼ ☺

INTERMEDIATE

Lycaste macrophyllum   ◼ ☺

INTERMEDIATE

One of the most robust species of the whole genus—its pseudobulbs are up to 4 in/10 cm tall, the leaves reach lengths of 24 in/60 cm (hence the Latin name, meaning "big-leafed"). The flowers are up to 4.8 in/12 cm across and stunningly beautiful. They consist of a white, red-spotted lip, three outer brown-and-red and two inner whitish tepals. The species' cultivation requirements do

This orchid is often labeled with its synonym of *L. skinneri*, and it is unquestionably the most decorative species of the whole genus. Its uncommon appearance is reflected in the species name—*virginalis* means virginal or untouched and naturally refers to the beauty of the plant. The 4 in/10-cm-tall pseudobulbs bearing two or three leaves reaching lengths of up to 6 in/15 cm do not differ in appearance from their closest relatives. On the other hand, the pinkish flowers can be 6 in/15 cm across with a shade-darker, purple-spotted lip. Collectors are also after the species' rare white-flowered variety (var. *alba*). Cultivation rules are identical with those of *L. aromatica*. The species blooms between the fall and spring and lives epiphytically in an area between Mexico and Honduras in altitudes of 6,560 ft/2,000 m and lower.

Lycaste virginalis

Masdevallia   ▢ ☺

CRYOPHILIC-INTERMEDIATE

Outside of the flowering period, many *Masdevallia* species are the spitting image of one another, and their appearance is far from striking. However, the more boring their green parts look, the more pleasantly surprising their wonderfully shaped and colored flowers appear! The "cornerstone" of the plants is an extremely shortened trailing rhizome giving rise to almost completely reduced sticklike remnants of pseudobulbs. Each of them bears a stiff succulent leaf of a spatulate or inverted lanceolate shape typical of

Masdevallia tovarensis

Masdevallia. The foliage is vividly green and glossy and forms dense tufts. The morphology of the flowers is quite uniform: they are dominated by sepals usually extended into long, thread-like tips and a tongue-shaped or conchoidal lip. They grow on stalks of varying lengths, always individually (rarely in pairs) and there are always a number of them on a plant at once. Representatives of the genus *Masdevallia* grow epiphytically, terrestrially or lithophytically on moist rocks. Their cultivation requirements may appear a little extraordinary, but they are manageable. As they mostly come from cooler, moist and shady regions, their roots are not well adapted to dryness. Therefore, they should be cultivated in a fine-

Masdevallia floribunda

Masdevallia picturata

Masdevallia ignea

grained substrate in flowerpots rather than on an epiphytic support. Place them in semi-shade in a well-
ventilated place and cool them by frequent misting
on sultry days. Do not divide the clusters too often.
Approximately 300 species of this systemically unstable and unprocessed genus have been described
(some of its representatives have been transferred
to independent genera of *Andreetaea*, *Dracula*,
Dryadella and *Trisetella*). *Masdevallia* orchids are
known to grow all over Central and especially South
America.

Masdevallia biflora

Maxillaria   ⊡ ◼ ☺

CRYOPHILIC-INTERMEDIATE

Maxillaria is a quite well known orchid genus but certainly not one of the most popular. Only a fraction of a total of its 300 species boast large, showy flowers that, however, grow on short spikes, which makes the plants useless in gardening. Furthermore, collectors are put off by the considerably large proportions of many *Maxillaria* species. Several small or otherwise attractive species can, naturally, be found even within this

genus; some of them are introduced in the photos. An overwhelming majority of *Maxillaria* orchids form pseudobulbs ranging in shape between ball-shaped and elongated egg-like varieties and attached to a trailing or ascending rhizome. The pseudobulbs usually bear one or two elongated, narrow leaves and are either crowded in a dense cluster or sparsely distributed on the long rhizome. Spikes bearing one flower each grow out of the bases of the pseudobulbs and do not surpass the

Maxillaria sp., Ecuador

Maxillaria rufescens

Maxillaria picta

Maxillaria tenuifolia

Maxillaria sp., Ecuador

leaves in length. Typically, the lip of the flowers is arched and tongue-shaped, usually bearing three inconspicuous lobes. The other tepals are also elongated, protruding widely into space and positioned in a similar manner as those of *Lycaste* orchids. *Maxillaria* orchids are epiphytes growing in medium elevations of tropical areas. Cultivation rules can be deduced from this. The plants should be mounted on branches or bark, while some large-flowered species can be placed in a small wooden basket containing an epiphytic mix. If you want the orchids to flower well, put them on a well-ventilated place with as much diffused light as possible. The genus *Maxillaria* is known to grow only in tropical America.

Maxillaria uncata

Maxillaria porphyrostele

151

Mediocalcar ☐ ⊡ ☺ ☺

INTERMEDIATE-THERMOPHILIC

Representatives of this genus that has not yet been very systematically described are beautiful dwarfed orchids and highly sought-after cultivation rarities. They are not attractive only for their unusual bell-shaped flowers but also for the extraordinary morphology of their bodies. The clustered plants form pseudobulb-like cylindrical stems that grow either out of a trailing rhizome or from the apex of the preceding shoot (see the plant with the yellow-and-orange flowers in the photo, resembling somewhat the species *M. decoratum*); the latter instance is much less common. 1-5 short, succulent leaves adorn the apices of the stems. One or several yellow-and-orange, white or red flowers grow on the spikes. Growing these small epi-

Mediocalcar sp.

Mediocalcar sp., New Guinea

phytes is not very difficult. Mount the plants in a layer of moss on a wooden support and place them in a warm (temperate in winter), moist environment. Flowers appear irregularly, mostly in the winter and spring. Most *Mediocalcar* orchids (a total of about 50 species) come from the medium altitudes of New Guinea.

Meiracyllium trinasutum ☐ ☺ ☺

INTERMEDIATE-THERMOPHILIC

The genus *Meiracyllium* includes only two species, both of which are splendid-looking orchids. They have reduced pseudobulbs and oval, intensely thickened leaves. The species *M. trinasutum* is somewhat smaller than its lower mentioned relative. Each of the dwarfed pseudobulbs bears a single reddish, 2-in/5-cm-long, oval or almost round-shaped leaf. The inflorescences number up to 6 flowers and grow out of the bases of the leaves. The flowers are 0.8 in/2 cm across, pinkish purple, and their lower sepals are grown together. The lip is a shade darker than the other tepals. The species is a true gem of any collection as it is exceptionally attractive even when not in bloom. Some problems in cultivation may be caused by mold attacking the newly forming shoots and root tips. Grow the plants epiphytically on a piece of durable bark (pine, cork oak) and supply sufficient amount of diffused light. *M. trinasutum* blooms between late spring and summer and is known to grow in Cuba, Guatemala, Salvador and Mexico.

Meiracyllium trinasutum

Meiracyllium wendlandii

Meiracyllium wendlandii   □ ☺ ☺

INTERMEDIATE

Compared to the previous species, this orchid is a little better-known and more common in collections. Its pseudobulbs are also intensely reduced and the storage function is overtaken by its highly succulent leaves. The name of the genus is derived from the Greek word *meirakyllion* (small boy) and obviously refers to the size of the plants. The species is almost undistinguishable from *M. trinasutum* in appearance, except its leaves are a bit longer and its spikes are more robust. Small differences can be observed in the morphology of the flowers: in the case of *M. wendlandii*, the lip is less saclike (that is, the bulging blunt protuberance is absent form its lower part) and the column is thinner at the base. The species blooms in the winter and its natural habitat is in Mexico and Guatemala.

Mendocella burkei   ▣ ☺

INTERMEDIATE

A member of a rather small (11 species) genus that contains medium-sized New World epiphytes with gorgeous flowers. *M. burkei* has 2.4 in/6-cm-tall elongated pseudobulbs ended with two belt-shaped leaves that reach lengths of 14 in/35 cm. As with the closely related genus *Zygopetalum*, the lateral parts of the new pseudobulbs give rise to a flower spike that is up to 8 in/20 cm tall and bears 3-5 showy flowers, 2.8 in/7 cm across. The forward-bent, broad lip is cream-white with a pinkish red base; the other tepals are greenish with a decorative brown marking. The plant can be grown either epiphytically or in a permeable epiphytic mix. The flowers appear in the winter and early spring. *M. burkei* comes from Venezuela and Colombia.

Mendocella burkei

Mexicopedilum xerophyticum

Microcoelia exilis

Mexicopedilum xerophyticum ◼ ☺

THERMOPHILIC

The dernier cri in the world of orchids! Its first speci-mens were discovered in the xerophilous vegetation of the Bay of Mexico coastal region only a little over a decade ago—in 1991. At first, the plants were consid-ered to be a new species of the genus *Phragmipedium* (or *Cypripedium*), but their external features called for establishing a brand new genus! The ground rosettes of the stiff, belt-shaped leaves can form lateral daughter shoots, the whitish flowers grow singly on a 14-in/35-cm-long scape and their proportions are minuscule (0.6-0.8 in/1.5-2 cm). There is little information avail-able on how to cultivate the species. The home of this surprising find is Oaxaca, Mexico.

tween the root bases and each of them measures up to 6 in/15 cm and bears up to 30 whitish flowers that open one by one. Their extraordinary appearance made *Mi-crocoelia* orchids highly sought-after plants, although they are quite rare in collections. Grow them in a semi-shady, considerably moist and well-ventilated place. To avoid the risk of mold, watering (and also temperature) should be somewhat reduced in the winter. The flowers appear irregularly, almost anytime during the year. The species is reported to grow in the area between equato-rial Africa, South Africa and Madagascar.

Microcoelia exilis ☐ ⊡ ☺ ☺

INTERMEDIATE-THERMOPHILIC

The genus *Microcoelia* includes about 27 miniature epi-phytes whose common denominator is a rare form of ex-istence—they are entirely leafless. The assimilation and storage functions of the leaves were taken over by the chlorophyllous, fleshy roots, as the case of the genera *Chiloschista* and *Polyrrhiza*. *Microcoelia* orchids have stems that are either extremely elongated or extremely shortened; *M. exilis* is an example of the latter type. Its intensely reduced stem (often not longer than 0.4-1.2 in/1-3 cm) gives rise to a large number of long, fleshy, flat-tened roots. They are silvery when dry, and green when wet. Abundant, semi-erect flower spikes are formed be-

Miltonia candida ◼ ☺

INTERMEDIATE

There is a considerable amount of confusion connected with the systematic classification of many groups of or-chids within the family *Orchidaceae*; this is caused by the vast amount of different shapes orchids assume, as well as their often unclear relations. The genus *Miltonia* is a good example of this phenomenon—the differences in the morphology of its flowers and those of *Odon-toglossum* orchids are minimal. The species *M. candida* has 2.4-in/6-cm-long, bifoliate pseudobulbs. Its leaves are thin and up to 12 in/30 cm long. The erect flower spike bears 3.2-in/8-cm-large yellow-and-green flowers with brown spots and a whitish oval lip that is purplish on

Miltonia candida

Miltonia clowesii

Miltonia flavescens

INTERMEDIATE

The plant's bifoliate, 2.8-in/7-cm-tall pseudobulbs are stored in a trailing rhizome; this morphological trait is featured on all *Miltonia* orchids. *M. flavescens* differs from the other species in the appearance of its flowers, which are whitish all over and sport extremely narrow, elongated tepals. The flowers (6-12 at a time) are arranged in a sparse erect raceme. The lip is adorned with an inconspicuous red marking. Cultivation requirements of the species are not different from those of the two preceding species. The plants bloom between May and August and are native to Brazil and Paraguay.

Miltonia flavescens

the inside. Cultivation of this epiphytic orchid is easy (see *M. clowesii*). The species blooms in late summer and comes from Brazil.

Miltonia clowesii

INTERMEDIATE

The appearance of its green parts makes *M. clowesii* look like the previous species; unlike *M. candida*, this species has a flower raceme that reaches a length of up to 20 in/50 cm and bears 5-10 flowers. The lip is purple with a tinge of white and typically shaped like a violin. This species is likeable not only in appearance, but also when it comes to cultivation. The best way to grow it is epiphytically on a largish support, in order to give the delicate, decorative roots on its fast-growing and eagerly branching rhizome ample opportunity to grow over the slab. Keep the clusters in a moderately moist and semi-shady environment. A winter rest break is unnecessary. The flowers appear between September and November. The plant is native to Brazil.

Miltonia regnellii
 (x M. clowesii?) 　　▣ ☺

INTERMEDIATE

A pretty and rather small *Miltonia* orchid that is also very attractive for cultivation. Its bifoliate pseudobulbs are elongated and egg-shaped, reaching lengths of 2-3.2 in/ 5-8 cm. The thin, soft leaves measure 6-10 in/15-25 cm. The flower raceme can bear 5-8 flowers that are 2 in/5 cm in diameter and arranged in two rows. The tepals are typically whitish; the plant in the photo has flowers adorned with brownish spots, which possibly makes it a botanical hybrid with the species *M. clowesii*. The broad wavy lip is light pink with a whitish base and dark venation. The plant should be grown in the same way as other Brazilian *Miltonia* orchids. The flowers appear in the summer. The plant was first discovered in eastern Brazil.

Miltonia spectabilis 　　▣ ☺

INTERMEDIATE-THERMOPHILIC

The species *M. spectabilis* is one of the "pedigree" representatives of the genus—its classification is, in comparison with other species—completely unquestionable, mainly thanks to its trailing rhizome bearing tall, flat, slim, bifoliate pseudobulbs, about 2.8 in/7 cm far from each other. Single flowers appear, simultaneously with

the new shoots, between the bases of the new leaves, and resemble pansies in shape. The flowers on a typical *M. spectabilis* are white with notably broadened, flat, purple lips adorned with yellow stripes and red venation. The color of the flowers varies; one of the popular

Miltonia spectabilis

Miltonioides reichenheimii

of 4 in/10 cm, while its thin leaves can be up to 12 in/ 30 cm long. The flower raceme bears numerous flowers and reaches a height of 24 in/60 cm. The large flowers, up to 2.4 in/6 cm across, are yellow with large brown spots. The delicate composition is complemented by a broad lip that ranges in color between light purple and white. Flowers appear between May and August. *M. reichenheimii* is native to the mountain forests of Mexico.

Miltoniopsis phalaenopsis

CRYOPHILIC

This species used to be considered a member of the genus *Miltonia* but it was later excluded on the grounds of its unifoliate pseudobulbs, as well as differences in the flower morphology. The white flowers with a lip adorned in red and yellow are, admittedly, rather small (up to 2 in/5 cm), but despite this they are exceptionally beautiful, resembling the flat flowers of pansies. Being a plant native to cooler mountain elevations, *M. phalaenopsis* needs to be grown in a way similar to the cryophilic orchids of the genus *Odontoglossum*. It requires plenty of diffused light, good ventilation, slightly lower temperatures all year round and a more substantial winter break. It blooms between July and October and has been found in Colombia.

Miltoniopsis phalaenopsis

color variations has dark red flowers (var. *moreliana*). *M. spectabilis* is beloved by orchid fans for its delicate beauty and durability of its flowers. It is widely used for creating resistant and gorgeous-looking "potted" hybrids. Grow it the same as *M. clowesii*. Flowers can be expected between the spring and summer. The plant comes from Brazil.

Miltonioides reichenheimii

INTERMEDIATE-THERMOPHILIC

As with many others, this orchid also used to be included in the genus *Odontoglossum*. In orchid literature, you can also come across it under the name *Miltonia reichenheimii*. It has oval, bifoliate pseudobulbs reaching lengths

Mormodes   ▣ ☹ ☺

CRYOPHILIC-INTERMEDIATE

Representatives of this peculiar genus closely resemble their relatives—*Catasetum* orchids. They have spindle-shaped pseudobulbs bearing 3-7 lanceolate, lengthwise

wrinkled leaves. After the pseudobulbs reach maturity, the leaves fall off. The flower spike appears during the period when new shoots are forming at the base of the pseudo-bulbs, and there are usually 5-10 flowers on it. The dioecian flowers of this genus (a feature that distinguishes *Mormodes* from *Catasetum* orchids) are characterized by the morphology of their lip: it is folded and markedly

Mormodes amazonicum

Mormodes sp., Bolivia

Mormolyca sp. ⊡ ☺

INTERMEDIATE

An insignificant genus numbering about 6 species that resemble *Maxillaria* orchids in appearance. The best-known member of the genus is *M. ringens*, which grows in an area between Mexico and Costa Rica; the species in the photo taken in Bolivia is rarer and its name is probably *M. gracilipes. Mormolyca* orchids are characterized by unifoliate pseudobulbs growing on a short rhizome. Their thin leaves are up to 12 in/30 cm long, same as the one-flowered spikes. The flowers are 1.2 in/3 cm in diameter with yellow, brown-striped tepals and a brown three-lobed lip. Grow them in the same way as *Maxillaria* orchids. The Bolivian plant in the photo blooms in the winter.

Mormolyca sp., Bolivia

arched. Orchids of this genus are very pretty and developmentally interesting plants and highly valuable collection items. As far as their cultivation is concerned, they are rather demanding and should be grown much like *Catasetum* orchids. Mount them on large wooden supports and provide them with ample watering, fertilization and indirect sunlight during the growth period. After the leaves begin to turn yellow and dry up, reduce temperature and cease watering completely. A total of about 25 species of this genus bloom mostly in early spring and are known to grow dispersedly throughout Central and South America.

Nanodes medusae

Nanodes medusae   □ · ☹ ☺

INTERMEDIATE

A characteristic feature of the genus *Nanodes* are its overhanging soft stems, slightly ascending on the ends and densely covered with two rows of short succulent leaves. The flowers positioned on the ends of the stems are yellow-and-green and up to 3.2 in/8 cm in diameter. They are dominated by a brown-and-red, fimbriated lip. This bizarre and highly sought-after species is not very easy to cultivate. The plants need a higher level of air humidity and good ventilation—this combination is impossible to achieve in hot summer days and the delicate stems or buds tend to dry up. Therefore, mount them in a thick layer of peat moss. The species blooms between July and August. It is native to Ecuador.

Nanodes megalospatha

Nanodes megalospatha   · ☹ ☺

INTERMEDIATE

This splendid overhanging orchid would certainly please many growers, if only it were more readily available and, above all, easier to cultivate. In the wild, *N. megalospatha* occurs in cooler locations with a high year-round rainfall, and grows over moss-covered tree trunks that are almost permanently moist. In culture, the plants are deprived of bacteriologically clean rainwater and fresh air, which makes them prone to molding, especially during the winter. In the summer months, on the other hand, they are damaged by frequent overdrying of their roots as well as by high temperatures. Instead of torturing the plant in cultivation, it is better to just view it growing in the wild—the plant in the photo grows in the winter in the foothills of the Ecuadorian Andes near the town of Baeza.

Nanodes porpax   □ ☺

INTERMEDIATE-THERMOPHILIC

This species is, with regard to the morphology of its body, the ultimate *Nanodes* orchid. Its crawling or ascending stems are foliaged with two rows of leaves. The plant is smaller than the previous species, which makes it a very lovable miniature. Its leaves are barely 0.8 in/2 cm long. The willingly branching soft stems produce numerous aerial roots and bear on their ends single, 1-in/2.5-cm-long flowers with a showy, reversed heart-shaped lip colored in brown-and-red. *N. porpax* is no

Nanodes porpax

cultivation stumper—it will settle for semi-shade and fairly frequent misting. It blooms in late summer and in the fall. It grows dispersedly over a vast area including Mexico, Panama, Venezuela and Peru.

Nanodes schlechterianum   □   ⊡   ☺

INTERMEDIATE-THERMOPHILIC

As with other *Nanondes* orchids, *N. schlechterianum* is by many botanists included in the maternal genus of *Epidendrum*. Classification of this particular species has one more peculiarity—the plant is often presented under its synonym, *N. discolor*. Its stems bear two rows of fleshy, soft leaves that reach lengths of up to 0.8 in/2 cm. The flowers are greenish brown with a pinkish brown lip; they are about 0.8 in/2 cm across and there are 1-3 of them per each extremely short terminal inflorescence. Cultivation does not differ from that of *N. porpax*. The plant blooms irregularly throughout the year—most often between the fall and spring. The species' geographical area includes Mexico, Panama, Colombia, Venezuela, Brazil, Peru, Trinidad, and other countries in that region.

Nanodes sp.   □   ⊡   ☺

INTERMEDIATE

There are many uncertainties in the taxonomy of this genus—a high number of small, plain-looking orchids grow in tropical America that are classified differently by different authors. Moreover, there is no general agree-ment as to whether the plants belong in the genera *Nanodes*, *Epidendrum* or, most recently, *Neolehmannia*. Be it as it may, the species in the photo (*N. barbeyana?*) is a pretty, clustered miniature, useful in small amateur collections as an "accessory" green epiphyte. The terminal flowers are whitish and have no decorative value to speak of. This undemanding plant should be grown in the same way as *N. porpax*. It blooms irregularly (mostly in the winter) and comes from Ecuador and other countries.

Nanodes sp., Ecuador

Neofinetia falcata

Nervilia aragoana

Neofinetia falcata ▫ ☺

CRYOPHILIC

The genus *Neofinetia* includes only one species that looks like a miniature version of an *Angraecum* or *Vanda* species. Its stiff, barely 4-6-in/10-15-cm-long stem bears two rows of tough leaves reaching lengths of 2.8 in/7 cm. Some 2-7 snow-white flowers appear on rather short flower spikes and are remarkable for their forward-bent spur that can be up to 1.6 in/4 cm long. In the wild, *N. falcata* grows epiphytically, but it can also be grown in a medium-coarse substrate in flowerpots. It requires the highest possible amount of light, but also a cooler environment and a winter rest. In the past, the plant was used to create hybrids with the genera *Vanda*, *Ascocentrum*, and even *Phalaenopsis*. The flowers appear between June and August. The species grows in an untraditional area—Korea and Japan.

Nervilia aragoana ▫ ☺

INTERMEDIATE

A peculiar terrestrial orchid, surviving by means of a 0.8 in/2-cm-tall underground pseudobulb in the underbrush of seasonally drier forests. During the growth of the inflorescence that bears 2-3 flowers, the plant has to do without its single egg-shaped or heart-shaped leaf with a showy brown-and-purple marking—the leaf does not develop until after the flowers fade. The flowers are about 1 in/2.5 cm across; their tepals are greenish yellow with lengthwise brown stripes of varying intensity. The lip is a shade lighter. The plant should be grown in a humic substrate in flowerpots. During growth, the plant needs moist semi-shade and ample warmth, while requiring absolute dryness and reduced temperatures in the winter. It blooms between January and April and comes from the Malayan Peninsula, northern Thailand, Laos and Burma.

Nervilia aragoana

Nidema boothii ▫ ☺

INTERMEDIATE

This small, undemanding orchid popular with collectors is the only representative of its genus. Its trailing rhizome produces club-shaped pseudobulbs that grow at distances of about 1 in/2-3 cm from each other and reach lengths of 2.4 in/6 cm. They bear one or two lineated leaves that are 6 in/15 cm long. Sparse inflorescences grow out of the apices of the new pseudobulbs. The plant's cream-white flowers are quite large and attractive. The species has no particular demands—it thrives on a wooden support in semi-shade. In the winter, you can reduce temperature and watering a little. The flowers appear in the fall and the plants come from Central America (an area between Mexico, Panama, Cuba and Surinam).

Nidema boothii

Notylia barkeri   □ ☺

INTERMEDIATE

A representative of a numerous (40 species) genus with plain-looking flowers arranged in quite showy raceme inflorescences. *N. barkeri* is not overly interesting with regard to cultivation and is only suitable for specialized botanical collections. It has tiny, flat, ball-shaped-to-elliptic pseudobulbs, and belt-shaped-to-oval, tough leaves that are

Notylia barkeri

up to 8 in/20 cm long. The plants usually don't reach their maximum possible proportions but still bloom, even if much smaller. The tiny, greenish white flowers grow in large numbers on an overhanging raceme. Grow the plant epiphytically in a medium-lighted and well-ventilated environment. The flowers appear in the spring. The species is known to grow in the warmer regions of Central America.

Oberonia sp.   □ · ☺

INTERMEDIATE-THERMOPHILIC

The whole genus of *Oberonia* is of absolutely no interest for cultivation—its flowers are no bigger than 0.04-0.08 in/1-2 mm. However, curiosity-growers might be intrigued by the peculiar iris-like morphology of these small orchids. The plant does not create any stems or pseudobulbs; its flat, pointed leaves grow out of one another. The overhanging inflorescences, consisting of dozens and hundreds tiny flowers, are sometimes compared to the infructescence of a European weed called "little mouse tail" (*Myosurus minimus*). Cultivation of these plants is not very complicated: these shade-loving plants must not be exposed to any extreme conditions due to their minuscule proportions. Epiphytic culture is recommended; when mounting the plants on a support, add a handful of moss to the roots. Some 200 species of this genus are widespread in eastern Africa, India, southwestern Asia and the Pacific Islands. The species in the photo taken in Thailand blooms in November and December.

Oberonia sp., Thailand

Odontoglossum kegeliani

CRYOPHILIC-INTERMEDIATE

The genus *Odontoglossum* used to be very extensive but it was gradually divided into a large number of independent genera (see the species *Lemboglossum cordatum*). The species *O. kegeliani* is one of about 50 remaining members of the original, "truncated" genus. It has flattened, uni- to trifoliate pseudobulbs reaching lengths of 2-2.8 in/ 5-7 cm; its elongated belt-shaped leaves are up to 10 in/25 cm long. Nice round flowers are 2.4 in/6 cm in diameter and are arranged in rich, sometimes branching, inflorescences that reach lengths of 10 in/25 cm. Greenish-yellow tepals are covered with several large brown-and-red spots. The medium-sized lip is white on the outside and brown-and-red on the inside and sports a white fimbriated edge. Grow the plant in a permeable epiphytic substrate and provide it with somewhat cooler, humid conditions and as much light as possible throughout the year. It blooms in early spring and comes from Ecuador.

Oncidium barbatum

INTERMEDIATE

One of the members of the vast genus *Oncidium* that have a "classic" look and are interesting to cultivate.

Oncidium barbatum

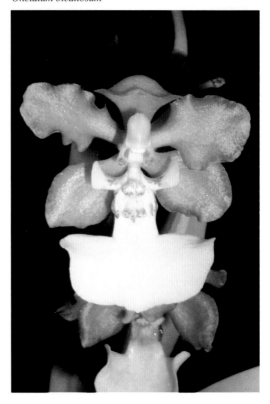

It forms at least 2.4-in/6-cm-long oval pseudobulbs ended with a single leaf that is 4 in/10 cm long. The flower spike bears 6-12 waxy flowers. A three-lobed lip stands out well against the tawny tepals, and has a five-toothed, fimbriated comb speckled with red dots (hence the name "*barbatum*"="bearded"). Cultivation of this epiphytic orchid is not complicated: mount the plant on a slab of bark or branch and hang it up in a well-ventilated semi-shady environment. *O. barbatum* blooms between March and May and was discovered in Brazil.

Oncidium bicallosum

INTERMEDIATE

O. bicallosum represents those *Oncidium* orchids that do not form pseudobulbs. The function of storage organs for these orchids is served by its unusually succulent, broad, oval, long-lived leaves. *O. bicallosum* produces a high number of flowers arranged in an erect, branched inflorescence. The flowers are brown-and-green with a lemon yellow broad lip. Grow the plant epiphytically in a somewhat dry, light environment. The species blooms between August and October and is native to Mexico, Guatemala and Salvador.

Oncidium carthagenense   ▣ ■ ☺

INTERMEDIATE-THERMOPHILIC

As with the previous species, *O. carthagenense* has no
pseudobulbs and stores water in its intensely thickened
leaves reaching lengths of over 16 in/40 cm. Their surface, much like the similar species *O. luridum*, is speckled with red dots. The shape of their ears earned the
plants the nickname "dog ears." The branched, flower
spike bearing many sparse flowers reaches a length of
5 ft/150 cm. The decorative flowers are 0.8 in/2 cm
across and their color is atypical by the genus' standard—they are whitish with reddish spots. The lip is
markedly three-lobed with a yellow-and-red base. Both
aforementioned species have identical, equally undemanding requirements; they are happy in a warm environment in a modestly shaded greenhouse. Excessive
humidity coupled with falling temperatures causes the
foliage to mold. The species blooms regularly and willingly between May and June and it comes from southern Florida, western India and Mexico.

Oncidium cebolleta   ▣ ☺

THERMOPHILIC

A species exceptional not only within the *Oncidium*
genus. The plant is special in that the function of water
reservoirs was taken over by unusual-looking cylindrical
(almost round in cross-section), stiff leaves that reach
lengths of 12 in/30 cm. They look a little like

Oncidium carthagenense

Oncidium cebolleta

a rat's tail—hence the nickname of other *Oncidium* orchids with similar morphology. The flower spike is overhanging, branched and up to 24 in/60 cm long. It bears
a few dozen 0.8-in/2-cm-large flowers. The flower lip is
yellow, while the other tepals are yellow-and-green and
densely covered with brown-and-red spots. This epiphyte often grows in intensely insolated places; it therefore requires as much light and warmth as possible. It
blooms between February and May and various forms of
it were discovered in Central America and Brazil.

Oncidium cheirophorum

INTERMEDIATE

A miniature representative of *Oncidium*—a genus rich in species and varieties. Its appearance, small proportions and low cultivation demands make it a very attractive collection item. The pseudobulbs are barely 1.2 in/3 cm tall and each bears a single, 6-in/15-cm-long leaf on their apices. The pseudobulbs' bases give rise to two delicate, branched flower spikes covered with

dozens of golden-yellow flowers that are 0.6 in/1.5 cm across. The fragrant flowers last for up to 6 weeks on the plant. The species' name is derived from the shape of the lip that resembles a pair of spread arms. Grow it as you would any standard epiphyte. The flowers appear in late summer and in the fall. The species is native to Nicaragua, Costa Rica and Colombia.

Oncidium crispum

INTERMEDIATE

This orchid is highly sought-after by cultivators. Its flowers are colored in an unusual way. The number and size of the flowers provide a stark contrast to the relatively small proportions of the plant. Its bifoliate pseudobulbs are flat, egg-shaped and 2-3.2 in/5-8 cm tall. The leaves are up to 8 in/20 cm long. The branched, overhanging inflorescence bears 25-30 flowers that are up to 2.8 in/7 cm across! Their tepals are chestnut brown with yellow edges. The lip is similarly colored with a yellow spot in the center. The species should be grown epiphytically, or—in order to achieve a higher number of flowers—in a coarse bark substrate in flowerpots. *O. crispum* blooms between the fall and spring and comes from Brazil.

Oncidium crispum

Oncidium hastilabium

INTERMEDIATE

A spectacular, largish species that is impossible to over-look. For a long time, it was incorrectly classified as an *Odontoglossum* orchid. The egg-shaped pseudobulbs of this epiphytic plant reach lengths of 8 in/20 cm and bear on their apices 1-2 elongated leaves that are up to 8 in/20 cm tall. The nearly erect flower spike reaches a length of 30 in/75 cm at the most. The showy flowers resemble representatives of the above-mentioned mother genus both in shape and appearance. Their short, pointed tepals are greenish and—mainly from the bottom to the mid-dle—adorned with conspicuous crosswise stripes and spots that range in color from chocolate-brown to wine-red. The end of the lip is white and heart-shaped with a purple base. The species has no special cultivation re-quirements. It will do better in a potted epiphytic sub-strate than on a support. It blooms in early spring and comes from the foothills of the Colombian Andes.

Oncidium heranthum

INTERMEDIATE

This small (medium-sized when in bloom) orchid boasts a rare, curious feature—"two-floweredness": its 28-in/70-cm-long, richly branched inflorescence bears a num-ber of tiny sterile yellow flowers (up to 0.2 in/0.5 cm across) and only a small number (1-3 per branch) of much bigger yellow-and-brown flowers. The pseudob-ulbs are elongated, up to 2 in/5 cm long, and each of the

two leaves reaches a length of 6 in/15 cm. This unde-manding epiphyte will embellish any collection; it hap-pens to grow for a long time and its inflorescence is im-mensely decorative and long-lived. The flowers are produced in the winter and spring. The plant inhabits rainforests over a vast area between Costa Rica on one end, and Peru and Bolivia on the other.

Oncidium hastilabium

167

mature, you can treat the plant to a brief dry break. The flowers appear between May and June. The plant originated in the rain forests of Guiana, Brazil and Peru.

Oncidium ornithorhynchum   □ ☺

CRYOPHILIC-INTERMEDIATE

The overall small proportions of this *Oncidium* species increase its collecting value, except that some people may find the flower's scent rather unpleasant. The pseudobulbs are egg-shaped, up to 2.8 in/7 cm tall, with two leaves in the apex. Several flower spikes jointly form the base of the pseudobulbs. They are richly branched, up to 16 in/40 cm long and literally covered with a profusion of somewhat unusual-colored, pink little flowers with yellow centers. This rather cryophilic species should be grown either in flowerpots or epiphytically and provided with a rest period after the flowers fade. It

Oncidium nanum

Oncidium jonesianum var. *pinotii*   □ ■ ☺ ☺

INTERMEDIATE

Another beautiful and highly sought-after orchid, a representative of the rat-tailed *Oncidia*. Its subulate leaves are round in cross-section, about 8 in/20 cm long and overhanging. The flower raceme bears 10-15 wonderfully-colored flowers and is also downward-oriented. The pure-white lip is yellowish at the base and speckled with red dots; the other tepals are broad, yellow-and-white with spots ranging in color between red and brown-and-red. Typically, the spots are very small; the *pinotii* variety in the photo has them fused into bigger spots. Grow the species in the same way as *O. cebolleta*, but make sure to provide extra shade and misting. The inflorescence develops between August and November. *O. jonesianum* comes from Paraguay, Uruguay, Bolivia and southern Brazil.

Oncidium nanum   □ □ ☺

INTERMEDIATE

This orchid is alternatively called "dog ears" (same as its enlarged "copy"—*O. luridum*), for such is the shape of its intensely succulent, tough, 3-6-in/8-15-cm-long leaves. The pseudobulbs were reduced and the short inflorescence grows out of the axils of the leaves from a shortened rhizome. The branched flower spike is not longer than the leaves and bears up to 20 tiny brown-and-yellow flowers, 0.6 in/1.5 cm across. Its proportions and low cultivation demands make *O. nanum* a highly sought-after rarity. Grow it epiphytically; after the leaves

blooms in the fall and winter and comes from Mexico, Guatemala, Salvador and Costa Rica.

Oncidium phymatochilum   ▣   ■   ☺

INTERMEDIATE

One of the record-breakers of the genus: its richly branched flower panicle reaches a length of up to 6.5 ft/ 2 m! The pseudobulbs are up to 4 in/10 cm tall and bear a single, 12-in/30-cm-long leaf. The flowers are 2 in/ 5 cm or smaller in diameter and are green with brown spots. The lip is whitish and strongly resembles a violin in appearance. Cultivation is not complicated but the plant's monstrous proportions make it somewhat unwelcome in small amateur collections. *O. phymatochilum* blooms between May and June and was discovered in Mexico, Guatemala and Brazil.

Oncidium proliferum   □   ▫   ☺

INTERMEDIATE

An impressive, "viviparous" epiphytic miniature—the bases of its flattened, egg-shaped and almost transparent, 1.6-in/4-cm-long pseudobulbs give rise to a trailing, rotary, segmented shoot reaching a length of over 6.5 ft/2 m that climbs the surrounding branches or just

hangs in the air. New daughter pseudobulbs eventually end their development on its individual internodes. Single brown-and-yellow flowers, about 1 in/2-3 cm across, grow on short spikes from the bases of the pseudobulbs. This orchid curiosity is not hard to cultivate: mount it in a layer of moss on a wooden support, allowing enough room for the shoot. The species requires relatively more light and moisture than average. It blooms irregularly, usually in the winter and spring, and comes from countries whose territories stretch into the Amazonian lowlands.

Oncidium proliferum

Oncidium pumilum

Oncidium sp., Mexico

Oncidium pumilum ▫ ☺

INTERMEDIATE

Another representative of "dog-eared" *Oncidia* that are highly-valued and typical of the genus due to the morphology of their inflorescences. The species lacks pseudobulbs and the function of storage organs was overtaken by the thickened, reddish, elongated, oval leaves. The overhanging inflorescence is regularly branched, with the lateral branches densely covered with miniature (0.3 in/8 mm across) red-and-yellow flowers. This epiphyte is somewhat more demanding of light and heat. Flowers can be expected between April and May. *O. pumilum* comes from Brazil and Paraguay.

Oncidium sp., Mexico

Oncidium sp. ▫ ☹

CRYOPHILIC

A fine alpine *Oncidium* orchid that is listed here as an ecological curiosity. Owing to the extreme ecological conditions reigning in its habitat (namely, the high elevations of Oaxaca, Mexico), it is almost impossible to cultivate. The plant forms gold-colored, flattened pseudobulbs ended with thin leaves. The flowers are up to 1.2 in/3 cm in diameter and quite showy thanks to their broad lemon-yellow lip. The species inhabits sparse semi-deciduous oak forests in altitudes below and including 9,800 ft/3,000 m; in cultivation, it therefore needs round-the-year coolness, a certain amount of UV-radiation and

170

near-perfect ventilation—a combination that seems impossible to achieve… The plant blooms in the spring.

Oncidium tigrinum ◨ ■ ☺

INTERMEDIATE

A very robust plant that is (or rather, was) sometimes grown for cut flowers due to its high number of flowers. It is not exactly fit for amateur collections. Its bifoliate pseudobulbs are up to 3.6 in/9 cm long; the leaves are three times as long. The plant's erect spike is usually unbranched and bears 15-20 sparse flowers that are up to 2 in/5 cm across. The brown-and-yellow tepals are dominated by a broad sulfur-yellow lip that is markedly narrowed at the base. This species is no "troublemaker" in cultivation. It blooms between September and November and was discovered in Mexico.

Oncidium tigrinum

Oncidium varicosum

Oncidium varicosum ◨ ■ ☺

INTERMEDIATE

O. varicosum is one of the most frequently cultivated orchids. Especially in the past it was often imported to Europe; nowadays, it has given way to more efficient hybrids. It is a "classic" robust *Oncidium* that forms tall (up to 4 in/10 cm), bifoliate pseudobulbs. Its erect, branched flower spike, often longer than 3.3 ft/1 m, bears up to a hundred yellow flowers with red-and-brown dots and a showy sulfur-yellow lip. The size of the flowers is highly variable but limited by 2.2 in/ 5.5 cm. Grow this species in semi-shade, epiphytically or in a flowerpot, and fertilize it more abundantly during the growth period. The plants sometimes "omit" to produce flowers: this is caused by excessive shade or, paradoxically, if the conditions that the plants are provided with are "too good" with no vegetation rest. *O. varicosum* blooms between October and February and comes from Brazil.

171

Ornithocephalus sp., Ecuador

Ornithochilus difformis

Ornithocephalus   □ ☺ ☺

THERMOPHILIC

The flowers of these orchids resemble a bird's head—hence the Latin generic name. Unfortunately, the flower shapes can only be admired through a magnifying glass, for the flowers are of miniature proportions. Collectors, however, usually admire the plants for the original shape of their leaf rosettes that are usually hanging "head downward." The delicate leaves are "strangled" at the base and arranged in a very attractive symmetrical fan. The axils of the leaves subsequently give rise to medium-long flower spikes with 4-15 flowers. These delicate epiphytic plants require somewhat moist conditions and their roots tend both to dry out and to remain excessively moist for extended periods of time. *Ornitocephalus* orchids should be grown in a shady, ventilated environment. The genus is widespread mainly in Central America; several species can also be found in South America.

Ornithochilus difformis   ▣ ☺

THERMOPHILIC

Outside of the flowering period, this rarely cultivated plant is indistinguishable from *Phalaenopsis* orchids. Its tiny (0.6 in/1.5 cm across) flowers are, nevertheless, of an absolutely different and interesting appearance. The base of the lip is a foothold for a short and massive wine-red spur; the lip is marked by a notable radial forking. A large number of flowers grow on an overhanging

spike. Grow the species epiphytically on a moss-covered support, providing fairly humid conditions and semi-shade. It blooms between May and June and comes from the Himalayas, Burma, Thailand, Laos and Vietnam.

Osmoglossum pulchellum   ▣ ☹

CRYOPHILIC

As with some others, this former member of the genus *Odontoglossum* was also assigned an independent genus—its atypically reversed flowers with an upward-pointing lip are a feature that this species shares with two other related species. The plant's egg-shaped pseu-

Osmoglossum pulchellum

Paphinia cristata

dobulbs reach a length of 2.8 in/7 cm and end with a couple of markedly narrow leaves reaching lengths of up to 12 in/30 cm. The flower spike is not longer than the leaves and bears up to 10 white flowers with a yellowish, red-dotted lip. Cultivation is quite problematic because the climate of the cool vaporous forests insolated with alpine sunshine is very hard to emulate (see *Ticoglossum krameri*). The beautiful flowers appear on the plants between October and December. The plant was discovered in Mexico, Guatemala and Costa Rica.

Paphinia cristata □ ☺ ☺

THERMOPHILIC

Its beautiful star-shaped flowers with typically pointed tepals make this genus (4 species) very interesting for cultivation. The narrow, oval pseudobulbs of *P. cristata* are barely 1.6 in/4 cm tall and each bears a couple of leaves reaching lengths of 6 in/15 cm. The delicate, almost transparent flowers are whitish with brownish spots or stripes. The end of the lip sports curious protuberances. *P. cristata* should be cultivated epiphytically and provided with ample watering during the vegetation

Paphiopedilum appletonianum

period. The flowers appear irregularly between the fall and spring. The plant grows over a vast South American area including Colombia, Venezuela, Guiana and also Bolivia, where the photo was taken.

Paphiopedilum appletonianum ■ ☺

INTERMEDIATE

Representatives of this vast Asian genus that is also "super-important" for cultivation are nicknamed "Venus's shoes" —for their lip is typically shaped like a shoe. Its edge, in contrast to the closely related orchids of an American genus *Phragmipedium*, is not notched. *P. appletonianum* is a quite rare and large collection item. It has a sessile leaf rosette (same as other *Paphiopedila*) with belt-shaped, marbled leaves possessing rounded ends. The flowers are up to 4 in/10 cm across and are borne singly on a thin spike to heights of 20 in/50 cm. They are green and purple with protruding petals that are somewhat broadened on the ends. Grow this species as you would other *Paphiopedilum* orchids. It blooms in early spring and comes from Ásám.

Paphiopedilum argus ■ ☺

INTERMEDIATE-THERMOPHILIC

Another robust and well-growing Venus's shoe. Its showy, light-colored, marbled leaves are up to 6 in/15 cm long. Its spike is unsegmented (an important distinguishing feature from the genus *Phragmipedium*); it bears a single flower and reaches a length of 16 in/40 cm. The massive flower is 3.2 in/8 cm across and its dominant feature consists predominantly of its diagonally downward drooping petals decorated with dark papillae. As far as cultivation is concerned, *P. argus* is a less demanding Venus's shoe that can be recommended to beginners. The species blooms in the spring and comes from the Philippines.

Paphiopedilum argus

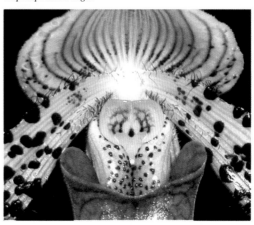

Paphiopedilum armeniacum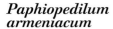

THERMOPHILIC

Although there have been disputes over the correct classification of some *Paphiopedilum* orchids, there is no doubt about the legitimacy of *P. armeniacum*—its pure yellow flowers with orange centers are almost unique within the genus. The species also exists in a rare and highly valued albino variety with snow-white flowers. The plant has leaves that are spotted and up to 6 in/15 cm long. The cultivation requirements of *P. armeniacum* do not differ much from the standard demands of the genus. This species was first described in 1982 and caused a huge uproar in botanical circles two years later, when it produced its first flowers in culture outside its home territory—China.

Paphiopedilum barbatum

INTERMEDIATE-THERMOPHILIC

This well-known and long-cultivated Venus's shoe is closely related to the species *P. callosum*. It is known among breeders as one of the parents of the first artificially cultivated hybrid of the entire *Paphiopedilum* genus (*P. harrisianum* in 1869). The plant has "cultivation-friendly" proportions—its marbled leaves are up to 8 in/20 cm long, while its one-flowered spike reaches a length of 10 in/25 cm. The flowers are 3.2 in/8 cm in

diameter and their dominant coloring consists of different shades of red; the upper sepal is white and embellished with 15 purple stripes, the lateral petals are also dark red (sometimes with whitish edges). The deepest shades of gray can be admired on the dark lip. Flowers appear in the spring months. The species inhabits moss-covered rock plates in shady mountain valleys in Malaysia and Thailand.

Paphiopedilum bellatulum

THERMOPHILIC

This species belongs in a systemically unclear Venus's shoe section termed *Brachypetalum*. The plants are highly variable as far as the details of the shape and color of their flower parts are concerned, which makes it practically impossible to determine what species, subspecies or even hybrids some discovered specimens happen to be. The photo presents, besides a typical specimen, also *P. conco-bellatulum*—a natural hybrid with the species *P. concolor*. The flower spike of *P. conco-bellatulum* is not longer than 1.6-4 in/4-10 cm, while its leaves reach lengths of 6 in/15 cm. Its white, purple-spotted flowers, make the plant a true gem of any orchid collection; unfortunately, its cultivation demands are quite high. In the wild, the sparse leaf rosettes of the species

grow in the cracks of limestone rocks in the warmest windy locations. The plants therefore need a maximum possible amount of diffused light, occasionally a somewhat dry break, exquisite ventilation and a little limestone grit added to the substrate. *P. bellatulum* flowers in the spring and comes from Burma and Thailand.

Paphiopedilum callosum

INTERMEDIATE

Indisputably one of the best-known Venus's shoes—a gorgeous and lively species that is quite easy to cultivate. It used to be imported in large numbers and, grown for cut flowers, same as the hybrid *P.* Maudiae. It is marked with high variability of the intensity of the marbling of its gray-and-green leaves and of the shape and color of its flowers. The flower spike is up to 14 in/35 cm long and bears a single flower with a brown-and-purple lip. *P. callosum* var. *subleave* has a beautifully enlarged upper sepal colored in an attractive combination of white, wine-red and green. The albinic form (var. *sanderae*) is one of the parents of the hybrid *P.* Maudiae. Grow the species in a standard mix consisting, for instance, of strips of peat moss, granulated Styrofoam, peat and beech wood shavings. If the roots of the repotted plants are healthy, you can also add a little beech soil or some other type of light soil. Plants whose roots are week or damaged ought to be planted in an inert mix of peat and Styrofoam. *P. callosum* requires a temperate environment, a slightly damp substrate and medium-deep shade throughout the year. It puts forth its flowers irregularly in the course of the whole year, mainly between March and June. It comes from Thailand and Cambodia.

Paphiopedilum chamberlainianum

Paphiopedilum ciliolare

Paphiopedilum chamberlainianum

THERMOPHILIC

A sizeable Venus's shoe with multi-flower spikes, a feature that is quite rare by the genus' standard. Each of its durable flowers opens only after the previous flower has faded and fallen off, which prolongs the time of flowering to many months. Its proportions render the species unsuitable for small amateur collections—its leaves reach lengths of 12 in/30 cm. The 20 in/50-cm-long spike gradually produces 3-10 flowers. They are very showy and resemble another multi-flowered species— *P. glaucophyllum*. Provide the plant with a warm, moist environment throughout the year, as it blooms almost continuously thanks to its different flowering strategy. It is native to Sumatra.

Paphiopedilum ciliolare

THERMOPHILIC

A likeable species with a rather unusually compact and small flower. It is quite rare in collections. Its leaves are about 6 in/15 cm long, and its approximately 8-in/20-cm-long flower spike bears a single flower with a white, purple-veined upper sepal and petals densely speckled with dark dots. It requires similar handling as other *Paphiopedilum* orchids but does not do extremely well in culture overall. It blooms between April and June and it is known to grow in the Philippines.

Paphiopedilum coccineum □ ?

INTERMEDIATE

A dernier cri in the world of Venus's shoes, and very handsome on top of that! It resembles *P. helenae* in appearance. Its intensely red-and-brown tepals have

greenish, slightly wavy edges. There is no information available on how to cultivate it. The species was discovered and described only very recently—in 2000. It was found in the Cao Bang Province in northern Vietnam, in the cracks of limestone rocks in the altitudes of 1,600-2,600 ft/500-800 m above sea level. It is unlikely to grow in its original natural habitat anymore, owing to the greed of some humans.

Paphiopedilum concolor

THERMOPHILIC

At first sight, this species is closely related to *P. bellatulum*, its life needs being also very similar. Two or three yellow flowers covered with red spots grow on spikes that reach lengths of 4.8 in/12 cm at the most. The

Paphiopedilum coccineum

176

Paphiopedilum concolor

Paphiopedilum curtisii

THERMOPHILIC

A very fine Venus's shoe—its flowers attract attention by their extraordinary large lip. Many botanists consider it a variety of *P. suberbiens*. For years, the species was known thanks to only two specimens that had been imported to Europe as far back as 1892 and had become the only original breeding material for a century to come! It was not until several years ago that this Venus's shoe was discovered in the wild again. Its leaf rosettes are of a standard appearance; the individual leaves are 10 in/25 cm long with a marbled surface and dark green nervation. The purple flower spikes produce a single flower reaching a height of 12 in/30 cm. The species is variable as to the depth of the color of its flowers featuring a purple-to-dark-purple robust lip. The upper sepal of each flower is whitish and decorated with lengthwise stripes ranging in color between green and purple; the drooping petals sport dark spots on a purple backdrop. Grow it in the same way as the other representatives of the genus. The plant blooms in the spring and comes from limestone rocks in central Sumatra.

Paphiopedilum curtisii

species' variety—*P. concolor* var. *striatum*—is colored differently: it has red spots arranged in circles running lengthwise through the center of the tepals. The species blooms between May and October. It comes from the warmest regions of China, Thailand, Burma, Laos and southern Vietnam.

Paphiopedilum concolor var. *striatum*

Paphiopedilum dayanum

Paphiopedilum dayanum ▣ ☺

THERMOPHILIC

Each leaf rosette of any *Paphiopedilum* orchid blooms only once in its lifetime; after that, it forms a lateral shoot and gradually dies. The species *P. dayanum* is no exception. Its white-marbled leaves are in the category of more sizeable leaves (they are up to 10 in/25 cm long); its one-flower spike reaches a length of 16 in/40 cm. The upper sepal of each flower is adorned with green-and-brown lengthwise stripes, while the lateral petals are purple. The plant blooms between May and June and comes from the warm elevations of northern Borneo.

Paphiopedilum delenatii

Paphiopedilum delenatii ▣ ☺

INTERMEDIATE

In the past, *P. delenatii* was an unattainable dream of many an amateur orchid grower. Nowadays, there are a sufficient number of specimens available that have been achieved by breeding; however, the prices still remain quite steep. No wonder—the flowers of this Venus's shoe are absolutely unique! The plant's leaves are fairly common—white-marbled and reaching lengths of up to 6 in/15 cm. The usually two-flowered spike is about 8 in/20 cm tall. The dominant feature of the white flowers consisting of a couple of broad petals and an extremely reduced upper sepal is a pink lip. Even though a temperate environment is recommended for cultivating these plants, good blooming is guaranteed if you treat the plant to at least a one-month-long dry period with temperatures below 50 °F/10 °C. The species blooms in the spring and is still reported to grow in the wild in northern Vietnam.

Paphiopedilum emersonii ▣ ▣ ☺

INTERMEDIATE-THERMOPHILIC

This Venus's shoe has an interesting history of discovery—the first specimen bloomed in 1986 against all odds in culture in California, and the beauty of its showy flowers immediately won the hearts of all cultivators. The species was first described on the basis of specimens "discovered" in

this way. The plant does not differ much from *P. hangianum* in the appearance of its flowers and green parts; there are important differences only in the color and shape of the flower staminodium. Likewise, the species' cultivation demands are quite high. Flowers appear in the spring and the plant comes from the province of Yunnan, China.

Paphiopedilum emersonii

Paphiopedilum esquirolei   ☺

INTERMEDIATE

A species with a peculiar feature consisting in that all the parts of its beautiful flowers are covered with hairs. *P. esquirolei* is sometimes considered a mere variety of a very similar "hirsute" species *P. hirsutissimum* (this "maternal" species is relatively more common in collections, certainly much more so than in its plundered natural habitat). The leaves are monochromatically green; the wiry spike brings a single flower to the height of 10 in/25 cm. The flower is up to 4.8 in/12 cm across and has an oval, brown-and-green upper sepal and metallic-glossy, purple petals. The lip is quite small in comparison with the other flower parts; it is yellow and covered with delicate dark red dots. Cultivation is not difficult; it is more of a problem to acquire the plant in the first place. Although it can also be grown in temperate conditions, you will induce the plant to producing more flowers by exposing it to cooler conditions in the winter. It blooms in the spring (between February and May) and is native to Laos.

Paphiopedilum exul

Paphiopedilum fairrieanum

Paphiopedilum exul   ⊡ ☺

INTERMEDIATE-THERMOPHILIC

A warmth-loving inhabitant of sun-drenched limestone rocks cooled by the sea winds. Its glossy green narrow leaves are arranged in a compact stiff rosette. A single flower grows on a 8-in/20-cm-long spike; the yellow-and-white flower is adorned with a marking similar to that of the widespread species *P. insigne*, but it is smaller and its upper sepal has dark spots only at the base. *P. exul* is a species with above-average light demands; during the winter, it should therefore be decelerated by reducing watering and temperature. It blooms between February and July and its natural habitat is in Thailand.

Paphiopedilum fairrieanum   ⊡ ☺

CRYOPHILIC—INTERMEDIATE

One of the few cryophilic species with an exceptionally bizarre-shaped flower. Its pale green leaves are only 4-6 in/ 10-15 cm long, while the slightly longer flower spike bears only one flower, 2.4 in/6 cm across. The upper sepal has sigmoid edges; the petals are oriented diagonally down at their bases, while their tips are turned vertically upward. The tepals are whitish (except the lip, which is brown-and-red) and embellished with pronounced purple venation. There are various color and size variations of this species, including a rare albino version (*P. fairrieanum* var. *bohlmanniana*). In growing the species, follow the same instructions as in the case of *P. callosum*. The flowers appear on the plants between June and September. The species comes from Bhutan and Asam.

Paphiopedilum fowliei   ⊡ ☺

INTERMEDIATE

A rather small and certainly not the most handsome Venus's shoe, with relatively little and dull-colored, but extremely durable flowers. The leaves are 4-6 in/10-15 cm long; the spike bears one flower and reaches a length of 6-8 in/15-20 cm. The upper flower sepal is broad and whitish with showy rainbow-like, purple-to-green stripes. The petals bear the same coloring and their edges are decorated with dark papillae. In cultivation, *P. fowliei* is an undemanding species. It blooms in the spring and comes from the Philippines.

Paphiopedilum fowliei

Paphiopedilum glaucophyllum

INTERMEDIATE

Another Venus's shoe with a multi-flowered spike. The flowers develop successively one by one on an axis reaching a length of up to 16 in/40 cm, which, sadly, makes it impossible to admire them all at once. *P. glaucophyllum* is a fairly robust species; its leaves are 10 in/25 cm long and 1.6 in/4 cm across; the flowers are about 2.8 in/7 cm in diameter and they are very handsome—the upper sepal

ranges in color between whitish, green and purple, the purple petals are twisted along a lengthwise axis and they are covered with dark papillae and a dark layer of hairs. The lip is white at the base, with a gradually intensifying purple dotting. Grow the species the same as other representatives of the genus (see *P. callosum*). The flowering season is, on account of the successive development of the flowers on one spike, very long—it lasts from the spring till the winter. The plant comes from Java.

Paphiopedilum godefroyae

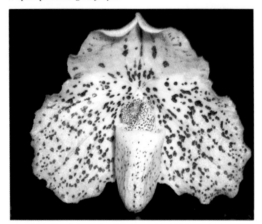

Paphiopedilum godefroyae

INTERMEDIATE-THERMOPHILIC

An orchid that is very closely related to the *P. bellatulum* Venus's shoe in kinship, appearance and ecological requirements—it is no wonder some botanists consider it a mere hybrid of *P. bellatulum* and *P. concolor*. To determine the species of a plant is sometimes too hard a nut to crack even for renowned experts. The flowers of *P. godefroyae* grow on a notably shortened spike (1.2-2 in/3-5 cm) and they are white-to-yellowish and covered with dark red spots of various sizes. The lip is white and almost spotless (in contrast, *P. bellatulum* has a markedly spotted lip). So as to develop well, the plants need to be grown in a limestone-enriched substrate and provided with an occasional drying-up, plenty of light and fresh air. Besides the well-known Krabi, *P. godefroyae* is reported to grow in some other places in Thailand, as well as in Borneo and southern Vietnam.

Paphiopedilum gratrixianum

Paphiopedilum hangianum

Paphiopedilum hangianum ▫ ▪ ☺
INTERMEDIATE-THERMOPHILIC

This Venus's shoe was not described until the late 1990s! It is similar-looking and closely related to another Venus's shoe—*P. emersonii* (differences are observable in the coloring and the morphology of the central part of the flower, known as staminodia). The leaves are belt-shaped, 10 in/25 cm long, and free of any sort of pigmentation; the spike is rather short and bears a single flower. The plant has white tepals, with purplish bases of the sepals. The flower's broad lip is cream-to-yellow colored. *P. hangianum* is a highly demanding and still rather obscure species. The plants develop extremely slowly and bringing the seedlings to a "flower-worthy" size takes a lot of patience and experience. The plant blooms in the spring and comes from northern Vietnam.

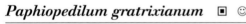

Paphiopedilum gratrixianum ▪ ☺
INTERMEDIATE

P. gratrixianum is an undemanding Venus's shoe of average beauty, attractive for cultivators for its fairly large flowers and very low cultivation requirements. Each flower reaches a length of up to 4 in/10 cm and grows singly out of a rosette of pure green leaves reaching lengths of 10 in/25 cm. The flowers resemble those of *P. insigne* in color, but their upper sepal is sparsely covered with noticeably bigger brown-and-red spots. The plant can be successfully grown even in a mixture of wood shavings and river (white) sand; it thrives on windowsills. The flowers usually appear between October and December. The species comes from Laos, northern Vietnam and Thailand.

Paphiopedilum haynaldianum ▪ ■ ☺
THERMOPHILIC

A showy, robust Venus's shoe with large flowers that reach over 6 in/15 cm in diameter. A rosette of 10-in/25-cm-long, pure green leaves gives rise to a flower spike reaching a length of up to 20 in/50 cm and bearing 2-5 flowers that open one after another. The coloring is a combination of green, brown and purple; the color shades are dull, providing thus a good backdrop for the large brown-and-red spots covering the extremely long petals. Interestingly, this species also grows epiphytically in its natural habitat; it should therefore be provided with a somewhat lighter substrate. It blooms in the spring and is known to occur in the Philippines.

Paphiopedilum helenae □ ☹ ☺

INTERMEDIATE

Even within the genus *Paphiopedilum* is it possible to find stunning miniatures; *P. helenae* is one of them. Its stiff, glossy green leaves are up to 3.2 in/8 cm long and its robust flower grows on an extremely short (1.2-2 in/ 3-5 cm) spike.

Paphiopedilum helenae

The upper sepal of the flower is greenish-golden-yellow, the petals are colored in a dull shade of brown-and-purple and the lip is purple red. There is also a highly valued color variation termed *P. helenae* var. *aureum* with flowers colored almost uniformly in yellow-to-orange. This limestone-loving, lithophytic Venus's shoe is not easy to cultivate; it is necessary to enrich the substrate in the flowerpot with big pieces of limestone. Flowers can be expected in the spring months; the plant was described in 1996 based on the specimens discovered in northern Vietnam near the Chinese border.

183

Paphiopedilum henryanum □   ☺

INTERMEDIATE

Its dwarf parameters and high cultivation demands make this plant resemble the previous species. It is a highly sought-after curiosity, mainly for its singular flowers. Its one-flowered spikes are up to 2.8 in/7 cm tall and grow out of compact rosettes of leaves reaching lengths of 4 in/10 cm. The flowers have a broadened, yellow-and-green upper sepal covered with brown-and-red spots of various sizes; the same spots also embellish the basal parts of the wine-red petals. The lip is intensely purple-and-red with a metallic shine. This Venus's shoe ought to be grown in a similar way as the previous one: both species must be provided with semi-shade and a well-ventilated environment. This attractive "mini-species" blooms in the spring and is known to grow in northern Vietnam.

Paphiopedilum herrmanii □ ☹ ☺

INTERMEDIATE

Toward the end of the 20th century, suddenly there was no end of newly discovered species of Venus's shoes—thanks to an improvement in the relations with the communist regimes in southwestern Asia. Western botanists have been allowed to move freely around Vietnam and China and they keep discovering and describing new species. However, their taxonomy is certainly far from flawless—many variable plants are interpreted differ-

Paphiopedilum henryanum

Paphiopedilum herrmanii

ently by different authors and there have been disputes over who was the first to describe them, whether they are pedigree Venus's shoes or mere varieties of other species, etc. One of the many recently discovered small species is *P. herrmanii* that was not described until 1995. Its narrow, belt-shaped leaves lack marbling and are about 6 in/15 cm long; the flowers grow on a rather short spike. Their upper sepal is red with a yellow edge and their petals bear a similar coloring. The showy pink lip resembles that of a closely related *P. henryanum* (a species that *P. herrmanii* is sometimes mistaken for). Grow it in a sandy mix enriched with limestone grit. The flowers appear between late winter and spring. The plant comes from northern Vietnam.

Paphiopedilum hookerae   ☺

THERMOPHILIC

A markedly thermophilic Venus's shoe suitable even for small indoor glass cases with a higher degree of humidity. It is a shame that *P. hookerae* is so hard to get (which, in fact, is a problem with most botanical species of the *Paphiopedilum* genus). The leaves are marbled and only 6 in/15 cm long. The stem is 2 in/5 cm longer and bears a single, medium-sized flower that calls for attention mainly by its two purple petals with metallic luster and delicate dotting. The other flower parts are brownish

184

green. The flowers open between April and June and the plant can be come across in the Borneo rainforests.

Paphiopedilum insigne   ▫ ◼ ☺

CRYOPHILIC-INTERMEDIATE

A true gardening "classic" among all botanical *Paphiopedilum* orchids; it used to be grown for cut flowers appearing in the winter, as well as for creating a number of efficient decorative hybrids. Nowadays, its fame has faded a little. The plant's pure green leaves are up to 10 in/25 cm long and arranged in large numbers in rosette clusters. Its one-flowered spike is about 8 in/20 cm long and bears one flower that is 4 in/10 cm across. The upper yellow-and-green sepal has a white edge and it is covered with red-and-brown spots. The petals and the lip are brown-and-red. There are a high number of color variations. In amateur conditions, this species is a little difficult to cultivate, as the plants require a cool environment with plenty of light and a maximum possible amount of ventilation throughout the year. You can enrich the substrate with a little soil component. *P. insigne* blooms in the winter and comes from the Himalayas.

Paphiopedilum insigne

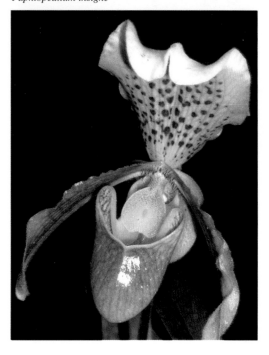

Paphiopedilum intaniae

Paphiopedilum krairitii

pearance very much; rather, it resembles *P. barbigerum* or *P. coccineum*. Its distinguishing feature from both latter species is the morphology of its flower column. There is no information available so far about the species' cultivation requirements. It is supposed to bloom in the spring and it is native to Thailand.

Paphiopedilum intaniae ▣ ■ ☹ ☺

INTERMEDIATE-THERMOPHILIC

A multi-flowered, rare and elegant representative of the genus, related to the species *P. randsii* and *P. philippinense*. Some 3-5 flowers grow on an erect flower spike that reaches a length of 20 in/50 cm and they all open at the same time. The plant's belt-shaped leaves measure 16 in/40 cm at the most. The yellow-and-green flowers have stripy elongated sepals and markedly extended, dotted leaves. The lip, too, is extended forward to look like a pipe, it is whitish at the base and light-brown-and-red on the end. This plant has to be grown in flowerpots enriched with pieces of limestone and in order to develop well, it needs a little more light than the other representatives of the genus. *P. intaniae* was discovered on limestone rocks in the southern part of Sulawesi, Indonesia.

Paphiopedilum krairitii ▫ ▣ ☺?

INTERMEDIATE-THERMOPHILIC

The name of this quite recently (2001-2002) discovered plant is only a working name and there has not been enough time for it to be scientifically proven! This brand new species was not discovered in the wild but in culture among imported specimens considered to be a Thai species *P. charlesworthii*. Paradoxically, the foundling does not resemble *P. charlesworthii* in ap-

Paphiopedilum lawrenceanum ▫ ▣ ☺ ☺

THERMOPHILIC

A very valuable albino form of this species (*P. lawrenceanum* var. *hyeanum*) is, along with *P. callosum*, a parent of one of the best-known and most frequently cultivated hybrids—*P.* Maudiae. *P. lawrenceanum* used to be grown for cut flowers; today, it is a little more rare. Its light-marbled leaves are up to 6 in/15 cm long, while its one-flowered spike measures 12 in/30 cm. The flowers of a typical specimen have a pink-and-white upper sepal adorned with purple stripes, the petals stick almost horizontally to the sides and they are purple with dark papillae on the edges. The lip is brown-and-red. This species is relatively easy to cultivate and it blooms between the spring and early summer. It was discovered in the northern part of Borneo.

Paphiopedilum lawrenceanum

Paphiopedilum leucochilum

INTERMEDIATE-THERMOPHILIC

This species is another example of the disagreement among botanical experts over the taxonomy of the Venus's shoe section of *Brachypetalum*. According to some botanists, *P. leucochilum* is an independent species; others claim it to be a mere local variety of the species *P. godefroyae*. One way or the other, it is a very pretty plant with whitish, red-spotted flowers growing on a short spike. Unfortunately, it is quite difficult to cultivate. Follow the same growing instructions as those applying to *P. bellatulum*. The plant comes from Thailand, Borneo and possibly also other parts of southwest Asia.

Paphiopedilum liemianum

INTERMEDIATE

This species belongs to the *Cochlopetalum* section of the *Paphiopedilum* genus, which suggests what the dominant feature of the flower is—its spiral-shaped (or, snail-shaped) twisted petals. Its belt-like leaves are flabby and green without any marking. Its flower spike grows continuously and can bear more than 20 flowers produced over a long period of time (up to one year). The upper sepal is very broad, dark green with snow-white edges. The twisted petals are turned upward. The robust purple lip is marked with metallic luster and speckled with delicate dots. The plant blooms in the spring (between March and May) and inhabits limestone rocks in the higher elevations of northern Sumatra.

Paphiopedilum lowii

THERMOPHILIC

This Venus's shoe with beautiful flowers is prevented by its bulkiness from becoming more widespread—its leaves

happen to reach lengths of 12 in/30 cm. The flower spike is up to 24 in/60 cm tall and bears 3-5 large flowers. The petals are abnormally elongated, purple on the ends and adorned at the base with a dozen red-and-brown spots. The lip is less showy, ranging in color between brownish-red and red. *P. lourii* grows both lithophytically and epiphytically in northern Borneo. It blooms between March and June.

Paphiopedilum lowii

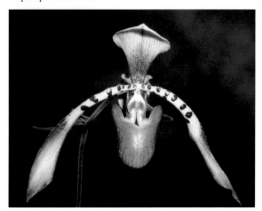

Paphiopedilum malipoense

Paphiopedilum jackii

Paphiopedilum mastersianum ▣ ☹ ☺

INTERMEDIATE-THERMOPHILIC

This Venus's shoe could serve as valuable material for breeders, as the coloring of its variegated flowers is almost free of the unwelcome brown-and-red shades. In spite of that, it has so far been only rarely used in hybridization. Its leaves with simple marbling reach

Paphiopedilum micranthum

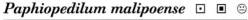

Paphiopedilum malipoense ▢ ▣ ☺

INTERMEDIATE-THERMOPHILIC

In spite of its attractive appearance, this species remained completely unknown until 1984; only after that year did it find its way to collections. *P. malipoense* is not easy to cultivate and the plants thus remain very rare. A similar species—*P. jackii*—that was not discovered until 1999, differs from the *P. malipoense* Venus's shoe only in minute details of the morphology of its flower column. Single greenish flowers grow out of rosettes of marbled leaves that reach lengths of up to 10 in/25 cm. They are greenish with a delicate red marking and a notably pouched robust lip adorned on the inside with a red decoration. Cultivation of this species should be left up to experts. The plants bloom in the spring and come from southwestern China.

lengths of 8 in/20 cm, while its one-flowered spike is up to 16 in/40 cm tall. Each of the large flowers has a green-and-white upper sepal, delicate purplish dotting on the broad tepals and a markedly purple lip. The species does not do very well in cultivation—it grows very slowly. The flowers appear between April and June. *P. mastersianum* comes from the Ambon Island.

Paphiopedilum micranthum ▫ ◼ ☺

INTERMEDIATE-THERMOPHILIC

Even though this species was described in China as far back as 1951, it was not allowed to cross the country's hermetically closed border until 1984. From that time on, its beauty made it a subject of very brisk trade, which soon caused it to become a very rare and endangered Venus's shoe. Besides *P. micranthum*, a photo also presents a specimen of *P.* x *fanaticum*—a botanical hybrid of the species in question and *P. malipoense*. The hybrid appears in the common habitats of both species in the border area between Vietnam and China. The species' leaves are marbled; its single flowers grow on 4-10-in/10-25-cm-tall spikes. Compared to the proportions of the plant, the flowers are quite large and domi-

nated by an abnormally big pale-pink lip. The other tepals are yellowish with dark red stripes. The species still survives in southwest China.

Paphiopedilum x *fanaticum*

Paphiopedilum Olivia

Paphiopedilum nivaeum   ▫   ☹   ☺

THERMOPHILIC

A significant and very easily discernible species of the *Brachylopetalum* section of the genus. Its flowers are unmistakably snow-white (hence "*nivaeum*") and covered all over with delicate red dots. The unusual color of its flowers was also used in breeding—see the hybrid in the photo bearing the name *P.* Olivia (*P. tonsum* x *P. nivaeum*). Another Venus's shoe—*P. ang-thong*—that is native to the eponymous islands on the east coast of Malaysia, is sometimes considered a mere subspecies of *P. nivaeum*. The leaves are up to 6 in/15 cm long, decorated with a dark marbling, and reddish on the underside. Its spikes bear one, rarely two flowers and they reach lengths of 4.8 in/12 cm. The flower lip is regularly egg-shaped. The species grows on limestone rocks in close proximity to the sea and therefore needs a lot of sunshine and a cool humid breeze. It does not do well in cultivation and develops only slowly. The flowers appear between April and July. The plant's habitat is the Malayan coast, mainly the Langkawi archipelago, Thailand.

Paphiopedilum ang-thong

Paphiopedilum parishii   ■   ☺

THERMOPHILIC

Despite its sizeable proportions, this Venus's shoe is very popular with cultivators, namely for its singular flowers. Its leaves are up to 12 in/30 cm long, monochromatically green and relatively stiff. The spike can reach a length of over 20 in/50 cm and it bears 3-6 medium-sized flowers (3.2 in/8 cm across). The disadvantage of their smaller size is compensated for by the fact that they all open at the same time. What makes the flowers attractive are their elongated, wine-red, decoratively twisted petals that can reach three times the length of the flower's greenish lip. Cultivation of this species is not different from the approach used for the whole genus. Exceptionally pretty flowers appear on the plants between April to July. The species comes from Thailand and Burma.

Paphiopedilum philippinense var. roebelinii ■ ☺

THERMOPHILIC

Another representative of the genus with "twisted ears" —its flowers are perhaps even more beautiful than those of the *P. parishii* Venus's shoe are. The appearance of the green parts is very similar in both species. Their yellow-and-red flowers are small (2.4 in/6 cm) and there are 3-6 of them growing on a long spike. Their impressively twisted, dark-red petals reach lengths of 5.6 in/14 (!) cm. The upper sepal is covered with dark stripes and the whole fantastic flower composition is complemented by a yellow-and-green lip. The plant blooms between June and August. It was discovered in the Philippines.

Paphiopedilum philippinense var. *roebelinii*

Paphiopedilum parishii

Paphiopedilum primulinum ▫ ◾ 😐

THERMOPHILIC

A species with untraditionally-colored, medium-sized yellow flowers and a spike reaching a length of 12 in/ 30 cm and bearing 7-10 flowers. The classification of this species is highly debatable since it was described in 1973 based on only a single discovered specimen. Many botanists consider it a mere subspecies of the *P. chamberlainianum* Venus's shoe. It was discovered in Sumatra.

Paphiopedilum purpuratum ▫ 😐 ☺

INTERMEDIATE

A tiny Venus's shoe suitable even for small amateur collections. Its place of origin is one of the features that make it a curiosity—it comes from what remains of the nature of Hongkong. Its leaves are 4 in/10 cm long, the showy flowers grow singly on 8-in/20-cm-long spikes

Paphiopedilum purpuratum

and they are faithful to their species name—their predominant color is purple in different shades. The plant blooms between June and August.

Paphiopedilum primulinum

Paphiopedilum randsii   ■ ☺

THERMOPHILIC

This Venus's shoe is epiphytic, quite sizeable and very charming when in bloom. Its leaves are up to 14 in/35 cm long, flabby and often hanging "life-lessly" downward from thick branches or tree crotches. The lip is brown-and-green; the other tepals are whitish and very notably decorated with vertical dark purple stripes. Grow the plant in a medium-light humic substrate in a suspended flowerpot. Do not ever let the substrate dry up completely. *P. randsii* blooms in the summer and comes from Mandanaa, Philippines.

Paphiopedilum rothschildianum   ▣ ☺

THERMOPHILIC

This species is considered by many cultivators of Venus's shoes to be the most beautiful *Paphiopedilum* orchid ever. *P. rothschildianum* is a robust Venus's shoe: its thin leaves reach lengths of 16-24 in/40-60 cm; the erect flower spike is up to 18 in/45 cm long and bears 3 or more sparsely arranged flowers that are up to 5.2 in/13 cm in diameter. Their decorative effect is enhanced by the fact that they all open at the same time. The white upper sepal is covered with dark-red stripes, the greenish petals point straight down and they are

adorned with brown-and-red dots. The lip color is brown-and-purple. The species has always been among the greatest gems of any orchid collection. It should be grown in the same way as other representatives of the genus. It blooms in the fall and is still reported to grow in the foothills of Mount Kinabalu, Borneo, where our photo was taken.

Paphiopedilum rothschildianum

193

Paphiopedilum spicerianum

⊡ ◼ ☺ ☺

CRYOPHILIC—INTERMEDIATE

This rather cryophilic species has its 'fingerprints" on the creation of hundreds of today's hybrid Venus's shoes; it is rarely come across in its "pureblooded" form. Its leaves are monochromatically green and they measure 10 in/25 cm or less. The brown-and-green flower develops individually on a 6-8-in/15-20-cm-long spike. It has two dominant features—a snow-white upper sepal with a pink central stripe and a similarly colored staminodium (a scutellar middle part of the flower bearing the reproductive organs). Grow the species the same as *P. insigne*. You will support its good flowering if you summer the plant in semi-shade outside the greenhouse. It blooms in the winter and comes from the Himalayas.

Paphiopedilum spicerianum

Paphiopedilum stonei

Paphiopedilum stonei

▣ ◼ ☺ ☹

THERMOPHILIC

During the flowering season, *P. stonei* is a very interesting species. Its upper flower sepal is white on the inside with irregular purple stripes, and purple with white edges on the outside (this coloring is observable only when viewed from the back). The equally large lower sepal bears the same appearance; both sepals are shaped like a seashell partly open around the other flower parts: a brown-and-white, red-veined and upward pointing lip, and brown-spotted petals reaching lengths of 6 in/15 cm. This interesting Venus's shoe is certainly not recommended for beginners, as its cultivation is similarly complex as the morphology of its flowers. It blooms between July and September and is native to the rainforests of northern Borneo.

Paphiopedilum sukhakulii

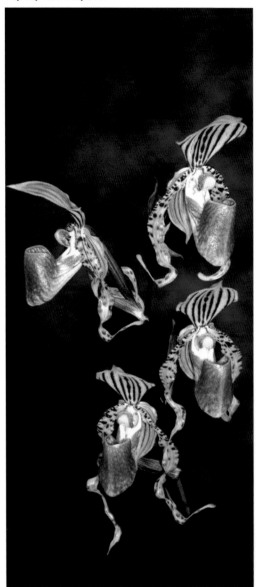

lively green petals. Their surface is covered with tiny dark spots. Grow the species like *P. callosum*. The flowers appear during a long stretch of time—between March and November. The plant comes from Thailand.

Paphiopedilum supardii

INTERMEDIATE-THERMOPHILIC

A lithophytic Venus's shoe with interesting flowers arranged in an inflorescence numbering 3-5 showy flowers. Their beauty is enhanced by the fact that they all open simultaneously. The leaves are dark green and reach lengths of 22 in/55 cm; the flower spike reaches a length of 18 in/ 45 cm. The green-and-yellow sepals are adorned with dark-brown lengthwise stripes, while the overhanging, twisted petals are covered with red-and-brown spots. The forward-protruding lip resembles a pipe and its color is brown-and-red. Cultivation is difficult—as with other lithophytic, limestone-loving species. The flowers appear on the plants in the spring and early summer, and the species is native to Borneo.

Paphiopedilum tigrinum

INTERMEDIATE-THERMOPHILIC

The flowers of this species are embellished with pronounced brown-and-red spots that are, judged by the standard of the genus, rather large and distributed on the flowers in a somewhat unusual way. In spite of this idiosyncrasy, the species passed completely unnoticed by botanists for a long time and was not described until the end of the 2nd millennium. *P. tigrinum* is a medium-sized Venus's shoe with thinner-than-average leaves free of any marking. The species should be cultivated in the same way as the other representatives of the genus that come from southwest Asia. The flowers appear in the spring and the plant is native to southern China.

Paphiopedilum tigrinum

Paphiopedilum sukhakulii

INTERMEDIATE-THERMOPHILIC

The discovery of this species has an interesting history—the first plants bloomed in the 1970 in Europe among the imported specimens of *P. callosum*. It is a popular species, quite widespread in collections; its positive qualities have been frequently used by breeders in the past twenty years. Its marbled leaves are only 8 in/20 cm long and the one-flowered spike is 8-10 in/20-25 cm tall. The main pride of the large flowers (up to 4.8 in/12 cm across) is a pair of markedly broadened and elongated

Paphiopedilum tonsum

a subject of disputes... *P. tranlienianum* is closely related to *P. barbigerum*. A specimen in bloom will attract attention mainly by the proportional contrast between the 2-2.8-in/5-7-cm-across, beautiful flower on a short spike on the one hand, and the 4-6-in/10-15-cm-large rosette of fully green, narrow leaves. This orchid grows on little limestone rocks and must be provided with the same environment in culture. However, this rare Venus's shoe is still completely out of an ordinary mortal's reach. We can only hope that it will be possible to admire its flowers opening in the spring in the species' northern Vietnam habitat even in the future.

Paphiopedilum venustum ⊡ ☺
CRYOPHILIC-INTERMEDIATE

This Venus's shoe seems quite flawless: it is decorative not only for its flowers but also its leaves; its proportions are ideal and the species' cultivation demands are manageable by any beginner. From the historical point of view, it holds one primacy: it was the first Venus's shoe ever to bloom in Europe (in England in 1819). The plant forms dense clusters of several leaf rosettes; the leaves are dark green, and

Paphiopedilum tranlienianum

Paphiopedilum tonsum ⊡ ▣ ☺
INTERMEDIATE-THERMOPHILIC

This Venus's shoe is still quite abundant in the wild—paradoxically thanks to its flowers that are not endowed with a very high decorative value! The plant is variable as to the coloring of its 8-in/20-cm-long leaves (each leaf is marbled on the top, while its bottom part can be either red or green), and flowers. The species' bronze-green flowers are characterized by sparse dark spots distributed mainly near the edges and in the axes of the petals. In contrast to an overwhelming majority of *Paphiopedilum* orchids, *P. tonsum* is not dependent on limestone subsoil. Grow it in the same way as other common Venus's shoes. The plant blooms in the spring and grows in Sumatra.

Paphiopedilum tranlienianum ⊡ ☺
INTERMEDIATE-THERMOPHILIC

A dernier cri in the world of Venus's shoes, that was not discovered until the end of the 2nd millennium. The plant was described in Germany under the name presented here, while in Vietnam it was ascribed the name *P. caobangense*. It goes without saying that the validity of the names is

red on the bottom. The spike bears a single flower and it reaches a length of 6 in/15 cm. The upper sepal is white with pronounced green stripes, the blunt-edged petals are wine-red on the ends and embellished with several conspicuous dark papillae. The lip is adorned with an intense brown-and-green marbling. Grow the species the same as *P. insigne*. The flowers are enjoyed in the winter. *O. venustum* comes from the Himalayas.

Paphiopedilum vietnamense   ⊡ ◼ ☺

THERMOPHILIC

P. vietnamense was not discovered until the end of the 20th century, and it serves as a sad example of the uneven match between commercial interests and nature conservation. The plants no longer inhabit its only known, Vietnamese habitat; shortly after the species was described, the specimens were dug up and sold underhand to the collections of Venus's shoe lovers, where they are now passed off as artificially cultivated specimens… The flowers of the species somewhat resemble those of *P. delenatii*—af-

ter all, both of these Venus's shoes are included in the same section termed *Brachypetalum*. Their upper sepal is light pink and the likewise light pink petals are conspicuously broad and oval. The lip is wine-red. The species should be grown in the same way as *P. delenatii*. The term of the flowering season is not yet known for sure; most specimens probably bloom in early spring.

Paphiopedilum vietnamense

Paphiopedilum villosum □ ■ ☺

CRYOPHILIC-INTERMEDIATE

Another example of a species that has been widely used for
hybridization of Venus's shoes; nearly all of the multiple
hybrids sold today are its partial offspring. The species is
variable both in the coloring of its flowers and in size: its
leaves reach lengths between 10 and 16 in/25 and 40 cm.
The plants form dense clusters of several leaf rosettes—the
flowers therefore appear in higher numbers. As these plants
bloom between the fall and spring, they are grown for cut
flowers. Each of their hairy flower spikes bears a single
flower to the height of 12 in/30 cm. On a typical specimen,
the upper flower sepal is brown-and-green with a white
edge. The subspecies *P. villosum* var. *boxalii* has its upper
sepal covered with marked dark spots, a feature mostly ap-
preciated by breeders. The petals are ocher brown. The lip
is colored in a pale shade of brown-and-red and sports
a delicate venation. Cultivation of *P. villosum* is easy, much
the same as *P. insigne*. However, the substrate in which you
grow the plant should not be enriched with soil admixture.
Outdoor summering is highly desirable. The species comes
from the submontane regions of Burma.

Paphiopedilum villosum

Paphiopedilum violascens

Paphiopedilum violascens □ □ ☺ ☺

THERMOPHILIC

A handsome Venus's shoe that has been cultivated for
a long time. Its marbled leaves are 8 in/20 cm long at
the most; its one-flowered spike is only a little longer
than that. The flowers are medium-sized; the upper
petal is white with purple-to-green venation. The
petals are also decorated with purple venation. The robust lip is periwinkle-green. *P. violascens* blooms between May and July and its origin is somewhat exotic:
it comes from a place little known by orchid lovers—
New Guinea.

species used to be included. Who could forget about the butterfly-like (hence the name of the genus), 4-in/10-cm-or-smaller flowers sparsely distributed on inflorescences bearing 2-5 flowers! The tepals are pink-and-white, the "chopped of" three-lobed lip is purple with yellow venation. This usually epiphytic or lithophytic plant thrives even in seemingly uninhabitable places, such as the sun-drenched rocks on the Andaman Sea coast (see photo). It follows that the species has exceptionally high warmth and especially light requirements. In the plant's natural habitat in Laos, Burma, Thailand and Himalayan foothills, the flowers appear between March and June.

Papilionanthe teres

Papilionanthe biswasiana

THERMOPHILIC

The representatives of the genus *Papilionanthe* are still known under the name *Vanda*; however, they have been excluded from this genus on the grounds of the big differences in the morphology of their bodies and flowers. Comparison with the genus *Vanda* is really not precise— the plants have thin spikes reaching lengths of 6.5 ft/2 m, only sparsely covered with thickened, 4-6-in/10-15-cm-long cylindrical leaves. *P. biswasiana* has 3-5 pink flowers growing on a shortish, horizontally-protruding spike; the flowers are, in contrast to the next species, rather small (2 in/5 cm across). The dominant feature of each flower is a long, downward pointing spur that is markedly thickened at the base and placed under the canopy of the pinkish tepals. Cultivation is not different from the rules that apply for the thermophilic orchids of the genus *Vanda*. Flowers appear on this species in February. The photograph was taken in Thailand.

Papilionanthe teres

THERMOPHILIC

Perhaps the best-known orchid not only within the genus *Papilionanthe* but also the genus *Vanda* in which this

Paraphalaenopsis laycockii

THERMOPHILIC

The orchids bearing this generic name used to be included in the genus *Phalaenopsis*. While their flowers corresponded with this classification, their succulent leaves of a completely different morphology did not— they are cylindrical and resemble the *Vanda* or, more recently, *Papilionanthe* orchids rather than *Phalaenopsis*. The fact that they were unrelated to the latter genus was later proved by the futile attempts to hybridize the two genera (while, a large number of lively hybrids have been created with the genus *Vanda*). Although *P. laycockii* is a beautiful plant, it is also highly unvigorous and difficult to cultivate. It needs an epiphytic support and more light than any *Phalaenopsis*. It blooms irregularly and comes from Borneo.

Paraphalaenopsis laycockii

Pescatorea dayana

INTERMEDIATE

The small genus *Pescatorea* is often mistaken for the genera *Huntleya, Bollea, Chondrorhyncha* and *Kefersteinia* (it is very hard to distinguish between them) and includes about 17 species with similar body morphology. The leaves are 6-12 in/15-30 cm long and arranged in a dense, firm, iris-like fan. Single fragrant flowers grow on short scapes from the base of the leaf rosette and they are very showy. The tepals are broad and symmetrical, the lip is small and inconspicuous, sometimes decorated with fimbriated protuberances. An overwhelming majority of the plants are epiphytes or occasional terrestrites, growing in a thick layer of organic material; that is why they should be mounted on wooden supports along with a tuft of peat moss. The plants need a relatively intensive light. *P. dayana* usually blooms in early spring and is known to inhabit montane elevations of the strip of land between Costa Rica and Ecuador.

Phaius tankervilleae

INTERMEDIATE

This species is the most valuable representative of its genus as far as cultivation is concerned, and it is also the best known. It grows usually in the ground, in the humus of sparse forests or between tussocks of grass in savannas. Its egg-shaped pseudobulbs give rise to an erect, 24-in/60-cm tall spike bearing 5-10 flowers. The purple flower lip is complemented with elegant brownish tepals. The decorative, durable inflorescences are sometimes grown for cut flowers. The recommended style of cultivation includes a rather heavy humic substrate, semi-shade and moderate round-the-year watering. The species blooms in the fall and winter. It was originally widespread only in southwest Asia, Australia and the Pacific Islands; later, by human intervention, it started growing also in Cuba, Jamaica, Hawaii and Panama.

Phalaenopsis amabilis ⊡ ◼ ☺
THERMOPHILIC

The genus *Phalaenopsis* is one of the most significant cultivation and breeding genera worldwide (see chapter Hybridization and Breeding of Orchids). And it was the large-flowered species *P. amabilis* that "signed" most of the important modern hybrids of this genus with its genes. The plant resembles other *Phalaenopsis* orchids in morphology. It has egg-shaped, fleshy, fresh green, sessile leaves reaching lengths of 12 in/30 cm. The erect flower spike bears 5-20 white flowers with the center adorned in yellowish and red. The middle lobe of the lip tapers off into two flagella. The species requires the same style of cultivation as *P. fimbriata*. It blooms between the fall and spring and is native to Indonesia, northern Australia and New Guinea.

Phaius tankervilleae

Phalaenopsis amabilis

Phalaenopsis amboinensis ⊡ ◼ ☺
THERMOPHILIC

All the botanical species of the genus *Phalaenopsis* require warm conditions and above-average air humidity; this quality makes them rather unsuitable for open-grown cultivation in an apartment. Unless you own at least a small indoor glass case or other equipment, in which the plants' needs could be satisfied, it is better to grow the large-flowered multiple hybrids instead, as they are much more resistant. *P. amboinensis* is one of the large-flowered species; its leaves are up to 10 in/25 cm long; its yellow flowers with pronounced crosswise spots reach 2 in/5 cm in diameter. This epiphyte blooms between April and August and comes from humid jungles of Ambon and Ceram.

Phalaenopsis amboinensis

Phalaenopsis aphroditae

that grow over the support into great distances from the shortened stem. Some 3-7 flowers appear on the overhanging flower spike and they are very showy. The greenish hue of the tepals gradually turns into brown-and-red color at the tepals' bases; the lip is shiny pink. The plant's cultivation requirements are the same as those of other *Phalaenopsis* orchids. The species blooms in the spring and is native to Burma and southern China.

Phalaenopsis celebensis

THERMOPHILIC

A very handsome orchid that is still quite rare in collections. The smaller proportions of the flowers are compensated for by their quantity—there can be up to 30 of them on the semi-erect or overhanging spikes. Orange-and-yellow spots on the lateral tepals and orange-and-yellow lineation on the lip complement the white color of the flower. The species blooms in the fall and it was discovered in Celebes.

Phalaenopsis cornu-cervi

THERMOPHILIC

When in bloom, this species has a very peculiar appearance—its slim flower spike turns at the end into a robust, enlarged, sometimes club-shaped, flattened flower spindle. The yellow flowers covered with brown spots are up to 2 in/5 cm across and they grow out of

Phalaenopsis braceana

Phalaenopsis aphroditae

THERMOPHILIC

This orchid resembles *P. amabilis* in appearance, except that it is a little smaller. Its flowers are white, 2.4-3.2 in/6-8 cm in diameter, with a yellow and purple marking on the red lip. The flagellated protuberances on the lip's middle lobe are very long and twisted. Grow this species in the same way as other *Phalaenopsis* orchids. Flowers can be expected in the winter. The plant comes from the Philippines and Taiwan.

Phalaenopsis braceana

INTERMEDIATE-THERMOPHILIC

A miniature and very decorative orchid with small leaves whose assimilation "debt" is well complemented by the photosynthesis of its numerous flat roots

Phalaenopsis celebensis

Phalaenopsis cornu-cervi var. *alba*

the spindle in long time intervals until they are pollinated; each flower lasts on the plant for up to several
months! The flower spindles are long-lived, and in addition to that, they repeatedly add in growth after
a while. An "albino" variety is know to exist—*P.
cornu-cervi* var. *alba*—with pure yellow flowers free
of brown spots. This popular orchid blooms between
May and August. It is native to Sumatra, Java, Borneo
and mainland Malaysia.

Phalaenopsis cornu-cervi

Phalaenopsis equestris var. *alba*

Phalaenopsis equestris

Phalaenopsis equestris

THERMOPHILIC

An exceptionally popular representative of the genus. Its only weak spot—small flowers—is compensated for by a large number of waxy flowers, as well as their durability. The plants form up to several branched inflorescences at once. *P. equestris* has oval, fresh green leaves reaching lengths of 6-8 in/15-20 cm. Each of its slightly arched, erect inflorescences consists of up to 15 flowers with a purplish lip and tepals colored in a light shade of pink. A white-flowered variety of *P. equestris* (*P. equestris* var. *alba*) is also known to exist. In cultivation, follow the same instructions as with other *Phalaenopsis* species; the plants do better in flowerpots. *P. equestris* blooms in late summer and comes from the Philippines.

Phalaenopsis fimbriata

THERMOPHILIC

A species with 10-in/25-cm-long leaves and 15-20 whitish flowers, 1.6-2 in/4-5 cm across, distributed on an arched flower spike. *P. fimbriata* needs, same as other *Phalaenopsis* orchids, to be grown in semi-shade and provided with a permanently high level of air humidity (therefore it is not very suitable for growing on a windowsill). An optimum round-the-year temperature is 75-82 °F/24-28 °C, and it can drop to 64-68 °F/18-20 °C only exceptionally in the winter, when the orchids undergo their vegetation rest caused by insufficient light. The substrate can be left to dry well between waterings but it should never dry up completely or remain overly moist. Grow this species in flowerpots, epiphytic baskets or on wooden slabs in a layer of peat moss (the latter possibility should only be resorted to in sufficiently humid and ventilated greenhouses). *P. fimbriata* blooms between April and August and comes from the islands of Java and Sumatra.

Phalaenopsis fuscata

THERMOPHILIC

This species is very rarely cultivated and not very well known. It has medium-sized (1.6 in/4 cm across) fleshy flowers with a spoon-shaped lip. Between 2-12 flowers grow on a shortish spike; the lip is yellowish or ocher yellow with brown-and-red lengthwise stripes, the other tepals are yellow on the ends and brown on the bases. The species should be grown in the same style as *P. fimbriata*. Flowers can be expected between March and April. The plant's habitat is in the Malayan Peninsula.

Phalaenopsis fuscata

Phalaenopsis fimbriata

Phalaenopsis gibbosa

Phalaenopsis gigantea ▣ ■ ☺ ☺

THERMOPHILIC

P. gigantea is the bulkiest species of the entire *Phalaenopsis* genus. Its leaves are up to 20 in/50 cm long, flaccidly over-hanging, bluish green. The suspended inflorescence is up to 1.6-in/4-cm long and bears 15-25 whitish flowers with brown-and-red spots and a tiny lip. The color of the 2-in/5-cm-large flowers is somewhat variable. The cultivation requirements are the same as those applied to other thermophilic *Phalaenopsis* species; because of the type of development and weight of its leaves, *P. gigantea* can only be grown epiphytically. It blooms between June and the fall and comes from Borneo.

Phalaenopsis gigantea

Phalaenopsis gibbosa ▢ ▣ ☺ ☺

THERMOPHILIC

A beautiful miniature closely related to a very similar species, *P. parishii*. When grown on a wooden slab, this epiphytic plant forms a multitude of assimilating roots whose overall area often surpasses the area of the small leaves, which are sometimes completely absent from the plant, or they are barely 3.2 in/8 cm long. The flower spikes reach lengths of 6 in/15 cm and there are 1-3 of them growing from the axils of the leaves; each of them bears 8-10 flowers (in culture the number of flowers tends to be lower). The flowers resemble those of a related species in shape; the lip is decorated with two more or less marked yellow-and-brown spots. Grow this species same as other *Phalaenopsis* orchids. *P. gibbosa* blooms in early spring and was discovered in Laos and Vietnam.

Phalaenopsis hieroglyphica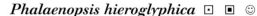

THERMOPHILIC

This orchid is closely related to the species *P. luedde-manniana* and it used to be considered its subspecies. The only difference is the color of the flowers—the crosswise stripes or dotting is more delicate and brown-and-red. It is slightly reminiscent in appearance of the Ancient Egyptian script (hence the Latin species name). Remarkably, its tepals do not fall off after pollination but instead they bulge and greenify a little, and they serve as a photosynthesis and storage organ until the seeds reach maturity. Grow the species as you would *P. fimbriata*; do not remove the faded flower spike, because it will bear more flowers, as well as daughter plants, in several years to come. The flowering season usually starts in the spring and in early summer. The species' habitat is in the Philippines.

Phalaenopsis x *intermedia*

THERMOPHILIC

The cross between the generic and species names of this orchid suggests that it is a hybrid, namely the first natural *Phalaenopsis* hybrid known in the botanical science. It originated in the nature of the *Philippines*, parented by *P. aphrodite* and *P. equestris*.

Phalaenopsis lobbii

THERMOPHILIC

A beautiful miniature suitable for small amateur greenhouses and indoor glass cases. The plant resembles *P. parishii* and takes up little space—its drooping leaves are barely 4 in/10 cm long. The flowers are small but showy and there are 3-8 of them growing on each short overhanging spike. The decorative look of the plant is enhanced by the fact that it forms several inflorescences at once. The snow-white flowers are vertically elongated and adorned with a broadened lip with a coffee-brown marking. The species blooms in the winter and spring and comes from the jungles in Southeast Asia.

Phalaenopsis lobbii

207

Phalaenopsis lowii

Phalaenopsis lueddemanniana var. *delicata*

Phalaenopsis lowii   ▫ ▪ ☺

THERMOPHILIC

Amateur cultivators sometimes mistake this species for a miniature small-flowered plant *P. lobbii*, owing to its similar sounding species name. *P. lowii* is a medium-sized orchid that outside of the flowering period resembles a smaller specimen of *P. amabilis*. Its 2-in/5-cm-across or smaller flowers also have a similar shape but they are colored in a light shade of pink and their purple column is extended like a beak. The lip is also purple and it lacks the pair of pendants characteristic of. *P. amabilis*. The erect, 16-in/40-cm-tall or smaller inflorescence bearing 5-12 flowers develops between July and October. *P. lowii* was discovered in Burma.

Phalaenopsis lueddemanniana

Phalaenopsis lueddemanniana   ▫ ▪ ☺

THERMOPHILIC

P. lueddemanniana is the most widespread botanical species in collections, thanks not only to its beautiful flowers but also its capability of easy vegetative propagation: after fading, its flower spikes repeatedly give rise to daughter plants. The flowers are highly variable, some former varieties are now considered independent species (see *P. hieroglyphica*). On a typical specimen, the flowers are fleshy, up to 2 in/5 cm in diameter, whitish with dense, crosswise purple spots. The flower lip is hairy in the central part. *P. lueddemanniana* is used in breeding for creat-

Phalaenopsis lueddemanniana var. *pulchra*

ing star-shaped flower types. Cultivation is easy and does not differ from other thermophilic representatives of the genus. The plant's faded inflorescences should not be removed by rule and the vegetatively created plants should not be separated until they grow several leaves and their own roots. The species blooms mostly in the spring and early summer. It comes from the Philippines.

Phalaenopsis parishii

Phalaenopsis modesta   ▫   ☺

THERMOPHILIC

This markedly warmth- and moisture-loving species "imitates" *P. violacea* in cultivation demands. Its extremely shortened stems bear relatively large fleshy leaves. The flower spike bears only one or two flowers at once but it keeps growing, which can significantly prolong the flowering period. The bases of the white tepals are embellished with crosswise, shiny purple stripes turning into compact spots; the identically colored lip is equipped with fimbriated protuberances on the end. The species is grown epiphytically or in flowerpots kept in a quite shady, moist place in a warm greenhouse. The flowers appear irregularly. *P. modesta* comes from Borneo.

Phalaenopsis parishii   ☐   ☺

THERMOPHILIC

A highly sought-after (and also given due recognition) miniature. *P. parishii* boasts only cultivation assets— small proportions, beautiful flowers and low demands. It does not differ from a related species *P. lobbii* in the appearance of its green parts, but it has prettier flowers; they are 0.8 in/2 cm tall, white with an extended, ocher-and-purple lip with a hairy center. This loveable orchid should only be cultivated epiphytically on a bare vertical support. The flowers are produced between May and June. The plant was discovered in Burma and other countries in southwest Asia.

Phalaenopsis schilleriana

THERMOPHILIC

By the standards of the genus, this species is extraordinary in two ways: the upper sides of its leaves are covered with decorative silvery spots, while the roots are conspicuously flat in the cross-section and they contain a lot of chlorophyll. The arched, branched inflorescence bears up to 30 pinkish purple flowers, 2-2.4 in/5-6 cm across. The lip is yellowish in the middle part and speckled with red dots, same as the lower tepals. Flowers appear between February and May. They are not very long-lived and fade fast if placed in a vase. The species can be grown either in a flowerpot or epiphytically (ideally in a layer of moss). The species comes from the Philippines.

Phalaenopsis stuartiana

THERMOPHILIC

This plant resembles the previous species in appearance—the upper sides of its leaves are also decoratively marbled. However, the flowers are colored differently—their upper half is pure white, their lower half (including the base of the lip) is yellowish with pronounced brown-and-red spots. Grow this species the same as you would the previous species that is more common in collections. *P. stuartiana* blooms in the winter and early spring and it is widespread in humid jungles in the Philippines.

Phalaenopsis venosa

THERMOPHILIC

An extremely rare species that cultivators obtain only with the greatest difficulty. Its leaves resemble those of *P. violacea* both in size and appearance. Its fragile-looking, showy flowers are 1.6 in/4 cm across and they grow (sometimes repeatedly) on a 6-in/15-cm-long spike bearing only a few of them. They are brown-and-red with green-and-yellow edges and a white center. The lip is tiny. Cultivation is similar to that of the above-mentioned related species; the plant requires more humid than average conditions throughout the year. It blooms in the summer and was discovered in Celebes, Indonesia.

Phalaenopsis stuartiana

Phalaenopsis venosa

riod, when some 2-4 large, star-shaped, symmetrical flowers distributed on a short, overhanging inflorescence begin to open. Their basic color is greenish white that gradually turns into dark purple, as you move closer to the center of the flower (this flower type is called "Malayan" after its place of origin). The flowers of the plants from Borneo are a lot more purple ("the Borneo type"). A white-flowered variation is also known to exist. *P. violacea* is ideal for humid, warm and modestly insolated indoor greenhouses. The seemingly faded flower scape repeatedly "wakes up" and should therefore never be removed after the flowers fade and fall off. The plant can be spotted in Borneo, the Malayan Peninsula and Sumatra.

Phalaenopsis violacea

THERMOPHILIC

Among orchid lovers, *P. violacea* has the reputation of an almost mystic species and a very pricey rarity. There is nothing remarkable about it outside of the flowering season: its extended, elliptic, 10-in/25-cm-long leaves are far from spellbinding. All this changes in the blooming pe-

Phalaenopsis violacea

Phalaenopsis wilsonii

THERMOPHILIC

P. wilsonii is still an extremely rare specimen of orchid collections. Lately, it has been classified as belonging in the genus *Kingidium*; its distinguishing features are, for instance, its peculiar-colored, sparse, deciduous leaves or the shape of its flower lip. The species is a wonderful looking orchid with very showy flowers. It creates a multitude of flattened aerial roots. Its flower spike measure 8 in/20 cm at the most and is able to carry 3-10 pinkish flowers with an impressive purple-and-yellow lip. Grow the species as other thermophilic *Phalaenopsis* orchids. This orchid blooms between March and June and it is only known to grow in China.

Phalaenopsis wilsonii

Pholidota chinensis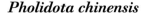

CRYOPHILIC-INTERMEDIATE

The genus *Pholidota* is a close relative of *Coelogyne* orchids. *P. chinensis* has slim, oval pseudobulbs reaching lengths of 2.4 in/6 cm and bearing two leaves. The individual flowers, about 0.8 in/2-cm-across and colored in whitish beige, do not have much decorative value but they are crowded in great numbers on a decorative overhanging tail-like inflorescence. The flower spike develops simultaneously with a new shoot. *P. chinensis* is an undemanding epiphyte with medium-strict light requirements. It can be cultivated on a wooden support or in a suspended perforated flowerpot. It blooms between March and May and its habitat is in southern China and northern Vietnam.

Phragmipedium besseae

Phragmipedium besseae

INTERMEDIATE

The splendid looking species *P. besseae* is a living proof that large orchids with showy flowers can be discovered in the wild even today. It was first found in Tarpato, Peru, but not until 1981. The discovered plants were transported in a non-blooming state to the U.S.A. where they all produced, to everyone's big surprise, shiny red flowers! Until that time, this color was unheard of in American Venus's shoes, and even the much more plentiful Asian Venus's shoes. Unfortunately, information about the location of the habitat leaked out and the specimens that occurred there were totally ravaged. Luckily, *P. besseae* (whose flowers were slightly more orange) was later also discovered in Ecuador. By now, the species has been propagated in sufficient numbers from seeds and it is no longer threatened with extinction. Several color mutations are known to exist, such as orange, yellow (var. *flava*) and many transitory variations; still, the original shiny red form is unbeatable in appearance. The cultivation rules do not differ substantially from those of other representatives of the genus (see *P. lindleyanum*).

Phragmipedium caudatum

INTERMEDIATE

The flowers of some of the representatives of the genus *Phragmipedium* are of comparable beauty with those of

Phragmipedium caudatum

Phragmipedium caudatum var. *walichii*

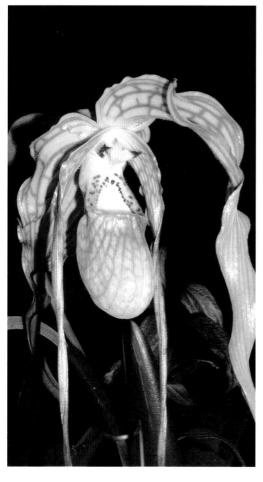

Paphiopedilum orchids; sadly, they are very short-lived and often fall off after only two or three days. Moreover, they open successively. The species *P. caudatum* is an exception in this respect—its flowers last longer and there can be more than one open at the same time. *P. caudatum* is among the most robust and most frequently cultivated *Phragmipedium* orchids. Its flower spike bearing two or three flowers reaches a length of 32 in/80 cm, while its leaves are up to 16 in/40 cm long. Its whitish flowers with a pronounced green venation are characterized by intensely elongated reddish ribbon-like petals—they are so long that they can even touch the ground! The species occurs in several varieties that differ in the coloring and shape of the flowers. Peculiar specimens were found in Ecuador that do not form a shoe-like lip; a detailed examination revelad differences in other traits as well and these specimens got the name *P. lindenii* (this species also exists in a standard form with a typical shoe-like lip). *P. caudatum* grows mostly in sandy soil or tufa on volcano slopes. It blooms in the fall and comes from Guatemala, Costa Rica, Panama, Colombia, Venezuela, Ecuador and Peru.

Phragmipedium chapadense

INTERMEDIATE

The New World genus of *Phragmipedium* is a "looka-like" of the strikingly similar looking Asian *Paphiope-dilum* genus. Both genera have flowers with that characteristic shoe-like lip that earned them the nickname "Venus's shoes". Besides geographical differences, some other differences can be observed between these two genera: for one, whereas *Phragmipedium* orchids are characterized by an ovary with three layers of casing, a segmented flower spike and revolute edges of the shoe-shaped lips; in contrast, *Paphiopedilum* orchids have an ovary with only one casing, their flower spike is not segmented and the lip edge is not revolute. *Phragmipedium* species are usually sizeable terrestrial orchids forming dense clusters of long, narrow, pointed leaves. *P. chapadense* has elegant flowers that appear on a 16-20-in/40-50-cm-long flower spike bearing two or three of them. Long wine-red petals that reach lengths of 6 in/ 15 cm and almost horizontally stick to the sides dominate the flowers. Grow the species in the same way as other orchids of the genus *Phragmi-pedium*. The plant was discovered in Brazil.

Phragmipedium Grande

INTERMEDIATE

In vain would you search for this flower in the wild—for it was created by an artificial hybridization of *P. cauda-tum* a *P. longifolium*. Thanks to its exceptionally low ecological demands (verging on indestructibility!), the hybrid literally became folk and is now often grown in orchid greenhouses. Its parents endowed it with robust proportions of leaf rosettes and flowers—the leaves reach lengths of 18 in/45 cm. Unfortunately, the decorative red-and-green flowers with long petals also inherited very short durability. The species should be grown as any standard representative of the genus. Flowers can be expected throughout the year.

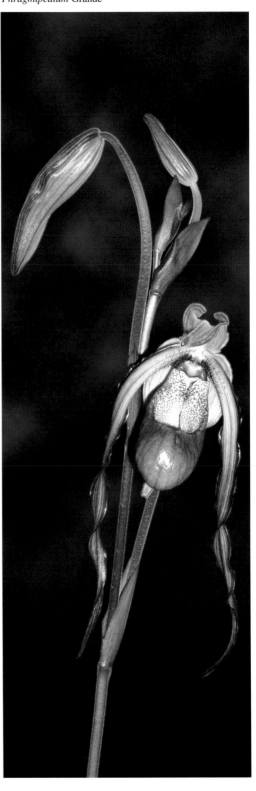

214

Phragmipedium klotzschianum

INTERMEDIATE

In the wild, the plants of this species can be spotted on water banks or in regularly flooded regions—their higher-than-average requirements of the moisture of the substrate must also be satisfied in cultivation. With its leaves reaching lengths of only 10 in/25 cm, *P. klotzschianum* is among the smaller representatives of the genus. Its compact leaf rosettes are usually pentafoliate; the flower spike bears two or three flowers and gradually acquires the length of 12 in/30 cm. The tepals are brown-and-red, the lip tends to range in color between yellow and yellow-and-green. Grow the species in semi-shade, the same as other *Phragmipedium* orchids; every once in a while, dampen the substrate thoroughly with rainwater. Flowers appear in the winter. The species is native to Guiana and Venezuela.

Phragmipedium lindleyanum

INTERMEDIATE

A fairly robust representative of the genus with usually pentafoliate rosettes. The individual leaves reach lengths of 20 in/50 cm. The plant's multi-flowered, erect and sometimes also branched, flower raceme is up to 3.3 ft/ 1 m tall. The flowers are 3.2 in/8 cm across, yellow or yellow-and-green with dull-red venation. The lip is usually yellow with a tinge of red and reddish venation. The outer side of the sepals is thickly covered with hairs. The plant occurs both in open and shady locations, mostly on rock plates covered with a layer of humic soil. It blooms in the winter and is native to Guiana and Venezuela.

Phragmipedium lindleyanum

Phragmipedium longifolium

Phragmipedium longifolium   ■ ☺

INTERMEDIATE

This is the largest of all *Phragmipedium* orchids—its leaves measure 24 in/60 cm and the inflorescence reaches a length of over 3.3 ft/1 m. The ladder-shaped flower spike bears up to 10 rather short-lived flowers, each of which opens only after the previous one has fallen off. The flowers are up to 6 in/15 cm in diameter and sport protruding, elongated green petals. The brown-and-green lip is smooth and relatively small. Although the plant's cultivation demands are low, its proportions make it somewhat unseemly and it is mainly used in breeding. The flowers appear irregularly. The plant comes from Costa Rica, Panama, Ecuador and Colombia.

Phragmipedium pearcei

Phragmipedium pearcei   ▣ ☹ ☺

INTERMEDIATE

This species' main asset are its beautiful and very fragile-looking flowers. Its leaf rosettes resemble those of other medium-sized relatives. The plant's relatively large flowers open successively on an erect multi-flower spike. The flowers parade a filigree green-and-white coloring complemented by brown spots on the edge of the lip. The elongated, downward pointing petals are reddish on the ends. This terrestrial or epiphytic species is relatively adaptive; after all, in the wild it grows in altitudes between 980-3,600 ft/ 300-1,100 m. It blooms in the summer and inhabits regions surrounding rivers in Peru, Ecuador, Colombia and Costa Rica.

Phragmipedium richteri   ▣ ☺

INTERMEDIATE

This orchid was described as late as in 1944 based on plants that had been cultivated in collections for several years before that: their owners took them for natural hybrids. The color combination on the flowers is very delicate—the pouched whitish lip is adorned with greenish venation on the outside and "agglomerations" of dark spots on the inside. *P. richteri* requires to be grown in a flowerpot filled with a light humic mixture of peat, Styrofoam, perlite, sand, moss etc. All the representatives of the genus need more diffused light than do *Paphiopedilum* orchids. The substrate should always be somewhat moist, and the plants will enjoy an occasional misting of the leaves, as well as a hearty dose of fertilizer. *P. richteri* blooms in culture throughout the year and it comes from Peru.

Phragmipedium richteri

Phragmipedium sargentianum ▣ ■ ☺

INTERMEDIATE

The leaf rosettes of this species usually bear seven leaves reaching lengths of up to 20 in/50 cm. The erect inflorescence bears 2-4 successively opening flowers. The basic color of the flower is green; the lip's green gradually turns into yellow, and the surface of the lip is speckled with red and green dots. The flower features a pair of petals that are purple on the edges and ends and reach lengths of 2.4 in/6 cm. The species has no particular cultivation demands. It is related to *P. lindleyanum*. The flowers appear irregularly (in most cases in late winter and in the spring). This orchid is native to Pernambuco, Brazil.

Phragmipedium sargentianum

Pityphyllum amesianum

Pityphyllum amesianum □ ▫ ☺

INTERMEDIATE

A special treat for the lovers of unconventional-shaped epiphytic orchids. The ends of its thickened pseudobulb-like stems are decorated with brush-shaped clusters of many delicate lineated leaves. Another 1-3 shoots are formed in the axils of the leaves; as the plant gradually extends and branches up, the leaf cluster assumes a very peculiar appearance. The species' whitish flowers are unfortunately quite plain and very minute (0.8-0.16 in/ 2-4 mm). *P. amesianum* is difficult to cultivate: mount the plant on a wooden support, propping it up with a layer of moss, and keep it in a moderately humid and well-ventilated environment throughout the year. If you allow the roots to dry up, the plant reacts by shedding its leaves irreversibly. The species blooms in the course of the whole year. The photo of one of its specimens was taken on the border between Venezuela and Colombia.

Platystele sp., Mexico

Pleione formosana

Pleione

CRYOPHILIC-INTERMEDIATE

Pleione is a genus of great consequence in cultivation. It includes mainly terrestrial cryophilic (to frost-resistant) species. In spite of this fact, *Pleione* orchids are included in the tropical section of *Orchidaceae*—their body morphology and life cycle makes them very similar to the tropical species. Moreover, the genus contains, among others, a group of rather thermophilic species (including one entirely tropical epiphyte, *P. maculata*). The plants form standard, firm, fleshy pseudobulbs of broad, conic or spherical shapes. The apices of the pseudobulbs give rise to one or two elongated, elliptical, rather flabby leaves with a marked lengthwise venation. The leaves are shed annually before winter. In

Pleione yunnanensis

Platystele   □ ▪ ☺

INTERMEDIATE-THERMOPHILIC

A clustered mini-orchid that forms masses of minuscule yellow flowers—their proportions are a good evidence for the nearly unlimited range of shapes and sizes that can be assumed by the plants from the family *Orchidaceae*. The entire small genus *Platystele* (a total of 6 species) is closely akin to the genus *Pleurothalis*. Its trailing stem forms multiple branches and each of its shoots is ended with a single, 1.2-1.6-in/3-4-cm-long leaf. The flowers of the species in the photo are arranged in a two-row flower raceme that is formed at the bases of the leaves and never surpasses the leaves in length. Each inflorescence bears a large number of 0.12-0.16-in/3-4-mm-large, successively opening flowers with a deep-yellow lip. After the flowers fade, the individual ovaries extend—even if not pollinated—and create a peculiar shape with comb-like protuberances on either side. The individual flower spikes sometimes survive for over a year, adding in growth and bearing on their ends new flowers that continuously open, one or two at a time. Thanks to this quality, the specimen in the photo has been continuously blooming for 12 years now! Cultivation rules are similar as those that apply to *Pleurothalis* orchids. The plant is, due to its minute proportions, in need of frequent misting and fairly humid conditions overall. The species was discovered in Palenque, Mexico, but specimens are known to grow also in other countries in Central and South America.

alpine species, single flowers develop in early spring simultaneously with the forming of new shoots (this group includes *P. limprichtii* a *P. formosana*); the more warmth-loving species do not bloom until the fall, when the leaves are shed (besides *P. maculata*, this section includes also *P. humilis*, *P. hookeriana*, *P. praecox* and other species). The flowers develop singly or in pairs on short spikes and are very decorative. Their lip is very decorative with lengthwise ribs and a fimbriated edge. The tepals are also attractively green and sometimes only partially open. Cultivation requirements are the same with both ecological groups—the vegetation period should be launched in early spring in a cool greenhouse (at temperatures between 50-65 °F/10-18 °C). Plant the bare pseudobulbs (unless they were wintered in a substrate) in broad ceramic flowerpots or bowls filled with a mixture of ground pine bark, grated Sty-

rofoam, perlite, charcoal, needles of coniferous trees and a little siliceous sand. For cryophilic species, you can add soil, but be aware of the risk of root molding. During vegetation, the plants need sufficient moisture, fertilizer, fresh, moving air and protection from direct sunlight. Toward the end of the summer, reduce watering somewhat, and start wintering the plants after they shed their leaves or, with "autumnal" species, after their flowers fade. Even though some of them are, if covered with a layer of quality snow, able to survive a cold winter, it is safer to winter them in cool greenhouses, cellars or refrigerators. If the pseudobulbs tend to dry up excessively during the storage period, it is recommended to place them in a plastic bag or cover them with peat. The orchids belonging to the beautiful genus *Pleione* can be spotted in alpine and submontane regions of India, China, Burma and Thailand.

Pleione maculata

Pleurothalis   □ · ■ ☺

INTERMEDIATE-THERMOPHILIC

A genus with a significantly high number of species (approximately 550) that are small or miniature in size, occasionally also very bulky. As the individual species produce plain, tiny flowers, they are of no consequence in gardening. However, they are useful as complementary collection plants—their proportions predetermine them to be cultivated in smaller amateur glass cases and greenhouses. The taxonomy of the genus is untransparent owing to the vast geographical area of its natural habitat, inconspicuous appearance and variability of the plants it includes. *Pleurothalis* orchids do not form pseudobulbs;

Pleurothalis grobyi

the inverted lanceolate, oval or spoon-shaped leaves grow out of a thin, trailing or intensely shortened rhizome on firm, reduced stems. The leaves sometimes assume a highly succulent character (the Brazilian species *P. teres* is a case in point). The flower raceme grows out of the leaf axils and bears a high number of minuscule flowers. The flowers are unconventional in morphology—the partially closed pair of sepals clearly dwarfs the tiny lip and other flower parts. *Pleurothalis* orchids are easy to cultivate, perhaps with the exception of the alpine lithophytic species. Grow the plants epiphytically on vertically suspended pieces of bark or sticks of elderberry. When mounting a species originating in humid, warm regions on a support, prop it up with a tuft of peat moss. The intensity of light, as well as watering dosages should be

Pleurothalis teres

Pleurothalis sp., Ecuador

Pleurothalis sp., Ecuador

based on the given species' place of origin. If that is un-known, you can partly guess it from the plant's morphol-ogy: small-sized species with not very firm leaves should be suspended in a rather humid, semi-shady environment and regularly misted, whereas species with more succu-lent leaves need more diffused light verging on direct sun-light and a cooler, drier break during stagnation. *Pleu-rothalis* inhabits the tropical regions of America between Mexico and Argentina.

Pleurothalis sp., Peru

Polyrrhiza funalis

Ponthieva maculata

Polyrrhiza funalis

INTERMEDIATE

The correct name for the representatives of this genus is in fact *Polyradicion*; however, the name under which they are known among cultivators is *Polyrrhiza*. These orchids are genuine floristic curiosities whose significance reaches beyond the borders of the *Orchidaceae* family! Orchids that belong to the *Polyrrhiza* genus and some other genera as well (see *Chiloschista, Microcoelia*, etc.) have lost the ability to form normal leaves. The indispensable photosynthesis takes place only in the chlorophyll contained in their succulent greenish roots. The flattened roots grow from an extremely shortened miniature stem and proliferate over the support or freely on their own, creating a nest-like shape. The flowers of *P. funalis* grow singly, they are quite large and greenish white. The lip is heart-shaped and boasts a greenish spur. Cultivation requires a certain amount of experience: mount the "root clusters" of the species (very lightly and with the utmost care) on bare wooden supports (elderberry is suitable, for instance) and hang them up in a well-ventilated place with a sufficient amount of diffused light. The plants require frequent misting, especially in the summer. *P. funalis* blooms in culture only very unwillingly; in its original habitat—Cuba and Jamaica—it flowers between February and May.

Ponthieva maculata

INTERMEDIATE

This species is not interesting for cultivation, but certainly attractive for botanists and curiosity lovers. It is one of the 25 species comprising a small genus of mostly terrestrial orchids. *P. maculata* grows epiphytically and occasionally even in the ground. It does not form pseudobulbs; its elongated leaves reaching lengths of 10 in/25 cm are arranged in a sessile rosette. The plant's raceme inflorescence is erect and consists of a high number of tiny flowers with blue-to-purple-spotted, whitish tepals

and a red or yellow lip. The thread-like roots of this orchid must never be left to dry up. The species blooms in the winter and spring and is widespread in an area including Mexico, Venezuela and Ecuador.

Porpax lanii

INTERMEDIATE-THERMOPHILIC

A delicacy for the lovers of miniature orchid curiosities. The genus *Porpax* is characterized by pseudobulbs whose top parts are completely flat and which are totally leafless during drought periods—the "sleeping" plants look really spectacular on branches or rocks. Not to mention their beauty when they open up! With the species *P. lanii*, super-short flower spikes grow on new shoots out of the axils of the pairs of leaves. Likewise, the brick-red flowers embellished with greenish marbling appear in twos. Their appearance is quite bizarre—the bases of their sepals are grown together, thus allowing the flowers to be only partly open. *P. lanii* should be grown as a normal epiphyte that is a little more demanding of light. After the new pseudobulbs mature, treat the plants to a substantial dry period. The species blooms between late fall and spring and comes from southeastern Asia.

Promenea xanthina

INTERMEDIATE-THERMOPHILIC

It is a shame that this representative of the small (both in the number and size of the species) genus *Promenea* never made its home in orchid collections, for it is a beautiful miniature—its pseudobulbs are only 0.8 in/2 cm long. The overhanging spikes bear one or two lemon yel-

Porpax lanii

low flowers with a red-dotted lip. In proportion to the size of the whole plant, they are literally enormous—2 in/ 5 cm across! *P. xanthina* is an epiphyte with medium-high light demands. It is more demanding of humidity and will therefore thrive in a light substrate in a small, suspended flowerpot or basket. The flowers open between May and August. As all the other members of the *Promenea* genus, *P. xanthina* is a native of Brazil.

Psychopsiella limminghei □

INTERMEDIATE-THERMOPHILIC

This gorgeous orchid used to be classified as an *Oncidium* for a long time until 1982, when was it excluded into an independent genus on the grounds of its different qualities (the shape and size of its green parts, the color of its leaves, as well as the anatomy of its flowers). *P. limminghei* is a fantastic-looking miniature "weighed in gold". Its barely 0.8-in/2-cm-long flattened pseudobulbs bear a single, 0.8-1.6-in/2-4-cm-long leaf adorned with red marbling. Both organs adhere to the support. The thin flower spike is up to 4 in/10 cm long and usually bears one flower. The flowers are 1.2-1.6 in/3-4 cm in diameter, their lip is light yellow and the other tepals are brown-and-yellow. Even though the opposite is sometimes claimed in orchid literature, this "teeny-weeny" orchid is not very easy to cultivate and is quite "moody". Grow it on a bare slab of bark or a branch in semi-shade. Stay away from higher levels of humidity in the winter months. Flowers appear between May and August and the plant comes from Venezuela.

Promenea xanthina

Psychopsiella limminghei

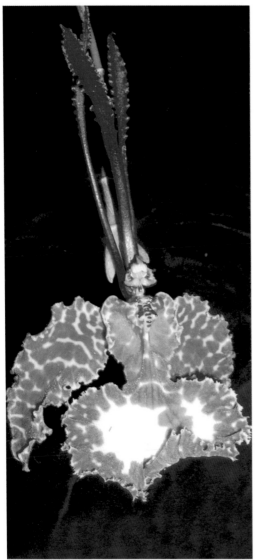

tenna-like erect trio of dark-red tepals resembling a butterfly's antennae (it is no coincidence that the generic name is derived from the Greek word "*psychi*" meaning "butterfly"). The wings of a butterfly can be seen in the lateral wavy, yellow-and-brown tepals. The broad lip is wavy, yellow in the central part and brown-spotted on the edges. The species should be cultivated in the same way as *P. papilio*. The plant blooms irregularly throughout the year. This collection gem is native to Costa Rica, Panama, Colombia and Ecuador.

Psychopsis papilio

INTERMEDIATE-THERMOPHILIC

Even though the genus *Psychopsis* was established as far back as 1838, its best-known and most beautiful representative, *P. papilio*, was not included in it until 1975. To this day, it is still sometimes classified as *Oncidium papilio*. Compared to the similar species *P. krameriana*, this plant is more robust and the upper part of its "butterfly" flower is flattened and bears typical "wings" on the column. Cultivation is not very complicated; both flowerpot culture and epiphytic culture are possible. The plants thrive in warmer indoor glass cases but need to be protected from excessive shade and dampness of the roots. These orchids bloom irregularly throughout the year; whatever you do, do not cut off the flower spikes, as they grow continuously and put forth flowers for many successive months or even years! *P. papilio* was discovered in the northern part of South America and also in Ecuador and Peru.

Psychopsis krameriana

INTERMEDIATE-THERMOPHILIC

P. krameriana is one of the species that were included in the *Oncidium* genus until 1982. Only then was it (mainly on account of the bizarre anatomy of its flowers) transferred by taxonomists to a small genus that now contains 5 species. The plant is a darling as to appearance, cultivation demands and proportions—its egg-shaped, 1.6-in/4-cm-tall pseudobulbs bear a single firm, elongated, elliptic leaf covered with red dots; single flowers appear repeatedly on 20-in/50-cm-long spikes (that is why the spikes should be removed). The flowers are real freaks of nature: they attract attention above all by an an-

Psychopsis versteegiana

INTERMEDIATE-THERMOPHILIC

This genus of beautiful butterfly-flowered orchids includes a total of 5 species that are very alike. *P. versteegiana* differs from the others, for instance, by some details in the morphology of its flower column, the smaller size of its flowers and, in contrast, its larger body proportions. Its unifoliate pseudobujeslbs measure 1.6-2.8 in/4-7 cm, while its leaves reach lengths of 12 in/30 cm. After the first generation of flowers fade away, the flower spike continues to branch out and reaches a final length of up to 3.6 ft/ 110 cm. The plant comes from cooler humid forests and is therefore, unlike the aforementioned species, a little more sensitive to higher temperatures. As the flower spike keeps growing, the plant blooms virtually the whole year round. The plant's habitat areas have not been exactly determined, as in many localities, the plant has been extinct for a long time. The latest findings have been reported in recent years from Surinam, Bolivia and possibly Ecuador.

Psychopsis versteegiana

Psygmorchis pusilla

Psygmorchis pusilla □ ☺ ☺

INTERMEDIATE-THERMOPHILIC

This species that used to be known as *Oncidium pusillum* was so unusual in appearance that it had to be excluded (along with another 4 similar species) into an independent species. The plant does not form pseudobulbs and its flat, only slightly succulent leaves are arranged in a fan-shaped rosette—botanists have a term for this: iridaceous morphology. *P. pusilla* is the ultimate miniature; the total length of the leaf rosette does not exceed 2-2.4 in/5-6 cm! The plant's super-short flower spikes usually bear a single yellow flower with the middle part dotted in red-and-brown. By virtue of its size, *P. pusilla* requires a rather frequent misting, medium-humid, moving air and a deeper shade. These are demands that can be satisfactorily met even in heated orchid glass cases. The flowers appear irregularly, mostly in the summer. This species is known to grow throughout a vast geographical area of tropical Central and South America.

225

Pteroceras
semiteretifolium □ · ☺

INTERMEDIATE-THERMOPHILIC

A wonderful-looking epiphytic miniature able to adorn any collection even when not in bloom. An extremely shortened monopodial stem confirms the plant's Asian origin. The stem is completely concealed from sight by swollen, compressed leaf bases. The highly succulent sticklike leaves are 2.8 in/7-cm-long or shorter, and arranged in a pretty compact fan rosette. The flower spike is even shorter than the leaves and bears a single flower with white tepals. The lip is yellowish with a pale purple marking. The flowers are only 0.8 in/2 cm in diameter, but since the plants create up to several spikes at once, the blooming season is an event to be celebrated. Grow the plant epiphytically in a place with plentiful light. In the wild, the flowers appear on *P. semiteretifolium* toward the end of the rainy season—that is, in September and October. The plant comes from Indochina, including Vietnam and southern Chinese provinces.

Pteroceras semiteretifolium

Renanthera monachica

Renanthera monachica · ■ ☺ ☺

THERMOPHILIC

Perhaps the best-known *Renanthera* species in European collections that belongs to a small genus (15 species), closely related to *Vanda* orchids. A common denominator of all the species is a firm monopodial stem bearing usually two rows of relatively short stiff leaves. The long, often-branched flower spike bears a lot of flowers. The spike of the species *R. monachica* measures 20 in/ 50 cm, while its leaves reach a maximum length of 5.2 in/13 cm. The inflorescence is about 8 in/20 cm long and consists of 10-15 showy flowers, 1 in/2.5 cm across. The tepals are yellowish or reddish and thickly covered with scarlet spots. The lip is almost imperceptible. In the wild, *R. monachica* grows epiphytically (on rocks only in exceptional cases) and in order to put forth flowers it needs direct sunlight. In culture, place the plant in an epiphytic basket with a permeable substrate and allow for a drier, temperate rest period in the winter after the flowers fade. The flowers appear only rarely—between the fall and spring—no matter how well you look after the plant. The species is native to the Philippines.

Renanthera matutina ■ ☺ ☺

THERMOPHILIC

As with a lot of its intergeneric hybrids, members of the genus *Renanthera* are popular mainly in commercial cultivation farms in the south of the U.S.A., Hawaii and the Malayan Peninsula. The plants are grown there over large areas under the open sky in order to produce at-

Renathera matutina

and-red tepals covered with brick-red spots; otherwise it does not differ in appearance or cultivation requirements from the previous species. It comes from Thailand, Malaysia, Java and Sumatra.

Rhyncholaelia digbyana

INTERMEDIATE

This species used to be classified as a member of the genus *Brassavola*, with which it shares only one trait—elongated neck-like ovaries. The appearance of its green parts is reminiscent much more of *Cattleya* or *Laelia* orchids. *R. digbyana* has only slightly thickened, elongated pseudobulbs bearing a single, impressively thickened leaf. The flowers are relatively large (up to 4.8 in/12 cm across) and very decorative with their cream-white lip fimbriated all along its edge. The rare variety, *R. fimbripetala*, has partly fimbriated edges even on its other petals and is valued especially highly. Although the heading informs us that this species is not easy to cultivate, it is not in fact hard to maintain in culture—but bringing the plants to bloom is any cultivator's graduation exam; for in the Temperate Zone, this orchid suffers from the lack of light in winter and therefore blooms only very rarely (between May and August). The species is one of the parents of most hybrids with *Cattleyas* (*Brassocattleya*). It is native to Mexico, Honduras and Guatemala.

tractive cut flowers. Hybrids with the genus *Phalaenopsis*, endowed by the genus *Renanthera* with a red color, branched inflorescences and robust proportions, are considered especially valuable. In Europe, this genus is cultivated quite rarely, although the very first epiphytic orchid ever to bloom on the Old Continent was the species *R. coccinea*! *R. matutina* has yellow-

Rhyncholaelia digbyana

Rhyncholaelia glauca   ⊡ ▪ ☺

INTERMEDIATE

This orchid resembles the aforementioned species in appearance but it is somewhat smaller and its green leaves are tinged with a deeper shade of gray. Moreover, its flowers are smaller in size and lack the impressive frilling on the lip, which is only modestly wavy. On the other hand, *R. glauca* is more willing to bloom, namely in early and high spring. Grow the plant as you would the previous species—mounted on a wooden slab. Repotting (or, should we say, re-mounting) should not take place too frequently—only when the plant begins to create new root tips. Faded specimens undergo a rest period—therefore they should be provided with sufficient light and air ventilation, as well as limited watering. The species was most often found in Mexico, but it also grows in Guatemala, Honduras and Panama.

Rhynchostylis gigantea   ▪ ☺

THERMOPHILIC

The genus *Rhynchostylis* contains only 4 species of orchids, nicknamed foxtails by American cultivators, for its characteristic overhanging dense flower raceme. The inflorescence surpasses in length the extremely shortened stem

Rhyncholaelia glauca

Rhynchostylis gigantea

that is covered with two rows of stiff, glossy, belt-shaped leaves reaching lengths of up to 12 in/30 cm. The color of *R. gigantea's* 1.2-in/3-cm-large flowers is highly variable—ranging between white and purple. Grow it in a sim-

Rhynchostylis gigantea, red form

ilar way to the members of the genus *Vanda*. On account of its overhanging inflorescences, it is recommended to mount the plant on an epiphytic support or place it in a suspended basket. *R. gigantea* blooms between October and November and grows in Burma, Thailand and Laos.

Rhynchostylis rosea   ◼ ☺

THERMOPHILIC

Another orchid resembling the genus *Vanda* in appearance. It is a copy of the aforementioned species in parameters but its flowers are smaller (0.8 in/2 cm), whitish, covered in sparse red-and-purple spots and sporting a purple lip. Several flower racemes can grow at once on one plant. Grow it in the same way as you would *Vanda* orchids. It blooms during a period favorable for cultivators—between October and February. *R. rosea* comes from the Philippines.

Rhytionanthos aemolum   ☐ ☺

INTERMEDIATE-THERMOPHILIC

This representative of tiny Asian orchids is characterized by bizarre-shaped flowers that make it interesting mainly for collectors of small epiphytic miniatures. The bases of its egg-shaped or elongated unifoliate pseudobulbs give rise to flower spikes that are covered with delicate spots and bear

5-6 peculiar-shaped orange flowers; their lateral tepals are grown together, forming a showy, downward-pointing "shoe". The lip is minuscule and of a light purple color. Cultivation of this species is no different from that of any standard thermophilic epiphyte, but the plant must be protected from excessive sunlight and drought! The time that the flowers choose to appear on old pseudobulbs is unfavorable for cultivators—September and October; (after that it is a difficult business for new pseudobulbs to develop, as the process takes place in the winter—a period poor in sunlight). The plant's home is in Thailand, Laos and Burma.

Rhytionanthos aemolum

Rodriguezia granadensis

Rodriguezia granadensis □ ☺

INTERMEDIATE-THERMOPHILIC

All the species included in this small genus (a total of 35) are relatively small and of attractive appearance. Their tubular flowers feature a pair of backward-pointing, elongated, sack-shaped lateral sepals resembling a spur. *R. granadensis* is a ravishing miniature. Its pseudobulbs are barely 0.8 in/2 cm long and they bear a single, 2-2.8-in/5-7-cm-long leaf of medium stiffness. The yellowish-white flowers grow on overhanging sparse racemes. This species is an epiphyte with small cultivation requirements (see *R*. sp., Bolivia). The plant blooms in the summer and fall and is native to Ecuador.

Rodriguezia secunda ▣ ☺

INTERMEDIATE-THERMOPHILIC

The Latin name of the species captures one special quality of its flowers: they are all arranged unilaterally—secundly—that is, distributed only on one side of an overhanging flower spike. The pseudobulbs of this species are bi- or trifoliate, 1.6-2.4-in/4-6-cm-long, while the medium-stiff, thin leaves reach lengths of 6 in/15 cm. The flowers range in color between pink and crimson. Numerous delicate aerial roots further enhance the decorative appearance of the plant. This orchid covers a vast geographical area—its various forms are reported to grow in both Central America (Panama, Trinidad) and South America (an area bordered by Colombia and Brazil). The photograph presented here was taken in Ecuador.

Rodriguezia sp. ⊡ ☺

CRYOPHILIC-INTERMEDIATE

This gorgeous plant resembles a Brazilian species *R. bracteata*, but it will have to wait longer for precise classification. Its barely 1.2-in/3-cm-long pseudobulbs bear stiff, thin leaves. Between 7-12 dark-purple flowers grow on an overhanging flower raceme. The purple lip is adorned with delicate dark veins and an elongated yellow spot at its base. Cultivation is not very complicated and can be carried out either in flowerpots or baskets filled with a very light epiphytic substrate (in which case make sure to prevent any harmful permanent excessive dampness of the roots), or on suspended supports. The culture environment should be ventilated and exposed to as much light as possible (while protecting the plant from direct sunlight attacking it from behind the glass!). Do not stop watering the plant even in the winter, as the plants continue to develop and the pseudobulbs may bloom repeatedly, up to several times a year.

Rossioglossum grande ▣ ☺ ☺

CRYOPHILIC-INTERMEDIATE

Up until thirty years ago, this orchid was included in the genus *Odontoglossum*; however, differences in the morphology of its flowers earned it (and three other species) a classification within an independent genus. It is a good example of the fact that large-flowered species of botanical orchids can be successfully cultivated even in an open-grown style in apartments. This species' pseudobulbs are up to 3.2 in/8 cm tall, flat, bi- or trifoliate, with sharp

Rossioglossum grande

Rodriguezia sp., Bolivia

edges. The leaves measure 14 in/35 cm, they are elliptically elongated and have a firm, leathery epidermis. Some 4-8 (under cultivation usually only 2-4) large, 6-in/15-cm-across or smaller flowers grow on an erect flower spike. The basic color of all the tongue-shaped tepals is yellow: furthermore, the sepals sport brown stripes and the petals have brown bases. The shell-shaped lip is whitish with brown spots. *R. grande* has some cultivation specifics which need to be observed for the plants to thrive and bloom. The basic cultivation rules consist in providing a well-lighted environment, standard care in the summer (that may include placing the plant in the garden) and, first and foremost, a cool (50 °F/10 °C) and dry period in the winter. If the plants are kept in an epiphytic substrate in flowerpots under these terms, they thrive all year even in dry apartment air. *R. grande* blooms between October and December and comes from Mexico and Guatemala.

Rossioglossum schlieperianum

INTERMEDIATE

Another extremely popular, large-flowered orchid of the highly esteemed genus *Rossioglossum*. The size and shape of its pseudobulbs is the same as in the case of *R. grande*; its leaves are shorter (up to 6 in/15 cm) and the flowers are smaller (3.2 in/8 cm in diameter). However, the 10-in/25-cm-long spike bears a high number of them, even under cultivation (up to 8). The flower tepals are yellowish, covered rather densely with brown-and-red spots (in some cases, the basic yellow color is almost concealed). The edges and base of the broadened, circular lip are fringed with red-and-brown spots—the shape of the lip is the distinguishing feature of the 4 species contained in the genus. Follow the cultivation instructions applied to the previous species but bear in mind that *R. schlieperianum* is more warmth-loving and the winter rest period therefore should not be too long. Flowers appear in the fall and also in the spring. The plant's natural habitat is in Panama and Costa Rica.

Rossioglossum williamsianum

INTERMEDIATE

A beautiful gem among orchids with showy flowers that cannot deny its relation to the elite *Rossioglossum* genus. The coloring of its brown-and-yellow flowers is subject to variation, which makes some specimens resemble *R. grande*. Differences from the latter species consist mainly in *R. williamsianum's* longer flower spike, somewhat smaller and more numerous flowers, more markedly orbiculate tepals, and a different shape of the flower column. This species is the most thermophilic of all *Rossioglossum* orchids, a quality that must be taken into account in cultivation. The plant can tolerate only a slight reduction in temperature in the winter. It comes from the lower elevations of Guatemala, Honduras and Costa Rica.

Sarcochilus hartmannii

INTERMEDIATE

S. hartmannii represents Australian orchids. Its extremely reduced, monopodial and densely-foliated stem bears two rows of leathery, 4-in/10-cm-long leaves. The flower spikes are multi-flowered and reach lengths of 8 in/20 cm. The flowers are 0,8 in/2 cm across with a yellow-and-red lip and they smell like honey. The narrowed bases of the other tepals are adorned with red dots. *S. hartmannii* should be grown in an environment with a good amount of light, with a slight reduction of temperature and watering in the winter. The species blooms between March and May and comes from New South Wales and Queensland, Australia.

Sarcochilus hartmannii

Sarcoglyphis mirabilis

Schoenorchis fragrans □ ☺

INTERMEDIATE-THERMOPHILIC

A fantastic living gem among orchids—these are the only words that do sufficient credit to the looks of this miniature species! Its stem reaches a length of barely a few centimeters; it bears a crowded bunch of extremely thickened, 0.6-in/1.5-cm-long or shorter leaves. Following the example of the infinitely bigger *Vanda* orchids, the leaves' axils even give rise to several short flower racemes at once. Each of the inflorescences bears 3-8 tiny purple flowers with a tinge of white and a long, sigmoidal lip. *S. fragrans* is an epiphyte requiring a lot of sunshine (but make sure to protect it from dehydration!). In the winter it does not get sufficient light—a reduction in temperature to 68 °F/20 °C will therefore do it good. The plant puts on its flower attire in late summer. It comes from southeastern Asia.

Schoenorchis fragrans

Sarcoglyphis mirabilis ▪ ☺ ☺

INTERMEDIATE-THERMOPHILIC

A handsome orchid of small proportions and noted for the decorative appearance of its green body parts. Its monopodial stem grows only very slowly; it is covered with two rows of extremely thickened leaves that are almost round-shaped in cross-section and sport a lengthwise groove. The delicate whitish flowers with a purple lip are 0.4 in/1 cm across and grow on a semi-erect flower spike that bears 5-12 of them. *S. mirabilis* is relatively demanding as far as air movement and sufficient sunlight are concerned. Grow it epiphytically, much like *Ascocentrum* orchids. Flowers appear on the plant between April and June and its natural habitat is in Thailand.

Schomburgkia tibicinis

Schomburgkia tibicinis

THERMOPHILIC

The genus *Schomburgkia* is impossible to overlook due to its showy flowers and robust, goldish-yellow bifoliate pseudobulbs. Its pseudobulbs are hollow, hosting friendly colonies of ants and are reputed to have once been used as primitive musical instruments by Native Americans (hence the Latin name "*tibicina*" meaning "flute player.") *S. tibicinis* has stiff succulent flowers colored in a sophisticated combination of brown-and-purple, yellow and whitish shades. The plants do not grow a lot of roots and therefore, ideally, they should be cultivated epiphytically on a somewhat large "head" of grapevine. Many growers complain that their specimens of *S. tibicinis* have refused to bloom several years in a row; this is caused mainly by insufficient direct sunlight and a repeated and frequent division of the clusters. The species flowers in late spring and comes from the countries of the Central American isthmus bordered by Mexico and Costa Rica.

Schomburgkia undulata

THERMOPHILIC

S. undulata resembles the previous species: it is also characterized by myrmecophilia (that is, coexistence with ants) —colonies of specialized ant species live in its naturally

Schomburgkia undulata

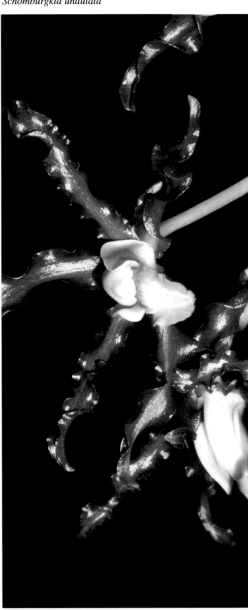

INTERMEDIATE

In the world of orchids, there are not many epiphytic species whose natural habitat is in Japan—anyone who owns a specimen of *S. japonica* should therefore be duly proud of it! Moreover, this species is a very pretty and small orchid. It is related to the genus *Aerides* (the generic name *Sedirea* was formed by reversing the spelling of the word Aerides), but outside of the flowering season, it resembles much more the orchids of the genus *Phalaenopsis*. Its extremely shortened stem bears two rows of fleshy belt-shaped leaves. There can be more than one spike growing at once, and each of them bears up to 12 relatively large showy flowers. The basic color of the flowers is white, providing a backdrop for conspicuous purple spots on the lip and the lower halves of the lateral sepals. This species can be grown either as an epiphyte, or in a flowerpot. Reduce temperature and watering somewhat in the winter. Flowers usually appear in early spring. This plant comes from southern Japan, Korea and the adjacent islands.

Sedirea japonica

hollow pseudobulbs with an "entrance" at the base. Their relationship can be described as a "mutually-beneficial co-operation": the orchid provides the ants with a dwelling and in return it receives nutrition from the ants' excrement, as well as their jealous protection from sundry pests. The apices of the plant's pseudobulbs give rise to a firm spike bearing 3-15 gorgeous brown-and-purple flowers, up to 3.2 in/8 cm in diameter. The three-lobe lip is lilac-to-white. Like the previous species, this epiphyte needs a maximum possible amount of light, especially in the fall when it grows new pseudobulbs. It blooms between May and June and comes from Colombia, Venezuela and Trinidad.

Seidenfadenia mitrata

Seidenfadenia mitrata

INTERMEDIATE-THERMOPHILIC

The only representative of the genus *Seidenfadenia* is interesting especially for the disproportion between the length of its monopodial erect stem and the partly overhanging leaves. While the length of the shoot does not exceed 4.8 in/12 cm, the fleshy leaves—semicircular in cross-section—reach

lengths of 16-36 in/40-90 (!) cm. Cultivators of this epiphytic species will also appreciate its fragrant attractive flowers growing in large numbers on a diagonally projecting spike. The flower spike is always shorter than the leaves. The flower is 0.5 in/1.2 cm across, with tepals colored in a combination of whitish, pink and purple, as with the lip, which is only a shade darker. *S. mitrata* ought to be grown epiphytically, with a maximum possible amount of diffused light and, during the vegetation period, hearty watering and fertilizer (much like *Vanda* orchids). It blooms between March and May and was discovered in Thailand and Burma.

Sigmatostalix radicans

INTERMEDIATE-THERMOPHILIC

A small orchid, of a value for miniature-collectors and growers with limited cultivation space. The species has a lot to speak for it: its proportions, as well as its vitality and the decorativeness of its fast-growing clusters. Unfortunately, the flowers are really tiny. The species is known also under the synonym *Ornithophora radicans* and is related to the genus *Oncidium*. Its small, elongated egg-shaped pseudobulbs end in pairs of grass-like leaves. The flower spikes are not very long and bear clusters of 2-10 whitish yellow flowers the size of 0.6 in/1.5 cm or smaller. The lip is yellow and the flower part in the middle, known as column, is purple. This orchid is extremely undemanding in cultivation; it will be happy if suspended on a small piece of wood or bark and provided with semi-shade and moderate watering. The flowers appear in late summer and in the fall. The species is a native of Brazil.

Sigmatostalix radicans

Sobralia crocea

Sobralia crocea

INTERMEDIATE-THERMOPHILIC

A feature shared by all *Sobralia* orchids are their long (up to 6.5 ft/2 m!), thin, gradually lignifying, reed-like stems. The leaves are lanceolate and stiff with a lengthwise waving. Beautiful flowers appear on the apices of the shoots and resemble those of *Cattleya* orchids in appearance. However, the rare and almost unknown species *S. crocea* is an exception that proves the above-mentioned "rules"! The length of its stems hardly ever exceeds 16 in/40 cm, its flowers are relatively small (1.2-2 in/3-5 cm across) and do not resem-

Sobralia sp., Ecuador – an epiphytic species

ble the shape of their large-flowered relatives. There are one or two of them growing on the ends of thickly foliaged, partially-overhanging shoots. The elongated, shiny orange tepals remain permanently half-closed and almost conceal the slightly paler tubular lip with a wavy edge. Besides its small proportions, the species *S. crocea* is also exceptional because of its epiphytic life style, which is not typical of the other *Sobralias*. In culture, it should therefore be mounted on a bark plate, propped up with a layer of moss and kept in a somewhat humid semi-shade. The plant blooms in the winter and spring and comes from Ecuador—our photo was taken in the vicinity of San Francisco de Borja, Ecuador.

Sobralia sp.

THERMOPHILIC

Sobralias, especially the terrestrial species, boast large, showy flowers with a tubular lip. However, they are extremely short-lived, which seems to be—along with their bulky proportions—a great obstacle in their becoming more popular in orchid collections. The taxonomy of the genus is still full of confusion; a genus relatively uninteresting for cultivation is probably not enticing enough for taxonomists. The species from Venezuela in the photo (*S. liliastrum*?) lives, as do most *Sobralia* orchids, as a ground-grower and is very similar in appearance to the well-known *S. leucoxantha*. Its stem is 20-40 in/50-100 cm long, which classifies the plant among the more "space-saving" plants. Its white flowers are up to 3.2 in/8 cm across and have a yellow tubular lip with a white edge. Terrestic species of the genus *Sobralia* should be cultivated in a sand-enriched humic substrate, provided with sufficient diffused light and good ventilation (that applies especially to sultry summer days). The presented terrestrial plant blooms in the winter and spring and comes from the foothills of the Venezuelan Andes, while the species in the other photo is an epiphyte and was photographed on the outskirts of the Amazonian Lowlands in Ecuador. The geographical area of the other *Sobralia* orchids is enormously large—they grow in a similar terrain all over tropical Central and South America.

Sobralia sp., Venezuela – a terrestrial species

Sophronitella violacea   □ ☹ ☺

CRYOPHILIC-INTERMEDIATE

This beautiful epiphytic miniature used to be classified as a member of the genus *Sophronitis*, but the shape of its flower lip and the presence of two lobes on the stigma earned it a place in an independent genus. Its unifoliate pseudobulbs grow on a trailing rhizome and they are 1.6 in/4 cm. The 3.2-in/8-cm-long stiff leaves are narrow and belt-shaped. One or two flowers appear on a short flower spike on the apex of a pseudobulb; their tepals are deep purple, resembling the more blunt-tipped, broader lip in coloring and length. Grow the species as you would *Sophronitis mantiqueirae*, while allowing higher average temperatures. The plant blooms in the spring and it comes from eastern Brazil.

Sophronitis cernua

nately, the 4-8 red flowers that appear on short spikes are relatively small (up to 1.2 in/3 cm across) and only partially open. The beauty of the species especially stands out when its sizeable clusters numbering dozens of pseudobulbs produce flowers on a mass scale. Cultivate this species as you would *S. mantiqueirae*, bearing in mind that *S. cernua* responds better to a slightly higher temperature. It blooms in early spring or in the fall.

Sophronitis coccinea   □   ⊗

CRYOPHILIC-INTERMEDIATE

The most splendorous and also the largest *Sophronitis* orchid, *S. coccinea* is the subject of a frenzied scramble among cultivators. Even though it possesses 2.4-in/6-cm-long extended oval leathery leaves, the species is included in the category of brilliant miniatures. The shiny red flowers growing singly on short spikes also have the largest parameters of the entire genus. Most highly-valued by cultivators are, above all, specimens of *S. coccinea* var. *grandiflora*, with flowers reaching 3.2 in/8 cm in diameter; collectors are also willing to dig deep in their pockets to obtain its yellow- or orange-flowered variations. Except for the species *S. rosea*, the entire genus is seasonally very cryophilic. Due to high cultivation demands, well-prospering specimens are a highly valued indication of exquisite cultivation work (to find out more about how to cultivate *S. coccinea*, see the following species). The species has served to create a large number of brilliant hybrids by crossbreeding with related genera *Laelia*, *Cattleya* and *Brassavola*. The plant blooms mostly between July and August, sometimes again between September and November. It comes from Brazil.

Sophronitis cernua   □   ⊗

CRYOPHILIC-INTERMEDIATE

The genus *Sophronitis* includes only 6 species that occur exclusively in Brazil. On the whole, these species are miniature orchids of a very attractive appearance including showy-colored flowers—little wonder they are highly valued and sought-after by orchid collectors! *S. cernua* is the second most frequently cultivated *Sophronitis* orchid. The basis of the plant is its trailing shoot that gives rise to egg-shaped, 1-1.2-in/2.5-3-cm-long pseudobulbs bearing a single, narrowly oval, thick, leathery leaf reaching a length of 1.2 in/3 cm. Unfortu-

Sophronitis coccinea

Sophronitis mantiqueirae

reduce their pseudobulbs, become stunted and bloom only very rarely. Under cultivation, the original dark red color of their flowers gradually turns into orange, owing to an insufficient intake of ultraviolet radiation. The roots are prone to molding, which is why the plants ought to be mounted on slabs of cork or pine bark. Some growers even succeed by placing the plants in small clay pots, always keeping the substrate sufficiently aired and well drained. Do not repot or transfer the plants too often. *S. mantiqueirae* blooms between January and February and comes from higher and very cool altitudes in Brazil.

Spathoglottis lobbii

INTERMEDIATE-THERMOPHILIC

The members of the relatively large (approximately 55 species) genus *Spathoglottis* are very much alike—most of them are terrestrial plants with small sessile pseudobulbs bearing 4-5 lengthwise waved, lanceolate leaves. Their erect flower raceme consists of a small number of very showy flowers—they are sulphur yellow with a red decoration in the center. The distinguishing feature of the whole genus is the shape of the arched flower column and the long lip (whose middle lobe is thin and intensely broadened on the end). *S. lobbii* requires cultivation in a pot containing a peat substrate enriched with clay, sand and Styrofoam. In the summer, place the plant in a fairly shady environment. *S. lobbii* blooms in the spring and comes from southwest Asia.

Spathoglottis lobbii

Sophronitis mantiqueirae   □ ☹

CRYOPHILIC-INTERMEDIATE

Another "wild dream" of all amateur orchid collectors, with enticing red and relatively large flowers! In appearance and proportions, it resembles *S. coccinea*, differing from it in the absence of red stripes on the leaves, a dissimilar time-span of flowering and a stronger cryophilia. Attempts to cultivate any *Sophronitis* orchids usually fail owing to the extreme ecological requirements of the plants. They need cool fresh air and plenty of light. Our summer months are the coolest ones in the plants' natural habitat—temperatures often drop to the freezing point there at that time of year. Therefore, plants in collections sometimes tend to gradually

Spathoglottis plicata   ☺

INTERMEDIATE-THERMOPHILIC

S. plicata is the most frequently cultivated *Spathoglottis* orchid, not only in collections but also in gardens and parks in the tropical regions around the world. Its popularity has gone so far that the plants transported from its original Asian habitat have begun to grow in natural habitats in Hawaii and southern Florida. The species re-sembles the previous one in the appearance of its green parts. Its flower scape overtops the leaves and is quite densely covered with 5-25 flowers that are 1.2 in/3 cm in diameter. The species is variable as to the color of its tepals—they can be white, pink or purple. The narrow lip is broadened on the end and yellow in the middle. *S. plicata* should be cultivated in the same way as the previous species. The plants bloom irregularly, mostly in the fall or spring, and they are native to the Philippines, Taiwan, Malayan Peninsula, Indonesia and New Guinea.

Stanhopea candida

Stanhopea candida

INTERMEDIATE-THERMOPHILIC

Anyone who has ever seen a *Stanhopea* orchid in bloom will find it hard to forget it! Orchids of this genus do not boast a very showy morphology of their green parts; all the more surprising it is to later see their often gigantic and always bizarre-looking fleshy flowers. The egg-shaped pseudobulbs of the species *S. candida* are slightly elongated into a pointed tip and they bear a single, up-to-12-in/30-cm long, stiff and lengthwise-waved elliptic leaf. The flower spike grows downward, measures only 3.2-4 in/8-10 cm and bears 1-3 pure white, 2.4-in/6-cm-across flowers with a bizarre-shaped greenish lip. The morphology of the flower is described under *Stanhopea* sp. on p. 246, the cultivation rules are the same as with *S. martiana*. Somewhat out of the ordinary, *S. candida* blooms in the spring. It comes from the lower altitudes of Bolivia, Colombia and Venezuela.

Stanhopea costaricensis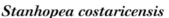

INTERMEDIATE-THERMOPHILIC

One of the most warmth-loving representatives of the whole genus. Its appearance is very much in accordance with the generic "paradigm," except the flowers are very beautiful and large—up to 4.8 in/12 cm in diameter. In addition to that,

Stanhopea costaricensis

there are up to six of them opening simultaneously on the 10 in/25-cm-long downward-pointing spike. Their coloring is unconventional: brown-and-red spots or circles stand out against a yellow backdrop on all the tepals. Two dark spots accentuate the middle part of the flower. Even though this orchid is easy to cultivate, it is still rare in collections. The flowering season opens in the spring and early summer. *S. costaricensis* was discovered in Costa Rica, as the species name suggests, but also in Panama and Nicaragua.

Stanhopea embreei ▣ ☺

INTERMEDIATE-THERMOPHILIC

After it was discovered, this plant was taken for the Mexican species *S. hernandezii* and it wasn't until later that it received its own name. It resembles other *Stanhopeas* in appearance. Its beautiful flowers with greenish-to-cream-white tepals are up to 4 in/10 cm across and grow in a sparse suspended inflorescence bearing 2-4 of them. The lip has a complicated morphology; it is whitish with delicate purple dotting on the tips and a dark orange base sporting two pronounced dark spots. Grow it in the same way as *S. martiana*. The flowers appear on the plant between late spring and summer. Its natural habitat is in Ecuador, in elevations between 1,640-3,300 ft/500 and 1,000 m.

Stanhopea embreei

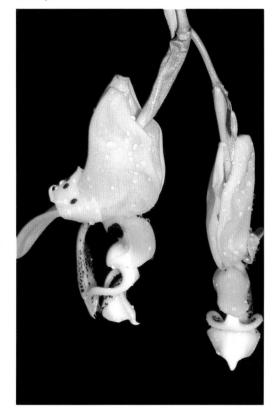

Stanhopea florida ▣ ■ ☺

INTERMEDIATE-THERMOPHILIC

Consider yourself lucky to come across a *Stanhopea* orchid in bloom in the tropical wild, as these plants are rare and their flowers extremely short-lived; even worldly field biologists count these encounters on one hand. The author of this book had one of these lucky days near the town of Baeza in the foothills of the Ecuadorian Andes. *S. florida* is a brilliant multi-flowered orchid with 2.4-2.8-in/6-7-cm-large, whitish, purple-spotted flowers. It is slightly more humid-loving than other *Stanhopeas*, otherwise the cultivation requirements are the same as for the whole genus. The plant blooms in January and February and, besides Ecuador, also inhabits Peru.

Stanhopea florida

Stanhopea jenischiana   ▣ ☺

INTERMEDIATE-THERMOPHILIC

This orchid is closely related to the species *S. oculata* and *S. wardii* — the appearance of its green parts is almost identical; slight differences can be observed in the morphology of its flowers. Cultivation rules are the same as those that apply to *S. martiana*. The plant blooms in the fall and is native to Ecuador, Venezuela, Colombia and Panama.

Stanhopea martiana   ▣ ☺

INTERMEDIATE-THERMOPHILIC

The appearance of *S. martiana's* green parts is similar to those of the other members of the genus *Stanhopea*.

Stanhopea martiana

A suspended flower scape bears two or three yellowish flowers that are up to 5.6 in/14 cm in diameter. Their greatest decoration consists of sparse purple spots and the same coloring of the bases of the tepals and the lip. The cultivation rules are almost the same for any *Stanhopea*. Potential admirers of these plants should pay careful attention to the location of the plants in a collection, to begin with: the robust, spindle-shaped foundations of future inflorescences are famous for their positive geotropism. Cultivators must take this quality into account. If you do not grow *Stanhopeas* epiphytically on bare branches or vertical slabs of bark, should plant them in spacious and relatively shallow epiphytic baskets. The substrate ought to be loose enough to allow the flower shoots to grow through it unharmed (a mixture of small pieces of pine bark, strips of peat moss, Styrofoam and similar ingredients is suitable). Cultivation in pots is absolutely not recommended. All *Stanhopea* orchids require a semi-shady and well-ventilated environment, regular watering and, when new pseudobulbs are forming, a good amount of fertilizer. Reduce watering during stagnation. The species *S. martiana* blooms in late summer and comes from Mexico.

Stanhopea oculata   ▣ ☺

INTERMEDIATE-THERMOPHILIC

Together with *S. tigrina*, *S. oculata* is the longest-cultivated species—both orchids were already among the "obligatory inventory" of any palm greenhouse in the pioneer times of gardening. The disadvantages of this species are the same as those of other *Stanhopeas*: a relative "bulkiness" of its medium-sized clusters, and a short durability of the flowers. *S. oculata* grows an

244

Stanhopea oculata

Stanhopea platyceras

Stanhopea saccata

INTERMEDIATE-THERMOPHILIC

A robust member of the genus, with bizarre twisted lateral protuberances on a whitish yellow lip. Its proportions make this plant rather unsuitable for amateur cultivators' small greenhouses. The sparsely flowered, spreading inflorescences bear occasionally 1, but more often 2-4 flowers with yellow tepals and a whitish lip. The tip of the lip is adorned with delicate dots. Grow this species, as you would *S. martiana*. The plant blooms in the summer and is still quite widespread in the humid rainforests of the northern part of South America including Mexico.

Stanhopea saccata

overhanging inflorescence reaching a length of up to 14 in/35 cm and consisting of 4-10 sparsely distributed flowers. The flowers are whitish with a tinge of yellow and delicate purple dots. The base of the lip is decorated with two showy brown-and-red spots. Grow this plant as you would the previous species. The flowers can be expected between June and September. The species is native to the countries of continental Central America—an area bordered by Mexico and Honduras, as well as to Colombia and Venezuela.

Stanhopea platyceras

INTERMEDIATE-THERMOPHILIC

This representative of the *Stanhopea* genus is still relatively rare in collections. Its proportions are rather large. The appearance of the pseudobulbs and leaves is the same as that of the related species. Between 3-6 waxy, tender blossoms grow on a 8-10-in/20-25-cm-long suspended inflorescence. Grow this species epiphytically or in a "sparse" wooden basket, much like *S. martiana*. The flowers appear in the fall. The plant's natural habitat is in the foothills of the Colombian Andes.

Stanhopea sp., Ecuador

Stanhopea tigrina

ters of unifoliate, dark-green pseudobulbs. In late summer, their bases give rise to a bizarre yellow-and-green sack-like shape covered with brown spots—a foundation of the amazing future inflorescence, as yet "unwrapped". And then comes the big moment: the opening of the fantastic, almost spooky-looking flowers, up to 6.4 in/16 cm in diameter. The basic color of the whole flower is pale yellow that provides a good background for impressive-looking and often coalescent brown-and-red spots. The flower racemes bearing 2-4 flowers are, in proportion to the other body parts, almost unnaturally large and the plant sometimes finds it hard to sustain all of its flowers—in fact, some of them die right before opening. *S. tigrina* should be grown in the same style as other *Stanhopeas*. The flowers can be expected at the peak of the summer. The species comes from Mexico.

Stanhopea wardii

Stanhopea sp. ◼ ☺

INTERMEDIATE-THERMOPHILIC

The pseudobulbs of this rarely cultivated unclassified orchid (possibly an atypical variety of the species *S. wardii*) are a characteristic feature of the genus—i.e., egg-shaped with a slightly elongated tip. They bear single, lengthwise extended elliptic leaves with multiple lengthwise waving that reach lengths of 14 in/35 cm. The inflorescence consists of 2-5 succulent yellowish white flowers with a yellow lip and sparse dark dots. All the flower parts are fleshy. The lip has a complex morphology; Expert botanists distinguish three parts on the lip: *hypochile*, *mezochile* and *epichile*. For cultivation, follow the instructions for *S. martiana*. The plant blooms in late summer and occasionally also in early spring; it comes from Ecuador and Colombia.

Stanhopea tigrina ◼ ◼ ☺

INTERMEDIATE-THERMOPHILIC

S. tigrina is the largest and best known of all *Stanhopea* orchids. It is also the most commonly included in orchid collections—one look at its sensational flowers will tell you why. Just like the other species, this plant forms sessile clus-

Stanhopea wardii

INTERMEDIATE-THERMOPHILIC

S. wardii is an unjustly neglected species with relatively small proportions when not in bloom. The flowers are 5.6 in/14 cm across or smaller, yellow-and-orange, covered with red dots. The overhanging inflorescence bears up to 10 of them. The base of the lip is embellished with two showy dark spots. The cultivation demands of this species are the same as those of other *Stanhopeas*. As its pseudobulbs are relatively small, you can grow it in an epiphytic basket or openly on a branch. It blooms in late summer, but only very irregularly in collections—usually not until the cluster has achieved certain proportions. The plants should therefore not be divided too often. The species is known to grow throughout Central America between Mexico and Panama.

Stelis

INTERMEDIATE-THERMOPHILIC

The genus *Stelis* is quite large—it contains about 270 species! But since these orchids are of an uninteresting appearance with inconspicuous flowers, few people know or grow them. They somewhat resemble orchids from the closely related genera *Pleurothalis* or *Masdevallia* in appearance. Their trailing rhizome gives rise to thin, stiff unifoliate shoots ended with spatulate or inverted lanceolate leaves. The extended flower spikes bear numerous flowers, usually arranged in two rows; the sepals on the

flowers form a triangular arrangement and their bottom parts are grown together. In most species, the sepals are whitish; it is much rarer for the sepals of a *Stelis* orchid to be colored in a different and more attractive way. The other flower parts are plain looking and small. The plants can be grown either epiphytically or in pots, following the instructions that apply to the aforementioned related genera. The genus *Stelis* inhabits the tropical regions of the whole American continent; the plants in the photo come from the Pululahua Crater, Ecuador.

Stelis sp., Ecuador

Taeniophyllum obtusum   □ ☺

INTERMEDIATE-THERMOPHILIC

This plant is an example of a leafless orchid with an extremely reduced stem (0.4 in/1 cm at the most!) and flattened assimilating roots. But in contrast to the showy-flowered genera *Chiloschista* and *Polyrrhiza*, it forms only minuscule, 0.12-0.2-in/3-5-mm-across, whitish or yellowish flowers that appear singly or in short sparse racemes. The proportions of the flower-producing "root rosettes" are usually very small—2-4 in/5-10 cm across. These small plants are sensitive to excessive dryness and other cultivation errors, which is why they are only recommended to staunch admirers of orchid curiosities for cultivation. The cultivation instructions to follow are mentioned under *Polyrrhiza funalis*. The plant blooms irregularly (mainly in the fall) and comes from Malaysia, Thailand, Cambodia and Indonesia.

Stenoglottis longifolia   ⊡ ▣ ☺

CRYOPHILIC-INTERMEDIATE

This terrestrial orchid, very decorative when in bloom, is not cultivated very often. Every year, its succulent roots give rise to rosettes of spotty, 3.2-4.8-in/8-12-cm-long leaves, and a flower spike reaching a length of up to 14 in/35 cm and bearing a lot (30-90) of tiny pinkish flowers with a forked lip. To cultivate this orchid, plant it in pots with an airy humic substrate. After the flowers fade, the above-ground body parts die, which is why the plant should be wintered in a cool and dry environment. *S. longifolia* blooms between August and October and is native to the Natalu semi-deserts of South Africa.

Tainia viridifusca   ▣ ☺

INTERMEDIATE-THERMOPHILIC

A representative of a large Asian genus of terrestrial or epiphytic orchids. Its trailing rhizome gives rise to unifoliate cylindrical pseudobulbs. The leaves are narrow and extremely long; the tall, erect inflorescence does not develop until they fall off. The flower raceme of *T. viridifusca* numbers up to 30 flowers, 1.4 in/3.5 cm in diame-

ter; the tepals are brownish and twisted lengthways a little. The whitish lip is inconspicuous and short. The
species should be cultivated in pots in a permeable epiphytic mix (enriched with humic complement) and provided with humid, warm semi-shade during vegetation.
After the leaves are shed, cease watering completely and
reduce temperature. Flowers appear in January. The plant
is native to Thailand.

Thunia alba   ☺

CRYOPHILIC-INTERMEDIATE

Orchids of the genus *Thunia* are characterized by very
long fleshy reed-like stems bearing two rows of foliage.
They grow from the ground and can only occasionally
climb on trees. Between 2-8 showy flowers appear on
the apical inflorescence. *T. alba* has pure white large
flowers; their tubular lip is yellow on the inside and resembles *Cattleya* orchids in its appearance and fimbriated edges. Its bulky proportions make this species
rather undesirable for cultivation. The plants require
a heavier-than-average soil substrate and a substantial
dry period (during which their aboveground body parts
die completely). *T. alba* blooms in the summer and
comes from India.

Tainia viridifusca

Thunia alba

Ticoglossum krameri

Tolumnia variegata

Ticoglossum krameri

CRYOPHILIC-INTERMEDIATE

The pseudobulbs of this species are oval, 2 in/5 cm long and bear a single, 8-in/20-cm-long leaf. The erect flower spike is only 8 in/20 cm tall with 2-3 sparsely distributed flowers. The elliptic tepals are pure white, the lip is pinkish-to-white. *T. krameri* should be grown epiphytically or in a suspended flower pot placed in a well-ventilated, shady and rather cool environment. On hot summer days, provide it with frequent misting and pour water on the greenhouse floor; alternatively, you can hang the plant in a treetop in your garden. In the winter, after the flowers fade, treat the plant to a short period of dryness. *T. krameri* blooms between the fall and spring and is widespread in Central America (including Panama, Costa Rica and Nicaragua).

Tolumnia

THERMOPHILIC

The genus *Tomunia* is extremely well known, especially the species *Tolumnia variegata*—the only problem being that it is known by the scientifically invalid name *Oncidium variegatum*. From *Oncidium* orchids, however, *Tolumnias* differ in the morphology of their green parts, some details in the flower morphology, as well as the number of chromosomes. In a flowerless state, the two genera are very much alike, and they are difficult to classify since they readily crossbreed (it was above all

Tolumnia scandens

Tolumnia sp., Cuba

human intervention that caused their unwanted approximation) in what is left of their natural habitat. Easy hybridization has produced many beautiful hybrids that are now more widespread in collections than the original species, and they are also more willing to bloom. Members of this genus (a total of about 30) form small, almost dwarfed pseudobulbs or short stems bearing fan-shaped leaf rosettes. The leaves with serrated edges and sharp-pointed tips have adapted to life in dry hot stations—they are very firm and tough. The showy flowers are colored in a combination of yellow, brown, red and white and they grow on wiry-stiff, often branched multi-flowered spikes. The lip dwarfs the other tepals by its proportions and it is often marked by a very complex, species-specific morphology. Grow these plants as epiphytes for best results; a potted culture is also possible but the plants tend to bloom less eagerly. During vegetation, it is necessary to ensure a maximum possible amount of sunlight, warmth and moving air—for instance, by summering the plant in the garden. During the winter stagnation, reduce temperature somewhat and cut down radically on misting that should be scanty in other times of the year. The plants bloom irregularly and come from the Caribbean islands.

Trias disciflora

Trias oblonga

Trias disciflora   □ ☺ ☺

INTERMEDIATE-THERMOPHILIC

The miniature curiosities of the genus *Trias* will captivate your attention much more with the morphology of their bodies than with their flowers; nevertheless, they still remain a target of interest for lovers of small epiphytic orchid curiosities. These mainly epiphytic plants form large dense nets of sessile, ball-shaped, 0.8-in/2-cm-across, vividly green pseudobulbs with a single elliptical succulent leaf. The flowers of *T. disciflora* are some of the largest and showiest in the whole genus. They are up to 0.8 in/2 cm in diameter and their light red basic color is densely covered with purple spots. The lip is atypically enlarged and catches the eye with its darker color and more delicate punctuation. In cultivation, follow the instructions given for the following species. The flowers appear early in the spring; the plant comes from Laos and Thailand.

Trias oblonga   □ ☺ ☺

INTERMEDIATE-THERMOPHILIC

The body morphology of this species gives away its genus. Its flattened pseudobulbs are barely 0.6 in/1.5 cm long and bear only a little longer, almost ball-shaped leaf. The flowers are species-specific: they have a trio (hence the Latin generic name) of well-developed green-and-yellow sepals. The other flower parts are intensely reduced. Grow the plant epiphytically, adding a little peat moss to the roots when mounting the plant on a support. Place the suspended supports in semi-shade and ensure above-average air humidity. During the winter stagnation, water the plant more sparingly. *T. oblonga* blooms in early spring and comes from Thailand and Laos.

Trichocentrum pulchrum

INTERMEDIATE-THERMOPHILIC

The entire genus *Trichocentrum* is very significant for cultivation and all of its 20 described species are considered beautiful orchids—a fact that is proven by the *Trichocentrum pulchrum*

Latin name of the species in question—*T. pulchrum* (i.e., "pulchritudinous, comely"). Its pseudobulbs are miniscule to the point of being nearly invisible among the elongated, fleshy leaves reaching lengths of 3.6 in/ 9 cm and sporting a round tip. Single white flowers grow on shorter spikes and are yellow on the bases of their lips. All the other tepals are decorated with length-wise stripes of delicate red dots. This orchid should be cultivated in the same way as the following species. It blooms in the summer (July, August) and is native to Venezuela, Colombia, Ecuador and Peru.

Trichocentrum tigrinum   · ☺

INTERMEDIATE-THERMOPHILIC

This species is the best known of all *Trichocentrum* or-chids. It resembles *T. pulchrum* in appearance, but its leaves are speckled with red dots. Its whitish tepals are thickly covered with red-and-brown spots. Their dark color provides a stark contrast to the broad lip that is white

Trichocentrum tigrinum

on the end and purple-and-red turning into yellow on the base. The whole genus is not only very attractive but also easy to cultivate. Grow the plants on a piece of bark or in a pot located in a moderately shaded, rather humid and well ventilated environment. As the plants do not stagnate in the winter, they still require watering—only slightly limited at this time; but beware of permanent excessive dampness of the substrate in the pot! *T. tigrinum* blooms between July and October and is native to Ecuador.

Trichoceros parviflora   □ · ☺

INTERMEDIATE

A representative of a small genus (5 species) of epiphytic or lithophytic orchids. Collectors seek these plants mainly because of their small proportions and intriguing body morphology. Single, almost ball-shaped pseudobulbs grow on long stoloniferous protuberances. Each pseudo-bulb is belted with two or more stiff leaves at the base. Flowers grow on sparse overhanging inflorescences from the axils of the leaves and they are quite attractive. *T. parv-iflora* has 1-in/2.5-cm-long or smaller yellow flowers with a red, intensely hairy base of the lip. The likewise hairy column in the middle of the flower bears two blunt horny protuberances (hence the generic name—"*tricho*" means "hairy", "*ceros*" means "horn"). Creating a culture for the plant is not very difficult but the lithophytic species gen-erally bloom very slowly and unwillingly under epiphytic cultivation. The plant blooms in early spring and comes from medium elevations of the South American Andes.

Trichoceros parviflora

Trichopilia fragrans

Trichopilia laxa

Trichopilia fragrans ▫ ◾ ☺

INTERMEDIATE

The pure white flower lips of this genus are often almost transparent; unfortunately, their beauty quickly passes—the flowers fade after only 2-3 days. Luckily, there are up to 2-3 usually two-flowered (rarely multiflowered) spikes growing successively out of the bases of the densely crowded pseudobulbs, which are elongated, flat, unifoliate and reach lengths of 4.8 in/12 cm. *T. fragrans* is an epiphyte with similar cultivation requirements as *T. marginata*. The plant blooms in late

fall and is widespread over a vast area including the West Indies, Venezuela, Colombia and Bolivia. The plant in the photo was found in the foothills of the Andes in the vicinity of Baeza, Ecuador.

Trichopilia laxa ▫ ◾ ☺

INTERMEDIATE

The flowers of *Trichopilia* orchids are characterized by a typically shaped, large and showy flower lip with a folded base. Unfortunately, the beautiful and relatively

Trichopilia marginata

Trichopilia sp., Venezuela

more frequently. *T. marginata* blooms between April and May and its natural habitat is Central America, an area bordered by Guatemala and Colombia.

Trichopilia sp. ▫ ◼ ☺

INTERMEDIATE

The taxonomy of the genus *Trichopilia* is full of uncertainties and confusion. Many plants discovered in the wild have been waiting to be named for years; many species are mistaken for others and some were described on the basis of a single specimen that was never found again. This is also the case of the unnamed Venezuelan and Ecuadorian orchid in the photo. Those who would like to grow these plants will not encounter any difficulties, except in actually acquiring them. The entire genus *Trichopilia* is not very demanding of light or air movement, which even makes it suitable for small amateur glass cases and greenhouses.

Trigonidium egertonianum ◼ ☺

INTERMEDIATE-THERMOPHILIC

Bizarre-shaped flowers— a great (but unfortunately the only) asset of orchids belonging in this genus, which contains a small number of bulky species (about 12). *T. egertonianum* has small (only 0.8 in/2 cm long or smaller) pseudobulbs, ended with thin leaves reaching lengths of 14 in/35 cm. Its small (0.8 in/2 cm across), cup-shaped flowers grow singly on thin scapes. The tepals are brown-and-white with lengthwise brown stripes and they completely conceal the tiny lip. Two conspicuous dark spots in the upper corners of the petals resemble a pair of eyes. In cultivation, this species requires epiphytic handling. The plant blooms in early spring but usually without much regularity. Grow it in a well-ventilated environment with a higher-than-average amount of light and humidity. It comes from Mexico and Colombia.

Trigonidium egertonianum

large flowers are quite short-lived. The species *T. laxa* has flattened oval pseudobulbs reaching lengths of 2.8 in/7 cm. Some 4-8 half-open flowers grow on an overhanging spike. They have pinkish tepals and a yellow-and-white lip. In cultivation, follow the instructions given for *T. marginata*. This species blooms in the spring and comes from Colombia and Venezuela.

Trichopilia marginata ▫ ◼ ☺

INTERMEDIATE

A beautiful species, also known by the name *T. coccinea*. It looks much like *T. laxa*, except its flowers are much larger (up to 4.8 in/12 cm across). The flower tepals, including the tubular lip, are whitish-pink on the outside and crimson red with a white edge (hence the Latin species name) on the inside. This plant can be cultivated epiphytically, but it will do better in a suspended flowerpot filled with a permeable epiphytic mix. Plants mounted on supports must be misted

Trudelia pumila

In proportion to them, the whitish flowers, 3-5 of which appear on each shortened spike, are unusually large—up to 2.4 in/6 cm in diameter. The stripes on the lip range in color between blood red and red-and-brown. The species' original habitat is in higher altitudes, and it can therefore be cultivated in cooler environment without any worries. Its requirements for light are, however, as high as those of the former "home" genus. *T. pumila* comes from the Himalayas and blooms in a time unfavorable for cultivators—between June and August.

Tuberolabium cotoense

INTERMEDIATE-THERMOPHILIC

A small-sized, darling orchid with flowers that smell like coconut. Until 1992 it was classified as a member of the genus *Saccolabium*. It has a shortened stem foliaged with two rows of stiff belt-shaped leaves reaching lengths of up to 4 in/10 cm. The species' small, durable flowers grow on a short, sparse inflorescence and are whitish with a purple marking on the lip. Grow it epiphytically in a somewhat humid semi-shade. The species blooms in the spring and fall and comes from the Philippines and Taiwan.

Trudelia pumila

CRYOPHILIC-INTERMEDIATE

Up until 1988, this orchid was classified by botanists as a *Vanda*; when it was later transferred into a newly-established genus, it was because of the shape and the different anatomy of its flowers. Its leaves are barely 4.8 in/12 cm long.

Tuberolabium cotoense

Vanda – Coerulea hybrid ▣ ■ ☺

INTERMEDIATE

A parent of the hybrid in the photo—the species *V. coerulea* — looks very alike and is one of the few blue-blossomed botanical orchids in the world. This quality has been used extensively in creating both interspecies and intergeneric hybrids. The parent plant resembles the following species in appearance, except that it is a little smaller. Its sky-blue flowers (5-15) with a darker, hairnet-like venation are up to 4 in/10 cm across and grow on an erect spike reaching a length of up to 16 in/40 cm. Grow it in baskets or large pots filled with smallish pieces of bark or with a coarse epiphytic substrate. This orchid must be provided with a relatively cool air and a maximum possible amount of light. Even with the best cultivation effort, the stems develop extremely slowly and the flowers appear very rarely and irregularly. This plant comes from Ásám, Burma and Thailand.

Vanda coerulescens ▣ ■ ☺

INTERMEDIATE

Members of the well-known genus *Vanda* that is highly significant in cultivation, are the most typical and the best-known representatives of monopodial orchids. Their interspecies and intergeneric hybrids are grown on a mass scale for cut flowers in orchid farms in the tropics (Hawaii, southwest Asia). All *Vanda* hybrids bloom unwillingly and irregularly owing to insufficient sunlight in the winter. The leaves of *V. coerulescens* are up to 12 in/30 cm long; the stem tends to be 16 in/40 cm long or even longer. Lilac blue blossoms are 1.2-1.6 in/3-4 cm across and their lip is adorned with purple and blue markings. In cultivation, this species has the same requirements as the previous one. It blooms between March and May and comes from Burma, Thailand, northeastern India and southern China.

Vanda coerulescens

Vanda tricolor var. *suavis* ■ ☺ ☺

INTERMEDIATE

A relatively undemanding and yet very handsome species. Unfortunately, it is only suitable for big collection greenhouses, as its monopodial stem covered with two rows of 12-18-in/30-45-cm-long leaves reaches a length of 4.9 ft/150 cm! Its overhanging inflorescence consists of 5-10 three-colored (see the species name), 2-2.4-in/5-6-cm-across fragrant flowers. On a typical specimen, the propeller-shaped tepals are white on the outside and yellowish with brown spots on the inside. The var. *suavis* in the photo has narrower tepals that are also whitish on the inside. In both cases, the lip is pink-and-purple. This species has the same cultivation requirements as other intermediate *Vandas*. It blooms in the winter and comes from Java and Laos.

Vanda tricolor var. *suavis*

Vandopsis lissochiloides ▣ ■ ☺ ☺

INTERMEDIATE-THERMOPHILIC

Representatives of this small genus (a total of 12 species) resemble the orchids from the genera *Vanda* and, especially, *Arachnis*. From the latter genus, *Vandopsis* orchids differ in the absence of a spur on the lower part of their lip. Their beautiful durable flowers endow these orchids with a great potential for both cultivation and breeding, but so far they are still rare in cultivation. The spike of *V. lissochiloides* reaches a length of over 3.3 ft/1 m and is foliaged with thin leaves reaching lengths of up to 20 in/50 cm. The inflorescence is erect and bears 10-20 blossoms that are 2.4-2.8 in/6-7 cm in diameter. The yellow tepals are thickly covered with brown-and-red spots and they are purple on the outside; the small lip has a purple tip. This species' cultivation requirements are the same as

those of the more warmth-loving *Vanda* orchids. Its natural habitat has not yet been precisely determined—findings have been reported from the Philippines, New Guinea (see photo), the Moluccas and also Thailand.

Vanilla aphyllum

INTERMEDIATE-THERMOPHILIC

This plant is closely related to the only utility orchid of the world—*V. planifolia*—whose unripe fermented ovaries are used in the food processing industry (genuine "vanilla sugar") and the cosmetic industry. The species *V. aphyllum* is not very significant in cultivation and only rarely grown as a curiosity in botanical gardens. An epiphytic or terrestrial species, *V. aphyllum* creates many-feet-long, segmented and very firm liana-like stems covered with small, elongated egg-shaped leaves. The stems produce long, strong roots from every knot. And it is the knots again that later (provided that the stems are well matured and exposed to sufficient light) give rise to green-and-yellow flowers growing on inflorescences bearing 1-4 of them. The reddish flower lip is tubular

with a fimbriated edge. *V. aphyllum* has some special cultivation requirements: first, place the plants in broad bowls filled with an epiphytic substrate; then direct the climbing shoots to other pots, flowerbeds, wooden supports or suspend them in the greenhouse. The plants need a lot of warmth and a maximum possible amount of sunshine. They bloom only when really well grown, between October and November. The species is native to the Malayan Peninsula (the photo was taken in Thailand).

Warmingia eugenii

Xylobium elongatum

Warmingia eugenii

INTERMEDIATE-THERMOPHILIC

This genus includes only two small species, close relatives of *Macradenia* and *Notylia* orchids. They are suitable mainly for amateur collections as unusual-blossoming curiosities. The better-known species of the two—*W. eugenii*—forms tiny pseudobulbs reaching a length of only 0.8 in/2 cm and bearing a single, 4-in/10-cm-long elongated oval leaf. The inflorescence is an overhanging raceme bearing up to 30 flowers the size of 0.8 in/2 cm or smaller. All tepals are snow-white, transparent, with fimbriated edges. *W. eugenii* is classified among shade-loving epiphytes and that is how it should be cultivated. The flowers appear in the fall. The plant comes from forests in eastern Brazil.

Xylobium elongatum

INTERMEDIATE

Representatives of this small (30 species) genus are anything but much-desired gems of orchid collections. Admittedly, their flowers resemble those of *Lycaste*

Xylobium sp., Ecuador

Zygopetalum mackaii

orchids in morphology and shape, but they are no match for them in color and size. The species *X. elongatum* is a little exception—its greenish and relatively large flowers sport a showy red-dotted tongue-shaped lip. A sparse, short, overhanging flower raceme grows (as with all the other *Xylobium* orchids) from the base of the 2-3.2-in/5-8-cm-long pseudobulbs that are foliaged at the top. *X. elongatum* is an epiphytic, occasionally also terrestrial species that should be grown in a suspended flower pot for best results. The plants have no special requirements. In the winter, remember to reduce temperature and watering a little. The species comes from the Colombian and Ecuadorian Andes.

Xylobium sp. ▣ ☺

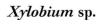

INTERMEDIATE

In contrast to the previous species, this one is a highly typical (and thus rather plain-looking) representative of the genus. Its pseudobulbs are robust, up to 3.2 in/8 cm tall, ended with one lanceolate, lengthwise-waved leaf reaching a length of 10 in/25 cm. The proportions of the plant are in stark contrast to the minuscule proportions of the tiny (0.4-0.8 in/1-2 cm across) red-and-white blossoms, densely crowded on an inflorescence bearing 5-8 of them. This plant blooms in the fall and comes from the foothills of the Ecuadorian Andes.

Zygopetalum mackaii ▣ ☺

CRYOPHILIC-INTERMEDIATE

If someone decided to put together a primer for or-

chid cultivation novices, she or he should by all means include *Z. mackaii*—so great is the renown and so widespread is the cultivation of this orchid. In recent years, it has even been offered on a mass-scale in supermarkets, including its pedigree variety. Considering the avalanche of rival hybrid orchids for sale, this is irrevocable proof of the beauty of its flowers. They are up to 3.2 in/8 cm across with a whitish lip adorned with purple venation. The lip is elegantly complemented by the quality brown-spotted green of the other tepals. The flower scape bears up to 8 flowers and reaches a length of 28 in/70 cm, which makes the species suitable (and it is indeed sometimes grown) for cut flowers. Cultivation requirements are similar to those of cryophilic *Cymbidia*, with an extra period of rest in the summer. During that time, deny the plant any watering for 8 weeks. *Z. mackaii* blooms in the fall and comes from mountain regions in Brazil.

Terrestrial Orchids of the Temperate Zone

In the minds of most inhabitants of the Temperate Zone in Europe, Asia and North America, orchids are associated with distant exotic countries. Very few people know that the natural habitat of these plants is not limited to the permanently warm tropical regions and that they even spread from those regions to extremely cool corners of the globe.

The fact of the matter is that orchids are virtually omnipresent on the earth's terra firma, with the exception of deserts and permanently glaciated arctic regions. Naturally, the rate of occurrence of *Orchidaceae* culminates in the tropics—the natural habitat of 90% of a total of 25,000 orchid species including not only the dominant epiphytic representatives of the family, but also a smaller number of ground-growers (known as terrestrial orchids). Admittedly, the number of species growing in an area rapidly decreases the further your travel from the equator; still, in the Temperate Zone of both the Northern and Southern Hemisphere, you can find hundreds of them—all growing in the "classic" style, that is, in the ground.

This chapter provides an introduction into orchids of the Temperate Zone of the Northern Hemisphere, with a focus on the European species. Compared to tropical species, terrestrial orchids may seem a somewhat plain poor relative at first glance, appearing like ordinary meadow herbs. But a closer look reveals their unusual, unique beauty. In addition, these are plants with very interesting and often almost incredible qualities and level of adaptiveness (for details, see the description of the individual species and genera).

The title of this chapter in itself is not quite precise— some of the orchids introduced here do not occur exclusively in the Temperate Zone but the area of their natural habitat stretches into the outskirts of subtropical regions or, in the opposite direction, beyond the Arctic Circle. In any case, they are known to grow in regions where temperatures drop so low in winters of various lengths that the growth of common vascular plants is ruled out. Consequently, these mostly perennial herbs (as well as other plant species) had to come up with an entirely different survival strategy than that used by the tropical epiphytic representatives of *Orchidaceae*. They settled down in a location where they have a chance to survive the harshest times of the year—in the ground.

That means that they do not grow continuously throughout the year, but only seasonally, while spending part of the year retracted in their underground organs—root bulbs or rhizomes. Pseudobulbs—a characteristic feature of most tropical orchids—are featured by orchids of the Temperate Zone only in

very exceptional cases (in genera such as *Malaxis* and *Hammarbya*). While the shoots of tropical orchids assume various forms (such as climbing, trailing, creeping, segmented), in terrestrial orchids they are always only erect with a spike or raceme inflorescence bearing various numbers of flowers. The flowers are, with a few exceptions, relatively small, but their morphology follows the same convention as the other *Orchidaceae*.

In contrast to the previous chapter, the following descriptions of individual orchid representatives will almost entirely omit cultivation instructions and the respective graphic symbols (including a specification of their temperature requirements, which are very similar in most species). The reason is simple: although some terrestrial *Orchidaceae* are very attractive in appearance, most of them cannot be replanted, let alone successfully cultivated on a long-term basis in artificial conditions.

This is caused by the extremely complicated and equilibrated ecological needs of terrestrial orchids. An overwhelming majority of these plants are firmly

Orchis purpurea, Czech Republic

Left: *Barlia robertiana*, Cyprus

fixed in mycorrhiza throughout their lives, mycorrhiza standing for a coexistence of their roots with the filaments of the "friendly" fungi that provide them with nutrition (for details see "A Mysterious Symbiosis" in the chapter "Characterization of Orchids").

Dependency on fungi is, especially for mature plants, much stronger than with tropical orchids. The slightest intervention into the chemistry of the environment close to or even rather distant from the terrestrial orchids' underground organs will cause a rapid and irreversible necrosis of the highly sensitive fungi and, subsequently, of the plants.

Of course, there are exceptions even to this rule: some mature plants are able to rely solely on their own assimilation apparatus; however, their cultivation is made impossible mainly by the strict legislative conservation measures practiced in many of the countries where these plants occur. Mycorrhiza and the overall sensitivity of terrestrial orchids is behind their rapid, and in many instances completely irreversible, fall into extinction that has taken place over the last 100 years. Especially in Europe—a region subject to heavy ecological exploitation and reshaping by the human hand—the once "global" natural habitat of some orchid species has been reduced to isolated, fragmented patches of land inhabited by highly enfeebled populations of a small number of specimens. Orchids had to give way to various processes: extending the area of arable land, amelioration, fertilization, acid rain, air pollution and general environmental pollution.

Furthermore, terrestrial orchids of the Temperate Zone cannot be propagated by seeds in artificial conditions—not even by aseptic sowing in vitro (if this is managed in spite of the low odds, transposing the acquired seedlings back into the natural environment is highly unprofitable and virtually impossible). This fact led practically all European countries to adopt severe measures for the conservation of their orchid species. Should anybody choose to exploit orchid bulbs for drug-using purposes, transplant them from what remains of their natural habitat, or even trade in them, they will be severely punished and their behavior must be condemned as an immoral and incredible act of barbarism.

The below-mentioned species cannot be anything more than a mere selection of the whole group of terrestrial orchids of the Northern Hemisphere, considering that there are about 215 orchid species known to grow in Europe and adjacent areas (and another tens or hundreds of species occurring in the Temperate Zones of Asia and North America). On account of the ecological fragmentation of the habitat of the presented orchid species, as well as their often striking variability, each photograph is accompanied by the name of the country in which the photo was taken, or to which the plant is native. With species that have been given English name, this name is given.

Anacamptis pyramidalis

PYRAMIDAL ORCHID

This very pretty orchid is the only representative of its genus. Its species name suggests the curious, pyramid-like shape of its partially open inflorescence.

The plant survives winters on a pair of almost ball-shaped, unsegmented bulbs. The stem reaches a length between 8-32 in/20-80 cm and bears 4-10 narrow lanceolate leaves that are up to 10 in/25 cm long. The plant's flowers range in color between light red and purplish red; the lip measures 0.4 in/1 cm and is markedly three-lobed. *A. pyramidalis* thrives mainly in the alkaline soil of relatively infertile mountain meadows, but can also be found in light forests. It blooms between April and August. The species is native to the Mediterranean region, from which it gradually spread out into the more northern parts of Europe and into western parts of Asia (including Central Siberia) and northern Africa.

Anacamptis pyramidalis, Czech Republic

Barlia robertiana

GIANT ORCHID

The genus *Barlia* is highly isolated within the family *Orchidaceae*, although speculations have been made about its relation to the genus *Himantoglossum. B. robertiana* (see photo on p. 262) is a typical Mediterranean thermophilic orchid. A pair of underground bulbs give rise to a robust stem reaching a length of 32 in/80 cm and bearing 2-5 elongated lanceolate leaves crowded in a rosette on the part of the stem near the ground. The plant's dense and rich inflorescence can grow to 9 in/23 cm in length. The flowers are colored in a complex combination of whitish-pink, purple, brown-and-red and greenish shades. The lip is three-lobed with the middle lobe sporting two points. In contrast to the species *B. metlesicsiana* (endemic to the Canary Islands), the lip of *B. robertiana* is somewhat greenish and its lateral lobes are bent backward. This species inhabits areas between and including light forests and infertile meadows; it grows predominantly in lowlands and hilly areas in dry or moderately humid alkaline soils. It blooms between January and May and grows all over the Mediterranean, except the southern part of the Adriatic.

Cephalanthera damasonium

WHITE HELLEBORINE

The genus *Cephalanthera* is widespread mainly in the Eurasian Temperate Zone, with only one non-green species occurring in North America. The name of the genus is derived from the Greek words "*kephale*" (head) and "*anthera*" (anther) and refers to the plant's forward bent apical anther. The pollen is, somewhat atypically, powdery, and thus not grouped into pollinia. Even though only 50% of the plant's roots are infected with symbiotic fungi, mycorrhiza is still vitally important for it. Completely non-green blooming specimens are reported to have been spotted in the wild. *C. damasonium* grows out of an underground trailing rhizome. The rhizome branches out a lot and creates adventive buds—that is why some localities often contain groups of vegetatively originated individuals. The stem tends to be 12-24 in/30-60 cm tall and bears 3-5 evenly distributed egg-shaped leaves with lengthwise grooves. The sparse inflorescence puts forth 3-20 cream-colored flowers with a yellowish lip. The flowers are capable of self-pollination and therefore open only very slightly. The species favors semi-shady-to-shady stations in forests, preferring alkaline soils. It blooms between May and July and is widespread all over Europe and Asia Minor.

Cephalanthera kurdica, Turkey

Cephalanthera longifolia

NARROW-LEAVED HELLEBORINE

This *Cephalanthera* orchid is remarkable mainly for the vastness of its natural habitat. It somewhat resembles the species *Cephalanthera damasonium* in appearance, but cannot be mistaken for it, since the thin, narrow, elongated leaves of *Cephalanthera longifolia*, usually arranged in two rows, reach lengths of 6.4 in/16 cm. Its flowers are snow-white. The species grows mostly in the semi-shade of light sparse forests and on the grassy edges of denser forests. Flowers appear on it, depending on the climate of the station, between April and July. The plant is known to grow in at least 40 countries—reports of its occurrence have come from Europe and an area bordered by Asia Minor, Caucasia, Persia and western Himalayas.

Cephalanthera longifolia, Czech Republic

Cephalanthera kurdica

C. kurdica is a beautiful, richly blooming *Cephalanthera* orchid nourished mainly by symbiotic fungi—its own assimilation apparatus is highly reduced. That is why the size of its rich inflorescence is in such striking disproportion with the size of its reduced leaves. *C. kurdica* grows 28-in/70-cm-long or shorter stems bearing barely-2-in/5-cm-long clinging or clasping leaves. The inflorescence is relatively sparse, but it consists of a high number of (up to 40) shiny pink, 1-in/2.5-cm-across flowers that open successively, starting from the bottom one. This species grows in light forests and shrubberies—especially in oak woods with a lot of undergrowth. It blooms between April and June and is native to southern Turkey, Turkish and Iraqi Kurdistan and western Persia.

Chamorchis alpina, Slovenia

Chamorchis alpina

ALPINE ORCHID

This alpine orchid earned its name by its tiny proportions (the Greek word "*chamai*" means "on the ground, low"). It is the only representative of its genus. It occupies a special place in the taxonomy of terrestrial orchids: it is strictly endemic to Europe. The species spends the best part of the year underground in the form of ball-shaped or oval bulbs. As it is able to create additional daughter bulbs and short shoots, it reproduces vegetatively and often grows in clusters. Some 4-10 almost lineated-to-grasslike leaves are arranged in a rosette near the ground; the center of the rosette puts forth a 2-6-in/5-15-cm-long flower spike. Between 0.8-2-in/2-12 minuscule flowers are arranged in a 2-5-cm-long inflorescence. The drooping brownish tepals form a helmet-like shape of the flower. The yellow-and-green lip is undivided and has a blunt tip. *C. alpina* blooms between July and August. It grows on stony or rocky infertile meadows and other similarly exposed alpine locations of the highest European mountains, where the species "climbs" to the altitudes of 8,900 ft/2,700 m above sea level. Besides the Alps and the Carpathians, it is known to grow in Scandinavia.

Comperia comperiana

This curiously-named orchid is remarkable chiefly for the intensely elongated thread-like points of its three-lobed lips. It is the only representative of an isolated genus unrelated to any other. It survives in the ground by virtue of its two ball-shaped bulbs. Its ground leaf rosette consists of only 2-4 extended oval leaves reaching lengths of 6 in/15 cm. When in bloom, the plant forms a flower spike reaching a length of 24 in/60 cm and bearing several gradually reduced clasping leaves. The sparse inflorescence is up to 10 in/25 cm long and consists of 20-30 showy flowers. The tepals are colored in greenish brown, the lip is mauve; both of its lateral lobes, as well as the two points on the middle lobe, are extended into super-thin twisted protuberances reaching lengths of up to 3.2 in/8 cm. The species grows in light coniferous or deciduous forests in alpine elevations. Flowers appear between May and July. *C. comperiana* inhabits only the edge of Europe (Crimea); the main area of its natural habitat is Asia Minor.

Comperia comperiana, Lesbos

Corallorrhiza trifida, Slovakia

Corallorrhiza trifida

CORALROOT ORCHID

An interesting representative of a genus of curiously, almost mysteriously growing, non-green orchids. The plants lack any chlorophyll and survive only by virtue of the fungal filaments that permeate through practically all the tissues of their underground organs. The whole genus *Corallorrhiza* is probably native to North America, with at least 15-20 species known to grow there (mainly in Mexico).

Corallorrhiza trifida got its generic name from a curious perennial underground rhizome that resembles ocean corals in appearance. In late spring, the rootless rhizome gives rise to one or more yellowish, 2.8-12-in/ 7-30-cm-long leafless stalks bearing sparse inflorescences with 2-10 tiny flowers. The tepals are colored in the same way as the spike; the lip is whitish, sometimes decorated with a few brown-and-red spots on the base. *Corallorrhiza* grows in shady humid forests, on damp bushy hillsides, in the tundra and similar locations. It is known to grow in elevations reaching 6,500 ft/2,000 m. Flowers appear on the plant between May and August. The species is also exceptional for the vast geographical area of its habitat—the Temperate Zones of Europe, Asia and North America.

Cypripedium

LADY'S SLIPPER

The name Venus's shoe, or lady's slipper, has already been used in this book to describe other (tropical) orchids: botanists also use it to refer to the terrestrial genera *Paphiopedilum* and *Phragmipedium*. These genera

Cypripedium calceolus, Czech Republic

are not very closely related to *Cypripedium*, but they do share some features: a very similar shoe-like shape of their flower spike and, above all, one crucial morphological detail—their flowers feature two functional stamens (in contrast to an overwhelming majority of other orchids that have only one stamen). This quality secures all these three genera a relatively special position among orchids of the world and scientists are not unanimous on whether these plants can be considered "pureblooded" *Orchidaceae* or if they ought to be excluded into an independent family.

Be it as it may, *Cypripedium* Venus's shoes are beautiful terrestrial orchids with usually very showy and large flowers. A vast majority of them grow in the Temperate and Cool Zones and their growth is therefore seasonal. They survive the harshest times of the year with the help of their thick, trailing and intensely branched rhizomes. Every year, the apical buds of the rhizome give rise to stems bearing staggered lanceolate foliage. The number of lengthwise grooved leaves varies according to the species and age of the given specimen; most often there are 1-5 leaves. The axil of the apical leaf subsequently gives rise to a single (rarely 2-3) flower, 1.6-4.8 in/4-12 cm in diameter. As with all other orchids, the tepals are arranged in two circles: the two lateral tepals in the outer circle are grown together into one two-pointed tepal positioned under the lip. The third tepal is oval-to-egg-shaped and pointed upward; the lateral inner tepals project to the sides and complement the showy, pouched lip resembling a baby's shoe.

Cypripedium japonicum, Japan

Cypripedium japonicum, Japan

Cypripedium orchids' flowers with complicated morphology are typical representatives of "trap flowers". Imprisoned in the inner structure of the flower, the pollinators—usually flying insects—are forced to move about in such a way that will guarantee pollination. At first, the insect is allured by the showy color of the flower. After landing on the smooth edge of the lip, it

slips and slides down into the pouch. After vain attempts to climb back up on the concave, slippery surface of the pouch, it is enticed by the light of the two apparent openings on the lateral walls near the base of the lip. On the way to the source of the light, the insect has to climb through a zone of "brittle hairs" until it finally catches sight of genuine light in the real "emergency exits." Right before leaving the flower, it rubs against the sticky pollen (not grouped into pollinia) on the anther. When the pollinator pays an involuntary visit to another flower, it touches the drooping stigma, rubs the pollen on it and only then picks up a new "load" of pollen on the stamens.

The development of the seedlings of Venus's shoes, from the germination of the seed to the first flowering, takes approximately 9-10, but often even 13-15 years! Luckily, the plants are also able to reproduce vegetatively, by a gradual branching up of the rhizomes. Mature *Cypripedia* are not overly dependent on mycorrhiza, and it is fairly easy to replant and further cultivate them. Unfortunately, this makes them an object of interest for rockery growers and collectors of curiosity plants. Since the vegetative propagation is very inefficient and the sowing in vitro method tends to fail under cultivation, the natural habitats of many attractive species around the world are almost completely ransacked. The species grown in garden cultivation include *C. calceolus* and *C. macranthum*, but mainly the North American species *C. reginae*, *C. parviflorum*, *C. acaule* and *C. arietinum*, the Japanese species *C. debile*, *C. japonicum* and, last but not least, the Himalayan species *C. cordigerum*. Some *Cypripedia* orchids entirely unknow to botanists and cultivators, including miniature unifoliate species, have recently been repeatedly imported from China.

Species of the genus *Cypripedium* are not ecologically overly specialized and can therefore be found in various biotopes, including lighter deciduous, semi-deciduous and coniferous forests, bushy and rocky hillsides, and infertile meadows in altitudes ranging from lowlands to alpine elevations. As they inhabit only the Temperate and Cold Zones in the Northern Hemisphere, their flowering takes place mostly between May and July.

The total number of *Cypripedium* orchids is about 50, but only three of them grow in Europe. Of these, the species *Cypripedium calceolus* plays "first fiddle", as it is widespread practically all over the continent (and Asia, including Japan) and also because it has no peer among all the other European orchids in the size and beauty of its 3.2-in/8-cm-across or smaller, bizarre flowers. The other two *Cypripedia* grow only on the very edge of Europe—in Russia *(Cypripedium guttatum* a *Cypripedium macranthum*, whose "real home" is in fact Asia including Japan, and also North America). All the representatives of the *Cypripedium* genus inhabit (with one Mexican exception) the aforementioned cooler zone of the Northern Hemisphere.

Cypripedium macranthum var. *speciosum*, Japan

Cypripedium montanum, U.S.A.

Dactylorhiza incarnata, Slovakia

Dactylorhiza incarnata

EARLY MARSH-ORCHID

Dactylorhiza orchids used to be incorrectly included in the genus *Orchis*. It wasn't until the 1970s that their full independence was finally acknowledged in botanical circles. Compared to the orchids of the genus *Orchis*, *Dactylorhizas* are a younger developmental group with the center of origin in Asia Minor. Anatomically, *Dactylorhizas* differ from *Orchis* species mainly by their finger-like segmented elongated underground tubers (hence the Latin name of the species—the Greek word "*dactylos*" means finger).

The species name of *Dactylorhiza incarnata* refers to the pale pink (skin-colored) flowers of the plant. It is a sturdy herb reaching a height of up to 36 in/90 cm when in bloom. Its stem bears 4-7 erect, yellow-and-green (somewhat washed-out during the flowering period), mostly spotless, elongated, lanceolate leaves. In proportion to the size of the plants, the inflorescence is relatively short (3.2-6 in/8-15 cm), but it is dense, consisting of 25-50 little flowers growing from the axils of the prominently large lanceolate scales. The tepals including the lip are decorated with a more or less dark-colored marking. The species is highly variable in appearance and is known to have many varieties and forms. As for a preferred habitat, it is fond of moister meadows and marshlands with alkaline foundation. It puts forth its flowers between May and July. *D. incarnata* is known to grow around Europe.

Dactylorhiza maculata

HEATH SPOTTED-ORCHID

This orchid used to be considered a mere subspecies of *D. fuchsii*: slight confusion still prevails over its taxonomy and data on its habitat, partly caused by the high variability and difficult determination of *Dactylorhiza* orchids.

Dactylorhiza maculata is an herb with flattened segmented underground tubers and a 6-24-in/15-60-cm-tall stem bearing a near-the-ground crowded rosette of 3-5 lanceolate leaves. From the bottom up, the leaves get smaller and narrower. An overwhelming majority of the flowers are decorated with pronounced brown-and-red spots. At first, the inflorescence is short, but it gets longer with time, bearing numerous flowers, 0.6-0.8 in/ 1.5-2 cm in diameter. Their color oscillates between light purple and white. The flowers form a broadened three-lobed lip with a showy marking made up of dark little round spots and lines. The species grows in forests, moors, infertile and somewhat damp meadows, and marshlands. It blooms between May and July and is widespread in Europe (in Russia its geographical area reaches into Middle Siberia) and rare in northern Africa (the Atlas Mountains).

Dactylorhiza maculata, Finland

271

Dactylorhiza majalis

MARSH-ORCHID

One of the best-known and still relatively abundantly growing European orchids. In spite of its high ecological adaptiveness, however, its numbers are alarmingly decreasing due to the ever-stronger pressure of human civilization. In the past, *D. majalis* was in many regions a true symbol and herald of the spring and people would often and successfully transplant it in their gardens.

When in bloom, *D. majalis* is a very decorative species. It occurs in a high number of varieties. The cornerstone of the plant are finger-like segmented underground tubers, which in early spring give rise to a thick, hollow stem reaching a height of 18 in/45 cm, covered with elongated egg-shaped or lanceolate leaves in the lower part, and smaller scale-like leaves in the upper part. The leaves are either green or thickly covered with conspicuous brown-and-red spots. The dense and relatively short inflorescence bears 20-35 pink-and-purple or purple flowers. The tepals are inclined or almost vertically erect; the lip sports a dark ribbon-shaped marking in its pale middle part and is divided into three lobes. The lip also consists of a short, blunt spur. *D. majalis* grows on damp meadows and stream swamps in medium and higher elevations (it was pushed out of most lowlands by human intervention). It blooms between May and August and is native to Europe, especially its western and Central regions.

Dactylorhiza majalis, Czech Republic

Dactylorhiza sambucina, Czech Republic

Dactylorhiza sambucina

ELDER-FLOWERED ORCHID

A remarkable and for several reasons a very exceptional *Dactylorhiza* orchid. Apart from being the smallest of the genus and one blooming in the earliest part of the spring, the most intriguing fact, and one very rarely seen with orchids, is that its specimens (even in a single location) appear in two completely different color variations. Besides the more abundant yellow specimens, larger populations also include plants with purplish red flowers!

Dactylorhiza sambucina winters on its two forked egg-shaped tubers. Its hollow stem is up to 12 in/30 cm tall (usually shorter) and covered with 4-7 elongated lanceolate spotless leaves. The edges of the tepals, the upper parts of the stem and the scales in the inflorescence are reddish-to-purple on the red-flowered plants. The inflorescence is dense, rich and short, and it bears 10-25 relatively large flowers. Apart from the aforementioned colors, the flowers can also be colored in white, pink or even a combination of yellow and purple. The lower scales that support the flowers are usually larger and surpass the flowers in length. The flowers are dominated by a very thick, long spur, attached to the back of the base of the unsegmented or only slightly three-lobed lip. The flowers smell like elderberry (hence the species name). For a habitat, *Dactylorhiza sambucina* prefers light forests and somewhat dry infertile meadows in medium and higher altitudes; it blooms between March and (in the coolest locations) July and grows only in Europe.

Epipactis palustris

MARSH HELLEBORINE

One of the prettiest and, when in bloom, showiest *Epipactis* orchids. In order to present itself in "full feather," it needs to grow in an unshaded environment with a high level of groundwater. It is the only European orchid able to survive an extended period even in completely flooded biotopes! Mature specimens are only a little dependent on mycorrhiza and can thus be relatively easily replanted and cultivated.

The wintering organ of the plant is (as with all the other representatives of the genus) a trailing rhizome covered with little protrusions. In the spring, its apical buds give rise to robust, 12-20 in/30-50-cm-tall stems bearing 4-8 elongated lanceolate, short, clasping leaves that are smaller, the higher on the plant they are positioned. The inflorescense is nutant (i.e., overhanging) at first, but later it straightens. The flower raceme consists of 8-30 brown-and-white flowers. The pointed tepals are brown-and-red with a tinge of green or (more rarely) of white. The lip is markedly divided into a flat, bowl-shaped, whitish, dark-veined hypochile, and a wavy, fan-shaped, pure white epichile. The species blooms between June and August and is native to Europe and Asia Minor.

Epipactis palustris, Czech Republic

Epipactis purpurata

VIOLET HELLEBORINE

Around the world, about 30-35 representatives of the genus *Epipactis* are known to exist, often insufficiently differentiated from each other; an overwhelming majority of them grow in the Temperate Zone of the Northern Hemisphere (mostly in eastern Asia) and there is only one species known to grow in Mexico. *E. purpurata* is among the species that are highly dependent on nutrition provided by fungal fibers. The surface of its foliage can therefore be reduced and the level of chlorophyll in the tissues can be low. Some extreme instances have been discovered that contained no chlorophyll whatsoever—such plants are completely purple-and-pink from top to bottom.

The plant's trailing, inclined, branched underground rhizome gives rise to several (up to 10) blue-and-purple

Epipactis purpurata, Czech Republic

stems reaching lengths of 2-4 in/5-10 cm. Like the rest of the plant, the leaves are "afflicted" with a partial loss of chlorophyll, they are blue-and-purple colored and extended. The inflorescence is up to 10 in/25 cm long, dense, rich, and consisting of 25-50 relatively large flowers. The tepals are drooping in a bell-like fashion, gray-and-green on the outside and yellowish- or greenish-white on the inside. The lip features a bowl-shaped, brown-and-purple hypochile that excretes a lot of nectar. The end of the lip (known as epichile) is purplish. *E. purpurata* has a passion for shady environments, and therefore occurs mainly in relatively dense forests of natural origin. It grows more rarely in spruce monocultures. It blooms between July and September and comes from Central and Western Europe.

Epipogium aphyllum

GHOST ORCHID

A somewhat mysterious orchid, both in appearance and life style. Its tissues lack chlorophyll and the plant is thus fully dependent on nutrition provided by fungal fibers (a process known as obligate mycotrophy). The plants survive in the soil by means of a rootless, intensely branched coral-like rhizome. The branching of the rhizome is the way the plant reproduces vegetatively; its natural habitat often reveals a picture of seemingly independent specimens, which are in fact connected together underground. In the summer, the apical buds of the underground organ give rise to barren, straight, hollow, transparent stems bearing fragments of intensely reduced leaves. The sparse inflorescence bears 2-4 pale-yellow-to-reddish flowers that possess a scent similar to bananas. The position of the flowers in the inflorescence is exceptional within the group of all European orchids—in their development, they do not undergo a process known as resupination (a 180° inversion) and, as a result, the lip is atypically pointed upward (see the generic name: in Greek, "*epi*" means "up" and "*pogon*" means "chin"). The rhythm of life

Epipogium aphyllum, Czech Republic

and sexual propagation of *Epipogium* orchids are still wrapped in mystery; sometimes the plants don't bloom for years and give no sign of existence. Moreover, they often bloom underground! The species inhabits shady deciduous forests and its geographical area is extremely large—including Europe, Asia Minor, the Himalayas, Korea, Kamchatka and Japan.

Gennaria diphylla

An unobtrusive green-flowered orchid that used to be classified as a member of the genus *Orchis*. It is the only representative of the genus *Gennaria* and one of the 8 orchid species inhabiting the Canary Islands. Its scape bears two staggered clinging leaves and a sparse inflorescence. It has a special ability to grow daughter underground tubers on root protrusions that expand to the distance of 3.3 ft/1 m away from the maternal plant. The newly formed specimens produce a single leaf and bloom after the lapse of several years. *G. diphylla* blooms between January and April. It grows in the western part of the Canaries and further east on Madeira, in the west Mediterranean, Sardinia and Corsica.

Gennaria diphylla, Tenerife

Goodyera repens, Slovakia

Goodyera repens

CREEPING LADIES' TRESSES

The main habitat of the genus *Goodyera* is southeastern Asia, and some individual species are dispersed in the Temperate Zone all over the Northern Hemisphere. *G. repens* is not a typical terrestrial orchid—its stoloniferous rhizomes trail along the surface layer of mosses and needles of coniferous trees. The rhizomes are intensely branched and give rise to entire groups of slender plants in natural locations. Another unusual feature of the life of this species is that it is an evergreen—new leaves are not produced until late summer and in the fall, they survive the winter and die only when a new generation of flowers begins to develop. The leaves are elongated and egg-shaped, arranged in small rosettes on the ends of the rhizome protuberances. The erect flower spike is 4-12 in/10-30 cm tall and bears 5-15 tiny, partially open and strikingly hairy white flowers. *Goodyera* orchids are happy in mossy coniferous forests and semi-shade. *G. repens* blooms between June and September and its natural habitat consists of scattered locations in Europe and Asia Minor.

Gymnadenia densiflora, Slovakia

Gymnadenia densiflora

FRAGRANT ORCHID

The genus *Gymnadenia* includes about 3 species, of which only 13 are known to grow in Europe, and the rest in the Temperate and Arctic Zones of Asia and America. The presented species was not acknowledged until the beginning of the 21st century; before that, it was considered a subspecies of a smaller *Gymnadenia* orchid named *G. conopsea*. The Latin generic name refers to the finger-like shape of the plant's underground tubers.

Gymnadenia densiflora, Slovakia

G. densiflora is a robust and highly variable orchid reaching a height of up to 3.3 ft/1 m. It winters on two deeply forked tubers. The lower part of its stem gives rise to a few elongated lanceolate, large, glossy leaves positioned close to each other, while the upper half of the stem gives rise to only small leaves resembling clinging scales. The inflorescence is dense and up to 12 in/30 cm long. It bears a high number (up to 150!) of fragrant, pink, purple-and-red or, rarely, pure white minuscule flowers. Another constituent of the flower is a 0.8-in/2-cm-long spur.

G. densiflora inhabits humid and damp meadows, marshlands and occasionally also light forests. It is known to grow in elevations up to 8,900 ft/2,800 m. It blooms between May and August and its natural habitat includes regions in Europe, Asia Minor, Caucasia, Himalayas and China.

Habenaria tridactylites

H. tridactylites is a rather inconspicuous and relatively rare orchid—it grows exclusively on the Canary Islands (mainly in the more humid western part of the archipelago). It represents a relatively large orchid genus: several hundred of its closest relatives grow chiefly in the tropical regions of the world. The main pollinators of the species are nocturnal butterflies.

The plant has two elliptic tubers stored underground, which give rise to a ground rosette of usually three elongated glossy leaves and a sparse inflorescence of tiny yellow-and-green flowers. The flower is dominated by its three-lobed, broadly forked lip—hence the Latin species name of the plant. It is the most plentiful orchid of the Canary Islands. From its original habitat—radically diminished laurel and erica forests—it "moved house" to new locations including man-made stations such as garden stone walls and house walls. The flowering period of this species is somewhat unusual—specimens growing in the lowest elevations bloom in an untraditional period of "spring"—starting in early November.

Habenaria tridactylites, Tenerife

Himantoglossum caprinum, Slovakia

Himantoglossum caprinum

H. caprinum represents one of the most bizarre genera of European orchids. The scientific name is derived from the Greek words "*himas*" (meaning "belt") and "*glossa*" (tongue). That clearly highlights the most distinctive feature of the entire genus—an extremely elongated, belt-shaped, decoratively spiraled middle strip of the flower lip.

The plants are robust and tall (up to 36 in/90 cm) with 7-10 lanceolate leaves diminishing in size the higher on the plant they are. The inflorescence is relatively sparse but it bears a high number (up to 50) of red-and-white flowers sporting cute little helmets and the aforementioned extended lips. *H. caprinum* blooms between May and July. Unlike with the previous species, its original habitat is centered around the eastern part of the Mediterranean and Asia Minor. From this area, *H. caprinum* spread out northward—only not by way of Western Europe, but through Pannonia, along the eastern part of the Alps. Until recently, the specimens from the sparse Austrian and Hungarian populations were considered the northernmost growing emissaries of *H. caprinum*; in 1989, however, the species was surprisingly discovered and identified in Slovakia, where it had long been mistaken for a smaller and earlier-blooming species, *H. adriaticum*.

Himantoglossum hircinum

LIZARD ORCHID

The genus *Himantoglossum* is marked by one interesting quality: all of its specimens (including those which grow a long way north of their original habitat) have retained their Mediterranean biorhythm and their leaves start growing out of the ground as early as in the fall. As a result, they are sometimes severely damaged by the freezing winter temperatures before the spring comes, and their flowers are almost dead when the flowering period begins!

H. hircinum is somewhat smaller than the previous species but otherwise very similar to it. Its flowers give off a strong goatish odor (hence the Latin species name). The plants inhabit sunny grassy hillsides, shrubberies and light deciduous forests, and they bloom as late as between May and July. The plant's original habitat consisted of the central and western parts of the Mediterranean, from which it gradually spread out all the way to the British Isles and the western regions of Central Europe.

Himantoglossum hircinum, France

Limodorum abortivum, Czech Republic

Limodorum abortivum, Czech Republic

Limodorum abortivum

VIOLET LIMODORE

L. abortivum is the only representative of its genus. The size, color and shape of its flowers ranks with the beauty of many smaller tropical orchids. However, its cultivation is out of the question—*L. abortivum* is fully dependent on "its own" fungi throughout its life and therefore extremely sensitive to any ecological changes in its environment. Moreover, it leads a somewhat mysterious existence. Underground, the species forms a thick rhizome with numerous, strong roots tangled together like a nest. This nest-like shape "sends" (not every year) a purplish stem above the ground that reaches a length of 110-24 in/25-60 cm. The leaves are reduced to resembling scales, they are brown-and-purple and completely clinging. The inflorescence is a sparse, erect 12-in/30-cm-long or shorter raceme bearing 5-20 purple or bluish flowers. The flowers often remain only partially open. In dry years, the stem is unable to push up from its relatively deep underground station, in which case both the flowering and the development of the seeds may take place underground! The seeds of *L. abortivum* are, along with those of *Cypripedium calceolus*, the largest among all European orchids—they measure a "breathtaking" 0.06 in/1.5 mm! The individual development of the seedlings is extremely complicated and slow: the plant does not appear above the ground until after 8-10 years of underground existence. *L. abortivum* inhabits light forests, bushy hillsides and infertile meadows. It blooms between April and July. It is highly ther-

mophilic and is known to grow mainly in southern Europe and northern Africa, stretching also to southern Persia.

Listera ovata

COMMON TWAYBLADE

If you chance to notice this unobtrusive herb with green-and-yellow flowers on your walk through a forest, it certainly won't occur to you that you have just encountered a genuine orchid. And yet, that is exactly the case! An interesting quality of this plain-looking plant is the extremely long time it takes for its seedling to reach maturity—between the germination and the first flowering there is often a lapse of up to 15 years! Luckily, the species propagates well also vegetatively—by growing adventive buds on its long roots. In spite of its slow development in the first few years, *Listera ovata* is very well prepared for life: it is one of the few members of the whole family *Orchidaceae* that is completely independent on the presence of symbiotic fungi in its tissues once it reaches maturity. This is why it is also highly adaptive ecologically.

The trailing underground rhizome of the plant gives rise to an up-to-24-in/60-cm soft stem with a hairy top. About a third of the way up from the bottom of it, it grows 2 almost opposite dark-green, broad, egg-shaped leaves. A sparse raceme inflorescence bears 20-80 yellow-and-green flowers with forward-bent tepals and

Listera ovata, Czech Republic

a notably elongated two-lobed lip. *L. ovata* can be spotted in somewhat shady meadow forests, on bushy sunny slopes or on meadows with various levels of dampness. Flowering takes place between May and July. The overall geographical area of the species is very large—it includes almost the entire Temperate Zone of Eurasia.

Neottia nidus-avis

BIRD'S-NEST ORCHID

Neottia nidus-avis, Czech Republic

An ecologically highly adaptive and relatively plentiful non-green orchid. Its almost leafless stems bear only the slightest traces of chlorophyll, and the plants are thus dependent mainly on the fungal hyphas present in their underground parts for nutrition. *Neottia nidus-avis* is able to "employ" a really high number of fungi, because its underground organs assume a really vast surface area: a short, trailing and slowly extending rhizome spends several years producing a massive nest-shaped cluster of succulent roots. Both scientific names of the species refer to the appearance of this cluster—the generic name (the Greek word "*neottis*" means "nest") and the species name (in Latin, "*nidus-avis*" stands for "bird's nest"). The seedlings of the species spend the first 5-8 years hidden underground storing nutrients, and only then can the flower-bearing stalk appear above the ground. After the flowers fade and the seeds mature, the rhizome dies, but the tips of some roots give rise to new individuals and the whole cycle can begin again. The plant's stalk is 8-16 in/20-40 cm tall and only sparsely covered with reduced leaves. The extended cylindrical inflorescence is dense and up to 5.2 in/13 cm long. The flowers are yellowish brown, pale yellow or, rarely, pure white. The species is also able to blossom underground! *Neottia nidus-avis* inhabits shady deciduous forests and blooms usually between May and June. It is plentiful in Europe, northern Africa and Asia Minor, its habitat extending into Middle Siberia and Caucasia.

Ophrys holosericea subsp. *holubyana*, Slovakia

Ophrys bombyliflora, Rhodes

Ophrys

The genus *Ophrys* is undoubtedly the most significant and interesting group of terrestric orchids both within and outside of Europe. Its members are highly unique—for the bizarre and unparalleled beauty of their flowers, as well as for the fantastic, incredibly perfect mechanism of enticing insect pollinators that is

Ophrys ataviria, Rhodes

almost unheard of in the entire realm of plants. As the individual *Ophrys* species are very alike with regard to the appearance of their vegetative parts and life style, they will all be introduced in a single passage.

The scientific name is of Greek origin—the word "*ophrys*" means "eyebrow" and metaphorically refers to this genus' condescending attitude to other plants. The first mention of this name was made in Plinius' History of Nature, which dates back to the 1st century AD. As it

Ophrys candica, Rhodes

Ophrys cretica, Crete

Ophrys epirotica, Greece

Ophrys fusca, Rhodes

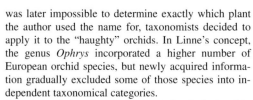

was later impossible to determine exactly which plant the author used the name for, taxonomists decided to apply it to the "haughty" orchids. In Linne's concept, the genus *Ophrys* incorporated a higher number of European orchid species, but newly acquired information gradually excluded some of those species into independent taxonomical categories.

The genus *Ophrys* is very young and quite isolated in terms of relations from other *Orchidaceae*. Its original habitat is in the Mediterranean, mainly its eastern part, in which about 40 species of *Ophrys* are known to occur, many of which form a huge number of subspecies. Only a few *Ophrys* species found their way to Asia and also northward to the heart of Europe.

All *Ophrys* species spend part of the year underground—they winter on a ball-shaped tuber which gives rise to a new bulb before and during flowering; in the following season, this new bulb serves as a resource organ for the new individual. As a result, there are two bulbs present on the plant during flowering. The underground organs rich in starch and mucilaginous substances used to be perhaps the most intensively collected component of a drug known as salep (a mixture of partially dried orchid tubers with a supposed aphrodisiacal effect). Reportedly, the underground parts of *Ophrys* orchids are being offered by Kurdish marketeers in Turkey and Iraq even today.

Ophrys garganica, Italy

Ophrys helenae, Greece

Most *Ophrys* orchids are characterized even in maturity by a medium-to-strong dependency on the presence of symbiotic fungi in their tubers and roots. That is why they grow only small, constricted leaves and why they cannot be replanted into gardens or new lo-

Ophrys helenae, Greece

cations. In many *Ophrys* orchids, their often bluish-green glossy leaves develop as early as in the fall and, if the temperatures are favorable, the plants continue to grow slowly even in the winter. The leaves thus tend to be very severely damaged by frost, especially in plants growing in the more northern and higher-elevated locations.

The flowers of *Ophrys* species surpass in the colorfulness and variety of shapes nearly all European orchids. Between 2-12 (very rarely more) flowers usually grow on erect stalks that are leafless on the top. It is the striking similarity of some of the flower parts to various insect species that made them so unique…

The above-mentioned similarity of some flower parts of *Ophrys* and the different shapes of insect bodies intrigued biologists for a long time, but remained a mystery until the early 20th century when Mr. Pouyanne, a Frenchman, noticed in Algeria in 1916 that the only "visitor" of the species *Ophrys speculum* is a hymenopterous stinging insect *Dasyscolia ciliata*. The flowers subject to his observation hosted exclusively the males of this species, who obviously were not

Ophrys insectifera, Slovakia

Ophrys kotschyi, Cyprus

searching for food and during their visits clearly carried out copulation movements! A new principle of flower pollination—known as pseudo-copulation—was discovered! In order to ensure the pollination of their flowers, *Ophrys* orchids use "sexual mimicry"—they imitate the females of certain insect species and make the confused male insects carrying out their sexual "practices" stick pollinia to their bodies and thus deliver pollen to other flowers on their future love-making expeditions. Every species of the genus *Ophrys* has its own "appointed pollinator" whom it imitates; the existence of the plant is thus fully dependent on the pollinator's sexual activity.

Alluring the males of the pollinator insect is not only a visual (optical) matter; the flowers "can do" much more: for 30-50 ft/10-15 m around, they are able to give off a highly specific scent (a mixture of terpenoids), which is very similar to that used by the real female insect ready for copulation in attracting a partner! It has been found out that a once "hoodwinked" male insect usually doesn't return to the "trickster" plant, nor to any other specimen of that species. That explains why the visits of the pollinators are so rarely observed and recorded by botanists. The successful pollination of a flower is a relatively rare event, owing to the high specificity of the whole process (which takes 3-4 weeks, in spite of the fairly long flowering season of *Ophrys* orchids); as a result, only as many as 5-10% of flowers in *Ophrys* populations are pollinated. Still, even that is enough (considering that each ripe capsule produces about 12,000 seeds) to keep the orchid populations in existence. In summary, it needs to be said that sexual mimicry is not a privilege of *Ophrys* species but that it is known to be used by other orchids growing in Australia and South America.

All *Ophrys* species inhabit sunny, warm and relatively dry locations without strong plant competitors. Specimen can be spotted in rocky, stony, only sparsely vegetated hillsides, on infertile meadows, in bushy Mediterranean societies known as "garrigue" and

Ophrys israelitica, Cyprus

Ophrys mammosa, Rhodes

Ophrys regis-ferdinandii, Rhodes

"macchio," and in light coniferous or deciduous forests. *Ophrys* orchids usually bloom in early spring or summer—depending mainly on the given location. In the Mediterranean, flowering takes place between February and March; Central European species pro-

Ophrys omegaifera, Rhodes

Ophrys sicula, Rhodes

Ophrys speculum, Italy

Ophrys tenthredinifera, Italy

duce flowers later, as could be expected—between May and July. The natural habitat of the genus is centered in and around the eastern part of the Mediterranean; many species' habitats extend into northern Africa, deeper into Asia Minor and warmer regions of Central Europe.

Orchis canariensis

The genus *Orchis* gave a name to the entire family (*Orchidaceae*). However, few people actually know how prosaic the Latin word "*orchis*" is: our ancestors believed in the aphrodisiacal (arousing sexual desire) effects of the tubers of *Orchis*—for their shape and their delicate roots closely resemble male testicles! And the word "*orchis*" translates nothing else but "testicle."

O. canariensis is a highly rare species endemic to all of the Canary Islands except the driest ones—Lanzarote and Fuerteventury. Two egg-shaped tubers of the plant give rise to a 6-18-in/15-45-cm-tall stalk bearing 2-3 elongated lanceolate leaves. The inflorescence is relatively short and consists of 5-20 flowers. The tepals are purple-and-red and usually decorated with a greenish marking in the middle. The lip is whitish with a dark marking along the edges. This species grows in relatively damp locations influenced by trade winds, i.e., usually on mountain slopes on the Canary Islands. The soil environment consists of a slightly alkaline substrate of volcanic origin. *O. canariensis* blooms between February and April.

Orchis canariensis, Tenerife

Orchis coriophora, Slovakia

Orchis coriophora

BUG ORCHID

Orchis coriophora is one of the unobtrusive yet valuable members of its genus. Its stalk is foliaged mainly in the lower part and is up to 24 in/60 cm tall. The flowers are barely 0.8 in/2 cm across; they form a dense and rich inflorescence and often smell like bedbugs (hence the species name). The tepals are brown, red, pink or greenish; the upper tepals droop a little to resemble a beak-shaped helmet. *Orchis coriophora* usually inhabits infertile meadows and light forests, but it has also been spotted in damper locations. It blooms, depending on the climate of its habitat, between April and June. Even though it is considered largely as a European species, it also grows in northern Africa and Asia Minor. This ecologically highly sensitive *Orchis* species is still relatively plentiful in southern Europe.

Orchis italica

NAKED MAN ORCHID

In spite of its name, this species is a typical Mediterranean species with a very extensive geographical area of occurrence. The wintering leaf rosettes consisting of 3-5 leaves give rise to a 8-20-in/20-50-cm-tall stalk bearing a shortened, sometimes almost ball-shaped inflorescence. The basic color of the flowers is whitish pink or, more rarely, purple (*O. italica* var. *purpurea*). The tepals are embellished with dark stripes, while the three-lobed lip boasts dark circular spots. Together, the tepals are shaped like a helmet resembling somewhat that of the species *O. tridentata*. *Orchis italica* grows in both infertile meadows and light forests, preferring dry-to-periodically-damp alkaline soils in warmer regions. It occurs in elevations up to 4,300 ft/1,300 m. Flowers appear between March and May. The species is widespread in the warm areas all over the Mediterranean.

Orchis italica, Italy

Orchis mascula

EARLY-PURPLE ORCHID

The aphrodisiacal effect of the tubers of *Orchis* and other terrestrical orchid species have not been proved by modern science; analyses have shown only the presence of starch substances. Even so, one can still come across older ladies in out-of-the-way Turkish markets, offering sexually dissatisfied men a drug named "tubera salep" (containing dry tubers of *Orchis*, *Ophrys* and other terrestric orchid species). Well, different strokes for different folks—everyone has their own recipe on how to live.

Orchis mascula is a beautiful orchid with a very wide ecological amplitude—that is why it is still relatively plentiful despite its gradually decreasing numbers. Also its appearance is highly variable; it occurs in several scientifically acknowledged varieties with different areas of habitat. The plant's ground lanceolate leaves are either spotted or spotless, the flower stalk is up to 24 in/60 cm tall. The purple flowers are arranged in a dense cylindrical inflorescence and have typically elongated lateral tepals that are bent outward on the ends. The broad flower lip is whitish at the base and covered with dark spots. The plants bloom between March and June. *Orchis mascula* inhabits areas between and including low elevations and alpine altitudes all over Europe—including the Iberian Peninsula, the Balkans, northern Africa and the British Isles. Reports of its occurrence have also been made in Caucasia, Iran and the Canary Islands.

Orchis mascula ssp. *signifera*, Slovakia

Orchis militaris

MILITARY ORCHID

Orchis militaris, Czech Republic

The species name of *Orchis militaris* refers to the appearance of the tepals, pinkish-to-white-and-gray on the outside, namely to the noticeable helmet-like shape that they form together. Specimens of the species are very robust—up to 28 in/70 cm tall when in bloom. Their egg-shaped, pale green leaves are crowded in the lower part of the stalk. A medium-sparse or dense inflorescence bears up to 40 flowers featuring—besides the helmet—dark-dotted lips resembling in shape the lips of *Orchis simia*.

O. militaris is among the most ecologically adaptive terrestrical orchids, which is why it was very plentiful in the past. It is also often (and successfully) transplanted into gardens. Today, it has become an endangered species, especially in continental Europe, due to a massive reduction of the area of its natural habitat. *O. militaris* is famous for its easy hybridization with other *Orchis* species. The plants inhabit infertile meadows or light forests with calcic, drier soils. It blooms between April and June, depending on the location. As to the area of natural habitat, it is one of the most widespread European orchids—it inhabits practically the whole of Europe (including northern Italy in the south and Sweden in the north, England in the west and Lake Baikal, Russia, Greece and Turkey in the east).

Orchis morio

GREEN-WINGED ORCHID

Some *Orchis*, form a ground leaf rosette in the fall and their leaves keep adding in growth slowly throughout the winter (except during periods with the lowest temperatures). The aboveground development of the plants is thus very long, extending to 7-8 months. The cause of this phenomenon consists in the Mediterranean origin of these species.

O. morio is quite variable in appearance and morphology; it creates a large number of subspecies and varieties. Its ground leaf rosette gives rise to a 4-16-in/10-40-cm-long stalk bearing 5-25 purple or, more rarely, pink or white flowers. The Latin species name refers to the unobtrusive brown-striped flower helmet resembling a clown's hat ("*morio*" means "clown"). The three-lobe lip is folded along the longitudinal axis and embellished with spots in the axial part. Its backward-pointed spur is 0.4 in/1 cm long. *Orchis morio* blooms between March and June. In the past, its adaptiveness made it one of the most widespread European orchids. As it is able to grow on both acid and alkaline soils, its area of habitat was virtually unbroken. Recently, it has been rapidly receding. The species is very rare and grows only in isolated locations. The overall area of natural habitat is quite extensive and includes Europe, northern Africa and Asia Minor.

Orchis pallens

PALE-FLOWERED ORCHID

The populations of *Orchis* species are marked by very irregular blooming: in some years, the localities are literally flooded with inflorescences, in other years in the same localities, the blooming specimens could be counted on one hand. This phenomenon is not easy to explain, as there are a number of factors acting at once. For instance, it depends on the number of specimens that reached maturity and their first blooming in a given year; on how regularly the species in question are actually known to bloom (for not all of them bloom annually); if the orchids' leaves were damaged in the previous year by agents such as pests, grazing cattle and mowing.

A good example attesting to the above explanation is the species *Orchis pallens*. Another point of interest is that it is the earliest to bloom of all *Orchis* species. Flowers appear on it as early as in mid-April and are therefore often damaged by frost. The ground leaf rosette consists of 2-4 elongated oval leaves; the flower spike is covered with 1-2 pouched leaves. A cylindrical inflorescence of medium density grows on a 6-14-in/15-35-cm-tall stalk and bears 15-30 sulphur-yellow flowers. The color of the flowers is relatively exceptional by the standard of the genus—yellow-flowered species are a minority among *Orchis*. (Other *Orchis* species featuring yellow flowers include *Orchis provincialis*, *Orchis pauciflora* and *Orchis laeta*). *Orchis pallens* inhabits semi-deciduous and deciduous forests, or the semi-shade of bushes on damp meadows. Flowers can be expected between April and June. It grows all over Europe and Asia Minor.

Orchis pallens, Czech Republic

Orchis palustris, Slovakia

Orchis palustris

BOG ORCHID

Orchis palustris is sometimes considered a subspecies of *O. laxiflora* and bears the name *O. laxiflora* subsp. *palustris*. It is a representative of wetland *Orchidaceae*. In appearance, it is reminiscent of a closely related genus *Dactylorhiza*, but its paired ball-shaped ground tubers give away its generic affiliation. A stalk of a specimen in bloom grows to a length between 6-24 in/15-60 cm; the leaves are elongated and only 0.8 in/2 cm wide. The species' inflorescence is usually somewhat sparse or of medium density and bears only a small number of large purple (or in rarer cases pink and even white) flowers. The lip is three-lobed with the middle lobe lengthwise extended. *Orchis palustris* inhabits alluvial and damp locations in the vicinity of rivers, lakes and in sparse reed growths. Its habitat is restricted to unpolluted, warm areas. It blooms between April and June. Its geographical area stretches between the northern part of the Mediterranean, and Central and Western Europe; it has also been spotted in Asia Minor and northern Africa.

Orchis papilionacea

PINK BUTTERFLY ORCHID

The plants in the photographs represent two out of three officially recognized varieties of this highly variable (and exceptionally decorative!) Mediterranean *Orchis*: var. *rubra* and var. *grandiflora*. The members of the genus are 6-16 in/15-40 cm tall and form only 2-3 elongated lanceolate leaves near the ground. Their inflorescence is either dense or sparse, usually bearing no more than 4-12 flowers. The tepals are bent forward, but do not form a helmet-like shape. They are colored in brown-and-red or purple with dark venation. The flower features a notably broadened lip adorned with dark stripes or lengthwise elongated spots that range in color between purple to deep purple (some specimens of the most beautiful variety *grandiflora*).

O. papilionacea blooms between February and May and inhabits the alkaline soils of infertile meadows, Mediterranean semi-steppe and bushy societies (known as garrigue and macchio) or light forests. The variety *rubra* in the photo is known to grow in the central part of the Mediterranean; sporadic findings have also been reported from Algeria and central Greece. The natural habitat of var. *grandiflora* stretches further east and west of the central Mediterranean region (the Pyrenean

Orchis papilionacea var. *grandiflora*, Italy

Orchis papilionacea var. *rubra*, Italy

Peninsula, Sicily, northern Africa etc.) This species also occurs in the remote region of Caucasia, in the form of its variety known as var. *caspica*.

Orchis pauciflora

Another representative of yellow-flowered *Orchis*. Besides the color of the flowers, it also stands out by the disproportion between the small leaf rosette and the large inflorescence. Between 4-9 leaves reaching lengths of only 1.6-2.8 in/4-7 cm are arranged in an unobtrusive ground rosette. The plant's inflorescence is usually sparse with few flowers and brought by the stalk to a height of 4-10

Orchis pauciflora, Greece

in/10-25 cm. The tepals are pale yellow and complement nicely the deep-yellow or greenish-yellow broadened lip. The lip's axial part is embellished with dark spots arranged usually in two rows. *O. pauciflora* is a hard species to determine—sometimes it is considered a mere variety of *O. provincialis*. It blooms between March and June, solely on the alkaline soils of infertile meadows and sparse bushy societies. Its natural habitat includes the central and eastern regions of the Mediterranean.

Orchis purpurea

LADY ORCHID

The number of species it contains makes the genus *Orchis* one of the richest in Europe—over 30 of its representatives are known to grow there. About 60 species of *Orchis* occur in northern Africa, the Canaries, the Mediterranean and the adjacent Asian area. The Mediterranean is also the original center of development of European *Orchis*.

Orchis purpurea is showy and robust. A specimen in bloom has the following appearance; a ground leaf rosette gives rise to 3-6 glossy, elongated egg-shaped leaves, and a stalk reaching a length of 90 cm and bearing another one or two relatively small clasping leaves on its lower part. The flower raceme is dense and rich. The flowers are equipped with a red-and-brown helmet and their whitish lip is covered with numerous tufts of red hairs. Two completely identical specimens are virtually impossible to find even in small, isolated populations. The species inhabits lowlands and hilly areas in warmer regions; it has a liking for calcic soils in forests and meadows. This orchid blooms between April and June, depending on the location. It is widespread in Europe, northern Africa and Asia Minor.

Orchis purpurea, Czech Republic

Orchis simia, Italy

Orchis spitzelii, Greece

Orchis simia

MONKEY ORCHID

It is immediately obvious at first glance where this orchid got its name from—a detailed analysis of the flower reveals a comical-looking elongated lip shaped like the body of a little monkey.

A specimen in bloom is 12-16 in/30-40 cm tall and bears broad glossy bluish leaves: the axil of the uppermost leaf gives rise to a dense spike consisting of dozens of flowers. An interesting feature of the inflorescence is that it does not start blooming from the bottom flower to the top ones (as is common with other orchids), but in the opposite direction. *O. simia* blooms between the beginning of May and June and is known to grow very rarely in calcic and loess soils all over the Mediterranean, in Caucasia and in the Iraqi part of Kurdistan, to name a few areas. Interestingly, it also rarely grows in the warmest enclaves of countries relatively far north influenced by oceanic climate, such as Holland, Germany, and even England.

Orchis spitzelii

SPITZEL'S ORCHID

A mostly mountain or alpine *Orchis*, interesting mainly for the extensive and scattered area of its natural habi-

tat. It is a relatively slender, unobtrusive orchid with narrow elongated leaves and a rather inconspicuous inflorescence. Its flower stalk is up to 20 in/50 cm tall or smaller; each of the 2-7 leaves arranged in a ground rosette reaches a length of 2.4-4.8 in/6-12 cm (and is about 1 in/2-3 cm across). A raceme inflorescence is usually dense and consists of 10-30 green-and-purple flowers. The green tepals are decorated with brown-and-red spots, while the spots on the pink-to-purple lip are dark purple. The species blooms between April and July, depending on the location. It inhabits light forests, dwarf mountain pine growths and mountain meadows in the elevations between 3,300 ft/1,000 m and 6,900 ft/2,100 m. It is fond of damp, alkaline soils. *O. spitzelii* is known to grow in the Mediterranean, in the Alps, the Pyrenean Peninsula, the Balkan Peninsula and Far Caucasia. Most of the individual locations are very distant from each other and thus perfectly isolated.

Orchis tridentata

TOOTHED ORCHID

Most *Orchis* propagate only vegetatively—by way of seeds. The development of one individual from a germinated seed to maturity is extremely long, taking up to 13-15 years!

O. tridentata is among the most ecologically sensitive and very slowly growing species. Its species name was derived from the "trident" protuberance on the end of its flower helmet. The plant forms ground leaf rosettes (usually as early as the fall) bearing 3-5 bluish green, elongated lanceolate leaves. A stalk bearing blooming flowers is only between 4.8-10 in/12-25 cm tall. The raceme inflorescence is intensely reduced and in the course of its development it changes its shape: at first, it is cone-shaped, later short and egg-like. The tepals arranged into a helmet are pinkish purple with a somewhat dark venation; the three-lobed lip is whitish-to-pinkish and covered all over with deep purple spots. *O. tridentata* blooms between March and June. It is a Mediterranean species that can also be found in Caucasia and Iraq. It inhabits sunny grassy meadows with calcic soils.

Orchis tridentata, Czech Republic

Platanthera bifolia, Czech Republic

Platanthera bifolia

LESSER BUTTERFLY-ORCHID

The genus *Platanthera* has its growth center in North America, an area with the highest number of the described species. Some of them spread from America all the way to Europe (such as *P. parvula* to Scandinavia by way of Siberia; or, *P. hyperborea* to Iceland via the southern tip of Greenland). At the same time, several representatives of this genus (which contains a total of at least 200 species) even grow in the tropics of the Northern Hemisphere!

Platanthera bifolia is a pretty, ecologically adaptive orchid with a strong fragrance. Mature specimens are only slightly dependent on nutrition provided by fungi and can therefore be easily replanted and further cultivated. The plant survives the winter with the assistance of two egg-shaped or elongated tubers, tapering off into a root-like protrusion. Both the blooming and sterile specimens usually form two almost opposite, broad, oval leaves. The flower stalk is barren, with only a few clasping leaves at the bottom, and capable of lifting the inflorescence into the height of 28 in/70 cm. The sparse but rich inflorescence is up to 10 in/25 cm long and consists of 15-35 green-and-white flowers. Among the attractive features of the elongated tongue-shaped unsegmented lip with a greenish end, is most importantly its 1.6-in/4-cm-long, hollow, semi-transparent spur containing nectar. The species grows in light forests, infertile meadows and moors in elevations between and including both lowlands and mountain altitudes: it thrives in both dry and damp soils of various make-up. It blooms between May and August and can be spotted growing in Europe, northern Africa, Asia Minor, Caucasia and Persia.

Platanthera hyperborea

ARCTIC BUTTERFLY-ORCHID

Especially the European lovers of terrestrical orchids will find this plant highly interesting—for of the entire area of Europe, the species grows only on cold, volcanic Iceland, an island apparently uninhabitable by orchids! *P. hyperborea* arrived there after a "miserable" journey from America over the southern tip of Greenland. Some experts classify it as a *Habenaria* species.

It has thickened beetroot-like roots. Its stalk is between 3.2-16 in/8-40 cm tall and bears 4-8 leaves, lanceolate ones at the bottom of the plant and increasingly smaller and more clasping ones, the higher on the plant they are positioned. The spur is relatively short. *P. hyperborea* grows on damp and alluvial meadows, on the moors, and also in wet forests in America. It blooms between July and August. Besides Iceland, it is known to grow in the cool parts of North America, as well as eastern Asia (Japan).

Platanthera hyperborea, Iceland

Serapias cordigera, Italy

Serapias cordigera

HEART-FLOWERED SERAPIAS

The Mediterranean genus *Serapias* contains relatively few (a total of 7) species, but it is highly remarkable for the atypical and unmistakable morphology of its fairly large flowers. The attractive appearance of the flowers consists mainly in the markedly elongated or enlarged middle lobe of the three-lobed lip, which resembles a stuck-out tongue in shape and often also its brown-and-red color. The upper part of the intensely hairy "tongue" is canopied by the upward pointed lateral lobes of the lip with their sides touching, and above all by the other dominant feature of the flower—a high, erect helmet made up of the remaining tepals.

S. cordigera survives the winter retracted in a pair of the plant's underground ball-shaped tubers. In February or March, these tubers give rise to several thin leaves and a flower stalk that is up to 20 in/50 cm tall, foliaged at the bottom and bearing 3-10 flowers. The middle lobe of the black-and-purple lip is broad and heart-shaped; the lateral erect lobes are almost concealed by the whitish purple helmet. *S. cordigera* inhabits light forests, the Mediterranean society of macchio, as well as damp meadows. Flowers appear between April and June. The species is widespread all over the Mediterranean region including the warm French coast of the Atlantic, and the Azores (except the islands of Flores and Corvo).

Serapias lingua

TONGUE-ORCHID

The likeness of the middle lip lobe of *Serapias* orchids to a stuck-out tongue is, in the case of *S. lingua*, also evident in both the English and the Latin name of the species ("*lingua*" meaning "tongue"). Furthermore, the species is interesting for its ability to form short underground shoots ended with daughter tubers—which is why it is often found growing in the wild in vegetatively formed groups. *S. lingua* is a rather slender orchid reaching modest heights of up to 14 in/35 cm during flowering. Between 4-8 elongated, lanceolate, 4.8-in/12-cm long or shorter leaves are concentrated in the lower part of the stalk. A sparse inflorescence is made up of 2-8 whitish-to-deep-purple flowers with embossed dark venation. The middle lobe of the lip is broader and shorter (up to 0.7 in/1.8 cm), blunt at the top and variable in color—often brick red or whitish-purple. The species grows in lighter forests or on bushy hillsides, as well as on relatively infertile, damp meadows. *S. lingua* blooms between March and June and can be found all over the Mediterranean region.

295

Serapias vomeracea, Italy

highly variable in color and shape. Botanists distinguish between several independent subspecies of this orchid, according to the size and shape of the lip. Robust scales protecting the bases of the flowers are, as with the helmets, colored in attractive, glossy pinkish shades with a markedly embossed red lengthwise venation. The middle lobe of the lip is lanceolate on the end (known as epichile), up to 1.1 in/2.8 cm long and often inverted. Its color ranges between brick red and brownish purple. *S. vomeracea* inhabits well-lighted and warm localities including the macchia, light oak forests, olive groves and damp meadows. It blooms between March and June. *S. vomeracea* is a highly variable species widespread in the form of at least 3 subspecies in the vast Mediterranean area. The southern foothills of the Alps represent the northernmost border of its natural habitat.

Spiranthes spiralis
AUTUMN LADY'S-TRESSES

This species has representatives almost all over the globe and contains some 60 species. Most of them grow in the Temperate Zone in the Northern Hemisphere. The Latin name of the genus (as well as the presented species) well captures a characteristic quality of these plants—their long erect unilateral inflorescence is intensely spiraled.
Spiranthes spiralis is a relatively unobtrusive herb growing out of two, three or four beetroot-like tubers. The flower stalk measures 2.8-12 in/7-30 cm, is covered with reduced, clasping, scale-like leaves, and never grows from the ground rosette of egg-shaped lanceolate leaves. This curious way of development, unheard of among European orchids, is caused by the fact that the rosette starts growing only after the formation of the inflorescence is already under way—in early summer; it then survives the winter and dies in early spring the following year. During its development, it gives rise to a new underground tuber that will produce flowers in the following season, again only after its "own" leaves have died. Between 6-30 flowers are arranged in a sparse, spiraled, unilateral raceme. They are small, partially open, white with a yellowish, wavy-edged lip. *Spiranthes spiralis* inhabits infertile meadows and pastures and light coniferous forests. It blooms relatively late in the year—between August and October and is widespread in Europe (chiefly the southwest), northern Africa and Asia Minor.

Trausteinera globosa
ROUND-HEADED ORCHID

This unobtrusive and relatively slender orchid used to be frequently mistaken for various other species, which caused numerous errors and inaccuracies in the information on its natural habitat in Europe.

Serapias vomeracea
LONG-LIPPED SERAPIAS

The flowers of *Serapias* orchids have been discovered to use another interesting strategy for attracting insect pollinators—the pronouncedly dark insides of the flowers serve as a cozy "cave" enticing certain insect species to spend the night. In the process, the careless guests are used as distributors of the pollen stuck to their little bodies!
S. vomeracea has a pair of ball-shaped tubers stored underground; in March, these tubers give rise to a few elongated, glossy green or reddish leaves and a stalk reaching a length of up to 24 in/60 cm. The upper part of the stalk ranges in color between pink and purple-and-red. The function of an inflorescence is served by a sparse raceme bearing 3-10 relatively large flowers,

Spiranthes spiralis, Czech Republic

Its tubers are elongated and unsegmented, with extremely short adventive roots. The leaves are not arranged in a ground rosette; instead, they are evenly distributed on the erect, sparsely foliaged, 10-20-in/ 25-50-cm-tall stalk. The largest and fully developed bottom leaves are elongated and lanceolate.

The function of an inflorescence is served by a dense, multi-flowered spike, at first pyramidal-round (hence the English name round-headed and the Latin name "*globosa*"), and later almost cylindrical. Tiny, dirty pink, red-and-purple or, rarely, white flowers are crowded in the inflorescence. The tepals are arranged in a helmet at the beginning of the flowering season, but later stand more apart. The lip has three deeply divided lobes and is only 0.2-0.3 in/5-8 mm long. It is adorned with delicate dark purple dots. *Trausteinera globosa* inhabits mostly damp infertile mountain meadows with alkaline soils and is known to grow in altitudes up to 8,200 ft/2,500 m. Flowers appear on the inflorescence between May and August. The plant is widespread in southern and Central Europe, as well as southwestern Asia.

Trausteinera globosa, Slovakia

Index

Selected Literature:

Bechtel H., Cribb P., Launert E., 1993: Orchideen Atlas, Ulmer Verlag, Stuttgart.

Buttler K. P., 1996: Orchideen, Mosaik Verlag, Munich.

Dušek J., Křístek J., 1986: Orchideje, Academia, Prague.

Haager J. R., 1992: Pokojové rostliny, Brázda, Prague.

Haager J. R., Ottová R., 1999: Orchideje v bytě, Ottovo nakladatelství, Prague.

Ježek Z., 1996: Na lovu mexických orchidejí, Moravské nakladatelství Květen, Brno.

Procházka F., Velísek V., 1983: Orchideje naší přírody, Academia, Prague.

Rakpaibulsombat S., 1992: Thai orchid species, Suriwong book centre, Chiang Mai.

Richter W., 1985: Orchideen, Neumann Verlag, Leipzig-Radebeul

Richter W., 1986: Orchideen Jahr, Neumann Verlag, Leipzig-Radebeul

Rysy W., 1992: Orchideen, BLV Gartenberater, Munich.

Zákrejs J., 1980: Orchidey, Príroda, Bratislava.

This book is due for return on or before the last date shown below.